ON THE NATURE OF
MUSICAL EXPERIENCE

ON THE NATURE OF
MUSICAL EXPERIENCE

Bennett Reimer and Jeffrey E. Wright, Editors

Center for the Study of Education
and the Musical Experience

School of Music, Northwestern University, Evanston, Illinois

CONTRIBUTORS

Paul A. Aliapoulios

Ian M. Alvarez

Anne Reisner Armetta

Judy Iwata Bundra

Donald E. Casey

David J. Elliott

Darlene L. Fett

David B. Fodor

Ellen H. Hostetler

Scott R. Johnson

John T. Langfeld

Eleni Lapidaki

Janet L.S. Moore

David L. Nelson

Doreen B. Rao

Bennett Reimer

John W. Richmond

W. Ann Stokes

Peter R. Webster

Steve F. Werpy

David A. Williams

Ramona Quinn Wis

Penelope Smith Woodward

Jeffrey E. Wright

David Zerull

ML
3845
·Ø62
1992

Published by the University Press of Colorado
P.O. Box 849
Niwot, Colorado 80544

10 9 8 7 6 5 4 3 2 1

The University Press of Colorado is a cooperative publishing
enterprise supported, in part, by Adams State College, Colo-
rado State University, Fort Lewis College, Mesa State College,
Metropolitan State College of Denver, University of Colorado,
University of Northern Colorado, University of Southern
Colorado, and Western State College.

Library of Congress Cataloging-in-Publication Data

On the nature of musical experience / Bennett Reimer and
    Jeffery E. Wright, editors.
        p.   cm.
    Includes bibliographical references and index.
    ISBN 0-87081-248-3 (alk. paper)
    1. Music — Philosophy and aesthetics.   2. Music —
Instruction and study — Research.   I. Reimer, Bennett.
II. Wright, Jeffery E.
ML3845.062 1992
781'.1 — dc20   92-10196
                                                       CIP
                                                       MN

The paper used in this publication meets the minimum requirements of the American National Standard for Information Sciences—Permanence of Paper for Printed Library
Materials. ANSI Z39.48–1984
∞

Jacket photo by Laurie Robare.

CONTENTS

PART II

FEATURES OF MUSICAL EXPERIENCE HELD IN COMMON AND IMPLICATIONS FOR RESEARCH

PART III

RECOMMENDATIONS AND POSTSCRIPT

INTRODUCTION

ABOUT CSEME

During the academic year 1983–1984, intensive discussions took place among the music education faculty at Northwestern University as to whether a major new initiative might be undertaken in regard to the way Ph.D. research was conceived. These discussions stemmed from a growing conviction that, among other issues, traditional ways of choosing and implementing doctoral dissertations in the field of music education were not in consonance with the modes by which scientific endeavors were most efficiently carried on. In science, individual research projects are typically linked to larger, coordinated efforts to solve pressing problems. Scientists commonly cluster in groups to which individual members can make special contributions, the group providing coherence and longevity for those contributions. Research centers exist by the hundreds, each focusing on an important issue or a variety of related issues that provide an essential structure for the accumulation of knowledge. The Northwestern faculty felt that music education research needed to be more scientific in the way it organized its efforts, because its typically atomistic, uncoordinated studies had not yielded, and likely would never yield, significant knowledge about the major problems of the profession.

These views about the need for structure in music education research were presented by Bennett Reimer, chair of Northwestern's Music Education Department, at the Music Educator's National Conference (MENC) national convention in Chicago (March 1984) in a paper titled "Toward a More Scientific Approach to Music Education Research."[1] In that paper, Reimer announced that, beginning with the academic year 1984–1985, doctoral research at Northwestern would be coordinated within the Center for the Study of Education and the Musical Experience (CSEME). The Center would attempt to provide several important features of an effective scientific research group:

1. Doctoral dissertations would focus around a central issue — that of the nature of musical experience and the ways it could be cultivated through education.

2. Each major mode of research — philosophical, historical, descriptive, experimental, as well as various combinations and offshoots — would be brought to bear on the central topic, reflecting:

   a. the need for the particular insights each research mode offers and the accumulative knowledge produced by the effects of one research mode on another; and

   b. the differing intellectual strengths of students, which must be honored and utilized as they choose research projects.

3. Specific problems chosen to be investigated would:

   a. deal with an important aspect of musical experience and its cultivation;

   b. link with previous studies, both inside and outside the Center; and

   c. reflect the particular interest and experience of the researcher.

4. The Center would encourage the study of particular issues requiring more than one person's research effort. This would lead to:

   a. longitudinal research; and

   b. simultaneous research studies organized by a single topic, either as coordinated but separate dissertations or as single, large dissertations to which several students contribute.

5. The Center would provide an ongoing, regular source of research training, professional enrichment, and communal support through its weekly meetings devoted to:

   a. dissertation proposal discussions, in which students' dissertation ideas were debated and monitored from earliest stages to their formal presentation to a faculty committee;

   b. dissertation work reports, in which students engaged in their projects would seek advice and counsel from the Center, and the Center members would be informed about progress being made and problems being addressed in all dissertations under way;

    c. Center research efforts engaging all members, students and faculty, in the production of a series of publications, jointly authored, on a variety of topics related to the Center's theme (the present study being an example);

    d. discussions of a variety of current issues in music education, arts education, research, psychology, aesthetics, and so on, as suggested by Center members;

    e. presentations by guest speakers on topics related to the ongoing work of the Center; and

    f. social activities enriching the sense of community among the Center's membership.

6. Structurally, participation in the Center would be required for all doctoral students in music education enrolled in full-time course work and expected for students remaining in the Evanston, Illinois, area after course work had been completed. Guest faculty members and doctoral students would be invited from other departments in the School of Music and from the university but would be expected to participate regularly. The Center would offer one course unit for each academic year's participation, although the unit could be waived at a student's request (so that an additional course could be fitted into each year of the program). All full-time music education faculty members would be expected to participate as regular members. A School of Music budget line for speakers and related expenses would provide basic financial support.

    In the years since its establishment, the Center has been guided by these principles and has added a variety of activities reflecting particular needs at particular times. These include discussions of the nature of the Ph.D. qualifying examination and how it might be improved, debates about fruitful Center research topics and how to organize such joint efforts, reports by individual members about their activities in the larger profession, discussions of ways to expand and enhance the teaching experiences of teaching assistants in the program, and so forth. While the main efforts are devoted to the group's research and individual students' research, an attempt is made to remain flexible enough to include other matters of interest and concern as they arise.

A much-hoped-for secondary benefit of the Center has, indeed, seemed to have occurred — the human benefit of being involved in a genuine community of scholars. Beginning doctoral students find themselves welcomed into a group in which people have achieved impressive scholarly foundations after only a year or two of membership, providing the beginners with inspiration, motivation, and encouragement. All doctoral students get to know the faculty not only as instructors but as colleagues who, too, are deeply involved in the process of learning. Research is allowed to be seen not as a mysterious process carried out in anxious isolation but as an active, shared engagement in systematic problem solving. Such problem solving requires not only the application of learned rules and regulations, but at times creative thinking, common sense, and leaps of faith as well, and the enterprise can be one of shared adventure among people who care about each member's success. The Center, it is felt, allows research to wear a human face.

THE CONCEPT OF MUSICAL EXPERIENCE

When a research center selects as the focus of its study the phenomenon of musical experience, it is choosing a subject of central importance to music educators and one that presents all the problems that usually beset umbrella concepts. Indeed, it would be difficult to find a term wider in application than that of *experience*. As Albert William Levi phrases it, experience is a "huge and all-inclusive term, as big as life, and almost as confusing. How is it philosophically possible to give some order and organization to this concept?"[2]

The most common way philosophers have attempted to bring some organization to the concept of experience has been with the use of division: they have divided the whole field into smaller parts and drawn distinctions between various types of experience. Levi reports that Saint Augustine provided the first major demarcation of the map of experience by dividing all the possibilities into three all-inclusive categories: experience of (1) Nature, (2) the Human, and (3) the Divine. These three categories can be further broken down, and Levi provides a table of the traditional categories usually drawn in philosophical discussion about types of experience.

Traditional Philosophical Categorization of Experience.[3]

	AREA OF EXPERIENCE	FIELD OF PHILOSOPHY
	The Knowing Process	Epistemology or Methodology
Nature	Matter in Motion Living Things	Philosophy of Nature or Philosophy of Science
	Mind The Universe As a Whole	Metaphysics or Cosmology
Man	Individual Decision	Ethics
	Social Living	Social Philosophy
	The Arts	Aesthetics
	History	Philosophy of History
God	God	Philosophy of Religion

From this table it can be seen that the arts were given a major category division called *aesthetics*. Although the validity of the category was rarely disputed, the basis for distinguishing the aesthetic from other types of experience varies confusingly from one philosopher to another. Despite the intuitive sense possessed by most of us that the arts provide a special type of experience, it has not been easy to identify the characteristics and components of aesthetic experience using the mode of philosophic reflection. Different philosophers have based their descriptions of aesthetic experience upon quite different aspects, and little agreement is found among their various theories.

Faced with such a multiplicity of accounts regarding the essential characteristics of aesthetic experience, it is possible to take three positions: (1) theorists can, like Marshall Cohen, argue that "there is no way of determining the precondition of all aesthetic experience just as there is no way of knowing what qualities such experience must bear";[4] (2) theorists can attempt to identify some necessary and/or sufficient conditions that enable us to say, with some justification, "this experience is aesthetic"; (3) theorists can follow the example of Nelson Goodman with regard to "symptoms of the aesthetic"[5] and make the more careful claim that an aesthetic experience is likely to be characterized by a mix of certain qualities rather than others, and that some of these features must be present for the experience to qualify as aesthetic.

Earle Coleman is one theorist who has chosen the second alternative.[6] Although he recognizes that wide variations can exist between one aesthetic experience and another, he argues that it still makes sense for theorists to seek one or more common denominators and defining characteristics that link the various kinds. His analysis offers three unifying earmarks or defining traits of aesthetic experiences: (1) trans-practical, (2) trans-mundane, and (3) trans-chaotic qualities.

The term *trans-practical* refers to the idea that in an aesthetic situation one apprehends the data offered by the art object for the intrinsic rewards provided by that apprehension itself, not for the usefulness of that information toward achieving some practical goal. The term *trans-mundane* means that an aesthetic experience stands out or apart from the usually undifferentiated continuum of everyday humdrum experiences. Finally, the term *trans-chaotic* refers to a common feature of aesthetic experiences: they are organized, unified, and coherent. The "phases or parts which make up the experience blend, fuse, coalesce, or stand in some clear relationship to each other":[7]

> To sum up, whenever an experience is characterized by trans-practical appreciation, trans-mundane significance, and trans-chaotic structure, it is an aesthetic experience. Unity and the extraordinary may both be present in a non-aesthetic experience, but only the presence of trans-practical appreciation insures that the experience is aesthetic.[8]

Although philosophers have used various qualifiers to distinguish aesthetic experience from other types of experience, John Dewey was critical of theories that made absolute distinctions. For him, the trouble with theories existing in his day was that they started "from a ready-made compartmentalization, or from a conception of art that spiritualizes it out of connection with the objects of concrete experience."[9] The disadvantage of this type of approach, he felt, is that compartmentalization tends to obscure perception of some of the patterns common to all types of experience. The goal of Dewey's analysis was to restore an understanding of the continuity between art and life, which he thought had been lost in many theoretical analyses of art. The aesthetic, in his theory, was a clarified and intensified development of traits that belong to every normally complete experience.

Dewey's use of the term *experience* needs to be explained because many authors since *Art as Experience* have been greatly influenced both directly and indirectly by Dewey's aesthetics. Dewey used the word *experience* in three different senses: (1) to refer to normal or everyday experience; (2) as a contrast to the memorable event of "having an experience"; and (3) in the sense that there are experiences that are dominantly aesthetic.

In the first sense of experience, Dewey argued that all ordinary experiences were potentially aesthetic. Coleman summarizes some of the features Dewey imputed to ordinary experiences:

> Normal experiences are said to be inchoate in contrast to *an experience*. Ordinary experiences are choppy, interrupted, dispersed. Dewey points out that in such experiences we do not attend to the connection of one event with what preceded it or with what follows it. Things occur, but they are not apprehended as constituents of a single, intact experience. Aesthetic quality is implicit but unrealized in ordinary experience or happenings.[10]

In the second sense of experience, namely, having *an experience,* the material, instead of being interrupted, runs its course to fulfillment; various ingredients are rounded out so as to reach a consummation. Coleman extracts some of Dewey's basic claims with regard to the term *an experience:*

> *An experience* always possesses unity; and Dewey holds that no experience is unified without having aesthetic quality. The unity of *an experience* is constituted by a pervading aesthetic quality. Aesthetic quality is that which "rounds out an experience into completeness and unity. . . ." *An experience,* therefore, always has explicit aesthetic quality as contrasted with ordinary experiences in which aesthetic quality is only implicit.[11]

How did Dewey distinguish between *an experience* that has aesthetic quality and an aesthetic experience in the full-fledged sense (an experience that is dominantly aesthetic)? An aesthetic experience is characterized by the same type of unity, completeness, and fulfillment of tendencies found in *an experience,* but it is controlled by different interests. The interest is not intellectual or practical, but perceptual.

Material qualities are brought into satisfying relations so that all the parts of an art work cohere to form an integrated whole. Dewey summarized his conception of the aesthetic in the following terms:

> An object is peculiarly and dominantly esthetic, yielding the enjoyment characteristic of esthetic perception, when the factors that determine anything which can be called an experience [unity, completeness, etc.] are lifted high above the threshold of perception and are made manifest for their own sake.[12]

Dewey's theory includes the three features proposed by Coleman but goes beyond them. First, Dewey held that the aesthetic experience is trans-practical but described it as trans-intellectual also. Second, not only is aesthetic experience trans-mundane, but so is having *an experience*. Third, both having *an experience* and the aesthetic experience are characterized by trans-chaotic quality; however, aesthetic unity and completeness are differentiated from intellectual or logical completeness. Not only is the aesthetic controlled by different interests, another distinction lies in the fact that emotion plays an important and essential role in achieving aesthetic unity. To do justice to Dewey's ideas, it would therefore seem necessary to add a fourth qualification of the aesthetic: aesthetic experience essentially involves feeling at one or more levels of response.

Dewey offered several descriptions of the role of emotion or feeling in art. In each of them it is clear that emotion guides creation, but Dewey was quite emphatic that emotion is not what is expressed. In an act of expression, the mind combines elements from many sources to construct a new object, and emotion is the moving and cementing force. "It selects what is congruous and dyes what is selected with its color, thereby giving qualitative unity to materials externally disparate and dissimilar. It thus provides unity in and through the varied parts of an experience."[13] Emotion is able to achieve this unity because any "predominant mood automatically excludes all that is uncongenial with it."[14] Emotion "reaches out tentacles for that which is cognate, for things which feed it and carry it to completion."[15] In art, emotion must operate. "But it works to effect continuity of movement, singleness of effect amid variety. It is selective of material and directive of its order and arrangement."[16] When an artist sets out to create a work of art, "the determination of the *mot juste,* of the right incident in the right place, of exquisiteness of proportion, of the precise tone, hue, shade, that helps unify the whole, is accomplished by emotion":[17]

> Emotional energy continues to work but now does real work; it accomplishes something. It evokes, assembles, accepts, and rejects memories, images, observations, and works them into a whole toned throughout by the same immediate emotional feeling. Thereby is presented an object that is unified and distinguished throughout.[18]

Unless the perceiver of an art object is aware of it as a whole unified by the same emotional feeling, the import of the art work is largely lost.

The relationship of aesthetic emotion to emotion in everyday life is also in keeping with Dewey's conception of the continuity between art and life. Emotion does not become aesthetic until it "adheres to an object formed by an expressive act."[19] Aesthetic emotion "is thus something distinctive and yet not cut off by a chasm from other and natural emotional experiences."[20] In these and similar passages, Dewey pursued his goal of distinguishing the aesthetic from other types of experience, yet at the same time showing how the quality of the aesthetic is rooted in everyday living.

Given that aesthetic experience, while related to experience in general, has identifiable features setting it apart as a subcategory of experience, the identification of its features as they are manifested in musical experience would seem to be both possible and desirable. Describing both general and particularized components of musical experience would help us understand what kinds of factors are operating when we experience music fully. More reliable information about both kinds of factors and how they interact with one another would be of great assistance to music educators, whose business it is to help students achieve their individual potential to experience music fully. The benefits of more detailed knowledge on this topic would be considerable on both a professional and a human level.

THE PRESENT STUDY

Soon after its inception, CSEME set about the task of finding a research topic that would be significant to the field of music education and would lend itself to the sort of group effort that was to be a major purpose of the Center. The first topic chosen was one that had been insufficiently researched in the past though it was basic to the field of music education and to the mission of CSEME: a description of musical experience itself. It is the purpose of the present study to make progress toward a better understanding of the nature of musical experience.

The first step of the study was to examine the views of musical experience expressed by a variety of musicians and other thinkers who had addressed the issue. The earliest Center discussions led to a listing of philosophers, aestheticians, composers, music theorists, and music educators who had written about musical experience. It was decided that the materials used in this research project would be primary sources — books, articles, and addresses written by the authors who would be included.

After the list was generated and preliminary research was conducted to ensure that each author selected for study had written enough about musical experience for an essay to be written on his or her views, Center members individually chose authors whose views most interested them. Each member thoroughly researched that author's views on musical experience and wrote an essay that followed an agreed-upon format in order to ensure consistency.

The authors included in Part I represent a broad array of ideas from a twentieth-century perspective. Obviously, many more ideas about musical experience exist in our century, and far many more have been expressed throughout Western history and in the history of other cultures. So those represented here must be understood as one small sample from a much larger population. (For this reason, Part III contains suggestions for further studies to expand the data base.)

Further, it would have been unrealistic to have attempted to incorporate everything written by each of the authors included in this study. Many of them have been extremely prolific, and all have dealt with many issues only marginally related to the topic of this research. An attempt was made to focus on those sources particularly relevant to the nature of musical experience, with the expectation that, even if some sources were missed, each author's key ideas about musical experience were likely to appear in those materials most directly concerned with that topic. Key ideas common among several authors would be discovered, even if some of those ideas had been treated additionally in other works by various authors.

The next step was for each essay writer to determine the key ideas about musical experience in the thinking of the author reported on. For some authors, the key features of musical experience were quite clear; for others they were not as explicit. Some authors identified many features; others identified only a few. Each essay writer prepared a short description on a four-by-six-inch card of each key feature of musical experience suggested by that author in preparation for an ongoing discussion at Center meetings.

Using a variation of the "constant comparison method of qualitative analysis,"[21] the Center divided the key features into broad categories. First, those of Bennett Reimer were used as categories because his essay generated the largest number of identified features and because, being present, he could guide the discussion as to how his features related to or did not relate to those of other authors. After each Reimer key-feature card was read, CSEME members read cards they felt related to it. If the Center was in general agreement about the strength of the relationship, the card was added to the category. After all the Reimer cards had been considered, the Leonard B. Meyer cards that had not yet been placed were set forth as categories with which other members' cards could be grouped. Meyer was used at that time because his essay also generated a large number of features and because this author was a familiar one to most participants. This process was continued for every author until every card had been placed or judged insignificant in terms of the total study.

Through this sorting process, the meaning of each broad category of concepts about musical experience was clarified. As new ideas of other authors were added and as the features were discussed, trends in thinking about most of the features began to emerge. Comparisons and contrasts between various authors' views also became apparent.

When this process was completed, clusters of identified elements were examined to see which could serve as bases for "feature essays." Many of the clusters of related features had enough entries to be obvious candidates for such treatment. Other features were addressed by fewer authors. In several such cases two or three small clusters seemed to fit together logically to form one essay topic with sufficient material. Finally, a few topics simply had not been discussed by enough authors to generate sufficient material for essays. These were removed from further consideration.

This entire process was complicated somewhat by the fact that the body of graduate students comprising the Center was in continual flux. As students left campus to pursue their careers and their degrees simultaneously, they occasionally left research projects unfinished. In some cases, these projects were taken up and completed by newer members of the Center. In other cases, the original essay writers worked on their own revisions from various locations across the country. CSEME thus served for many as a link to the university even after they left the Evanston area.

After the feature essays had been completed, the task of drawing implications began. Each essay writer (or student or faculty member assigned an essay written by a student no longer in residence) generated a list of possible research issues the essay suggested. In Center meetings these were discussed, refined, and given the structure found in Part II.

Introductory materials for the study had been generated during its initial phases. These were brought up to date, and the entire manuscript as completed to that point — Introduction, Part I, and Part II — was reviewed by all Center members, individually and in group discussions, in order to generate the final part that contains conclusions and recommendations.

This research summarizes the individual ideas of authors who have significantly addressed the nature of musical experience from a wide variety of viewpoints and then presents a series of essays that serve to synthesize their individual ideas. Included are both notions with which few thinkers about musical experience would disagree and others that are clearly individual views. Points of agreement and disagreement among authors are obvious. Some authors write brilliantly, some passionately, some pointedly about the musical experience; others may write with less conviction or specificity, but nonetheless have something worthwhile to say about what characterizes musical experience.

The study represents the cooperative research efforts of a group of scholars who are deeply committed to clarifying the nature of musical experience. It is shared in hopes that it will be worthwhile for the cause of music education, which exists to advance the musical experience of all people.

NOTES

1. Bennett Reimer, "Toward a More Scientific Approach to Music Education Research," *Council for Research in Music Education Bulletin* 83 (Summer 1985).
2. Albert William Levi, *Varieties of Experience: An Introduction to Philosophy* (New York: The Ronald Press, 1957), p. 7.
3. Ibid., p. 11.
4. Marshall Cohen, "Aesthetic Experience as Lacking Any Common Denominator," in *Varieties of Aesthetic Experience,* ed. E. J. Coleman (Lanham, MD.: University Press of America, 1983), p. 254.
5. Nelson Goodman, *Languages of Art* (Indianapolis: Bobbs-Merrill, 1968), p. 252.
6. Earle J. Coleman, "What Is Aesthetic Experience?" in *Varieties of Aesthetic Experience,* ed. E. J. Coleman (Lanham, MD: University Press of America, 1983) p. 12.
7. Ibid., p. 16.
8. Ibid., p. 19.
9. John Dewey, *Art as Experience* (New York: Capricorn Books, 1958, first printed in 1934), p. 11.
10. Coleman, *Varieties of Aesthetic Experience,* p. 128.
11. Ibid., pp. 128–129.
12. Dewey, *Art as Experience,* p. 57.
13. Ibid., p. 42.
14. Ibid., p. 67
15. Ibid.
16. Ibid., p. 69.
17. Ibid., p. 70.
18. Ibid., p. 156.
19. Ibid., p. 76.
20. Ibid., p. 78.
21. Barney G. Glaser, *The Discovery of Grounded Theory* (New York: Aldine DeGruzter, 1967), pp. 101–115.

ACKNOWLEDGMENTS

The editors are grateful to the many students and faculty members who made important contributions to this book subsequent to the writing stage — proofreading, reference-hunting, bibliographic cross-checking, and so forth: Isaac Amuah, Susan Bolanis, Dr. Donald Casey, Scott Cohen, Rob Dunn, Marian Dura, Maud Hickey, Eleni Lapidaki, Dr. Carol Richardson, Carlos Rodriguez, William Smith, Dr. Peter Webster, and Paul Woodford. W. Ann Stokes contributed valuable text material in addition to her author chapter. The support of the Northwestern University School of Music administration, for this book and for all the other activities of the Center for the Study of Education and the Musical Experience, is heartily acknowledged.

Bennett Reimer and Jeffrey E. Wright

PART I

SELECTED AUTHORS ON
MUSICAL EXPERIENCE

MONROE C. BEARDSLEY
(1915–1985)

SOURCES

Monroe Curtis Beardsley taught philosophy at Yale University, Mount Holyoke College, Swarthmore College, and Temple University. He was widely published in the fields of logic and criticism in addition to philosophy. Beardsley maintained a career-long involvement in aesthetics, including memberships in the American Academy of Arts and Sciences and the American Society of Aesthetics (where he served as president 1967–1968). He also served for thirteen years as book review editor for *The Journal of Aesthetics and Art Criticism*.

In *Aesthetics: Problems in the Philosophy of Criticism* (1958), Beardsley presented his philosophical rationale for an object-centered theory of art criticism. The theory proved controversial and generated a wave of new thinking and writing in a field that had been moving along relatively unchallenged. After that, Beardsley's writings in the arts were characterized by thoughtful attention to the arguments of his critics, as he continued to refine the ideas set forth in *Aesthetics*. Other Beardsley essays relevant to this discussion include:

1. "On the Creation of Art," published in *Aesthetic Inquiry: Essays on Art Criticism and the Philosophy of Art* (1967), edited by Monroe C. Beardsley and Herbert M. Schueller;

2. "Understanding Music," from *On Criticizing Music: Five Philosophical Perspectives* (1981), edited by Kingsley Price; and

3. *The Aesthetic Point of View: Selected Essays* (1982), edited by Michael J. Wreen and Donald M. Callen, which is a collection of
Beardsley's essays in aesthetics and art criticism published after the
1958 *Aesthetics*. Part IV, "Some Persistent Issues in Aesthetics:
Further Reflections" (pp. 283–370), was written expressly for the
1982 publication.

GENERAL ORIENTATION TO AESTHETIC EXPERIENCE

The theory of art criticism set forth in the 1958 *Aesthetics* arose
from Beardsley's dissatisfaction with popular trends in the standard
practice of art criticism. As he saw it, critics were using two kinds of
reasons to justify their statements about art works: *genetic* reasons,
which focus on artists and how they accomplish their creative ends;
and *affective* reasons, which refer to audience response to completed art
works. Statements made for genetic or affective reasons are *external
statements,* because they pertain to the causes and effects of art works.
Beardsley would have had critics evaluate art works neither according
to how they were created nor according to audiences' deeply felt
reactions to them.[1] Rather, he would have advised critics to attend
exclusively to the art object and its unique qualities and relations. In
his 1958 *Aesthetics,* Beardsley established the basis for an object-centered art criticism.

Beardsley's object-centered art criticism utilized *internal statements*
in an attempt "to discover, first, what is true of the parts, and, second,
how the parts contribute to the peculiar qualities of the whole."[2]
Following is an introduction to Beardsley's "parts-wholes" analysis:

> Any part of a sensory field is . . . a complex if further parts can be
> discriminated within it. An absolutely homogeneous part of the
> field is partless, and such a partless part may be called an *element* of
> the field. Analysis stops with the elements.[3]

> A musical composition, or auditory design, is a complex event, and
> its elements are smaller events, little — though sometimes momen-
> tous — changes that are occurring simultaneously and successively.
> For the purposes of critical analysis, these changes can be described

by their termini, for a change is always *from* something *to* something — from loud to soft, from low to high, from sweet to harsh. The termini of musical changes are sounds, and these we shall here regard as the elements of music.[4]

Qualities of elements are *local qualities*. One is not always conscious of these qualities when one experiences art. When elements combine to form complexes, the complexes take on *new* qualities that were not qualities of the constituent elements. It is these *regional qualities* that let one perceive sensory information in art works as aesthetic phenomena. Regional qualities depend, for existence as well as character, on relations within and between those elements and complexes that make up aesthetic objects. The quality of a complex is a function of both the elements and their relations, so that if either is rearranged the existing regional quality may change or disappear.[5] Regional qualities of complexes can each be more or less: *extensive* — a quality may prevail over a larger or smaller portion of a sensory field; *intensive* — a quality may exert a greater or lesser influence on relationships between parts; *persistent in time* — a quality may characterize a single relationship or a series of events.[6]

This is the base from which Beardsley developed an object-centered language to be used in art criticism. He wanted critics to devote most of their effort to *describing* art works according to the characteristics of their regional qualities. Beardsley did acknowledge, however, that critics are called upon to provide value judgments about art works. He thus devised a set of three criteria for making evaluations. The three were presented in his 1958 *Aesthetics* as the general canons of internal criticism: the canon of unity, the canon of complexity, and the canon of intensity.[7] Over time, the criteria were refined in definition and renamed the *triadic principle*. In "The Relevance of Reasons in Art Criticism," one of the essays in the collection published in 1982, Beardsley offered a refined version of his three criteria:

> To put this triadic principle directly, I say that a feature of an artwork is a normatively explanatory feature with respect to its degree of aesthetic value (so that a reason citing it is judgmentally relevant) if and only if it is

1. *unifying* or *disunifying:* that is, its presence causally contributes toward increasing or detracting from the work's coherence or completeness; or

2. *complexifying* or *decomplicating:* that is, its presence contributes toward giving the work range, scope, variety, subtlety, contrast, or depth, or restricting it in one of these respects; or

3. *intensifying* or *enfeebling* of the work's affirmative [or life-enhancing] regional qualities.[8]

Those people-oriented (genetic, affective) concerns, which Beardsley considered external to the practice of art criticism, he nevertheless acknowledged to be issues of great philosophical consequence. He devoted career-long efforts to delimiting and clarifying people's relationships with art, from the making of art works to the apprehension of the work made. Those experiential aspects that figured prominently in Beardsley's writings in aesthetics are examined next.

FEATURES OF AESTHETIC EXPERIENCE

1. *It is best to speak of the aesthetic in experience, since "aesthetic experience" in its fullest sense is only rarely attained and fails to account for much aesthetic commerce with things.*

By 1969, with the publication of "Aesthetic Experience Regained,"[9] Beardsley had brought his pleasure-based definition of aesthetic experience as far along as he felt it could be developed:

> I propose to say that a person is having an aesthetic experience during a particular stretch of time if and only if the greater part of his mental activity during that time is united and made pleasurable by being tied to the form and qualities of a sensuously presented or imaginatively intended object on which his primary attention is concentrated.[10]

After 1969, Beardsley began to call into question the use of "pleasure" as the primary defining feature of aesthetically characterized experiences. As the twentieth century progressed, much of what was being hailed as art seemed to dwell outside of the pleasure category. An alternative defining point was needed, one that would accommodate modern developments in art-making and performance but still make the necessary discrimination between aesthetically characterized experience and other kinds of experience.

Beardsley abandoned the single defining point in favor of a set of five criteria of the aesthetic character of experience. The five criteria are best applied as a family, but for the sake of usability Beardsley conceded that an experience could be deemed aesthetic in character if it had the first of the five features and at least three of the others, including preferably the last:

1. *Object directedness.* A willingly accepted guidance over the succession of one's mental states by phenomenally objective properties (qualities and relations) of a perceptual or intentional field on which attention is fixed with a feeling that things are working or have worked themselves out fittingly.

2. *Felt freedom.* A sense of release from the dominance of some antecedent concerns about past and future, a relaxation and sense of harmony with what is presented or semantically invoked by it or implicitly promised by it, so that what comes has the air of having been freely chosen.

3. *Detached affect.* A sense that the objects on which interest is concentrated are set a little at a distance emotionally — a certain detachment of affect, so that even when we are confronted with dark and terrible things, and feel them sharply, they do not oppress us but make us aware of our power to rise above them.

4. *Active discovery.* A sense of actively exercising constructive powers of the mind, of being challenged by a variety of potentially conflicting stimuli to try to make them cohere; a keyed-up state amounting to exhilaration in seeing connections between percepts and between meanings, a sense (which may be illusory) of intelligibility.

5. *Wholeness.* A sense of integration as a person, of being restored to wholeness from distracting and disruptive influences (but by inclusive synthesis as well as by exclusion), and a corresponding

contentment, even through disturbing feelings, that involves self-acceptance and self-expansion.[11]

2. *"An artwork is an arrangement of conditions intended to be capable of affording an experience with marked aesthetic character — that is, an object (loosely speaking) in the fashioning of which the intention to enable it to satisfy the aesthetic interest played a significant causal part."*[12]

Beardsley's definition of an art work does not rule out that natural and technological objects often provide aesthetically characterized experiences. Nor does the definition exclude as works of art objects in which intentions other than aesthetic (religious, political, technical) may have played some part.[13]

However, Beardsley warned against over-inclusiveness. Though art works are objects fashioned with skill, it would be a mistake to call *every* skillfully fashioned object a work of art. Neither should artistic status be conferred on natural objects.[14]

3. *Aesthetic value is the value something possesses by reason of its capacity to impart, through cognition of it, a marked aesthetic character to experience.*

The term *cognition* is used here to indicate the accurate and adequate apprehension of an object's qualities and relations, including any semantic properties it may possess. To apprehend accurately is to see what is actually there in the object. To apprehend adequately is to take in enough of what is there so that further discoveries would not noticeably affect the degree to which the experience is aesthetic.[15]

Those qualities that count directly in estimations of aesthetic value are an object's regional qualities. Local qualities enter value discussions only as they combine to form regional qualities.[16]

4. *"Each individual process that eventuates in a work of art generates its own direction and momentum. For the crucial controlling power at every point is the particular stage or condition of the unfinished work itself, the possibilities it presents, and the developments it permits."*[17]

Beardsley contemplated the genesis of art works in an often-printed essay, "On the Creation of Art" (1967). There he identified two phases of the so-called creative process that alternate throughout the process. During an *inventive phase* (traditionally called *inspiration*) new ideas are formed in the preconscious and appear in consciousness. A *selective phase* follows, which is "nothing more than criticism."[18] In the selective phase, the conscious chooses or rejects each new idea after perceiving its relationships to what has already tentatively been adopted. That is how the crucial controlling power lies within the realm of possibilities presented by the unfinished work.

It was not Beardsley's intention to demean the artist with his object-centered analysis, for people are the makers of the world's wealth of art works. Still, the finest qualities of art works cannot be imposed on them by force — the artist can only manipulate the elements of a medium so that *they* will make those qualities emerge:

> When in this way the artist makes plain to us over and over the marvellous richness of nature's potentialities, he also presents us with a model of man's hope for control over nature, and over himself. Artistic creation is nothing more than the production of a self-creative object. It is in our intelligent use of what we are given to work with, both in the laws of the universe and in the psychological propensities of man, that we show our mastery, and our worthiness to inhabit the earth.[19]

Even in his essay devoted to the creative process, Beardsley reminded his readers that *how* the artist's mind works has no bearing upon the value of *what* the artist produces, and thus holds no place in the practice of art criticism: "What I want to say is that the true locus of creativity is not the genetic process prior to the work but the work itself as it lives in the experience of the beholder."[20]

5. *It is the fictive character of art works that sets them apart from works of nature or technical objects.*

An art object is a physical object, fashioned from materials that had already existed in some form before being manipulated with aesthetic intent.[21] An art object is also a perceptual object, because new forms and qualities emerge during the manipulation of materials that were not indigenous to those materials.[22]

The art object as a physical-perceptual entity has much in common with other objects, human as well as natural. Other human objects, for example, can be said to share physical origin with art objects. Natural objects, though dissimilar in physical origin, are often regarded with that absorption in forms and qualities, or object-directedness, that people give as a matter of course to art objects.[23]

That which distinguishes art works, then, from works of nature and objects that are merely tools or machines is their fictive character:

The fictive character consists in a false seeming (a playfully false seeming, not a deception), in purporting to be something it isn't, in putting on an act or show. . . . I include the cheerful melody that trips along as though it had not a care in the world, somewhat like a person, though not really one — moving in a time that is not the time of the physical world. . . . The fictive character of art works . . . enables them to feature, to flaunt, the expressive or aesthetic qualities that are in a *special* way our mark on the world around us.[24]

Through the creation of art works, the earth is humanized. But if art works are to carry out their function of reconciliation of humans with their world, they must be allowed to occupy their own special field of influence:

We have to approach them in something like a suppliant mood, setting aside for the moment concerns about their cultural connections, their causes and effects — though not, of course, their semiotic aspects, their meanings and references, when such they have — if they are to realize their potentialities and serve us well in their fashion.[25]

6. *Music is not capable of pointing beyond itself to specific events, emotions, images, or psychological states.*

Following the publication of the 1958 *Aesthetics,* Beardsley expressed dissatisfaction with popularly accepted theories of musical meaning. In his early book Beardsley examined the signification and expression theories. He suggested that music does not essentially function as a natural sign, whose reference is established by cause and effect, or as a conventional sign, whose reference is commonly agreed upon. Nor does music "express" particular psychological states or emotions.[26]

In *Aesthetics,* Beardsley was able to propose the first stages of an alternative explanation:

A musical passage is a *process,* and so is a sequence of ideas and feelings that passes through a person's mind. Qualitatively these processes are very different in many respects: there is nothing in music to correspond to the distinction between the thought of a triangle and the thought of a circle, or between disgust and distaste. But music and mental life both have features that belong to process as such: tempo, variations of intensity, impulsiveness, relaxation and tension, crescendo and diminuendo.[27]

Music, then, is no symbol of time or process, mental or physical, . . . it *is* process. And perhaps we can say it is the closest thing to pure process, to happening as such, to change abstracted from anything that changes, so that it is something whose course and destiny we can follow with the most exact and scrupulous and concentric attention, undistracted by reflections of our normal joys or woes, or by clues and implications for our safety or success.[28]

Those musical qualities that *do* resemble qualities of human beings, or their states of mind, traits, actions, or activities may be called *human qualities*.[29] Beardsley suggested that metaphors, carefully applied, can help us to name these human (regional) qualities, since we have no other suitable language tool for describing our existence in art works. For example, in an early attempt Beardsley coined the term *kinetic pattern* to describe the most fundamental aspect of musical form. He defined kinetic pattern as the pattern of variation in intensity of movement, or propulsion, in a composition. Beardsley proposed experiential metaphors to identify four qualities of kinetic pattern commonly perceived in Western traditional music: *introduction quality* — the music sounds promissory of something coming up; *conclusion quality* — a sense of approaching finality; *exhibition quality* — a sense that an important musical event is happening "right now"; and *transition quality* — the music introduces a sense of temporary uncertainty or inconclusiveness, and seems to be on foot from one exhibition to another.[30]

There is potential danger in using metaphors in this way. They could be misunderstood to claim that music depicts, expresses, or refers to feelings and ideas. A distinction therefore must be maintained "between *describing* music as having certain human qualities and *interpreting* music as signifying or referring to the things they resemble."[31]

7. *Music is uniquely qualified to provide us with patterns, or modes, of continuation.*

Late in his career, Beardsley discussed again at length the nature of music's significance for people. In the 1981 essay "Understanding

Music" he further developed the idea of music as process or change: "Music is change, and in a sense it is nothing more than change in its myriad forms and ways, and in this respect it is a mirror or match for some of the most fundamental features of our personal lives and social histories."[32] "Music, we might say, is in essence *continuation:* the question is always where it will take us next."[33] Both change and lack of change are modes, or patterns, of continuation: "That something remains constant (for some time) is a fundamental and pervasive character of our experience, too."[34]

In music, it is the modes of continuation that have fictive character. Although nothing is *really* happening to the listener, the perceived continuations nevertheless have power to affect him or her because:

> Suspense is disturbing in whatever form it assumes, and the release from it correspondingly heartening and gladdening. So, too, disintegration is threatening, reversal astonishing, loss of power and drive unsettling, delayed fulfillment anxiety-producing, missed opportunity poignant; but growth is encouraging, revival inspiriting, arrival satisfying.[35]

This is why a person can be moved again and again by the same music work; the special kinds of continuation it exhibits can be full of significance even when one knows it by heart.

Monroe Beardsley concluded "Understanding Music" by suggesting, tentatively, that music may have the power to instruct us:

> The music-work does not need to refer to anything else besides its own aesthetically notable qualities in order to play its role in helping us understand our world and cope with it. Here is where the infinite subtlety, variety, and plasticity of music come into play. Music can make extremely delicate distinctions between kinds of continuation, between two slightly different forms of ambiguity or of headlong rushing or of growth. It thereby can sharpen our apprehension of such differences, and give us concepts of continuation that we might miss in ordinary experience, under the press of affairs, but yet that we can bring to experience (as "models," perhaps) with fresh perceptiveness and clearer cognitive grasp.[36]

Ellen H. Hostetler

NOTES

1. Monroe C. Beardsley, *Aesthetics: Problems in the Philosophy of Criticism* (New York: Harcourt, Brace, and World, 1958), pp. 457–461.

2. Ibid., p. 77.

3. Ibid., p. 83.

4. Ibid., p. 97.

5. Ibid., p. 83.

6. Ibid., pp. 85–86.

7. Ibid., p. 466.

8. Monroe C. Beardsley, *The Aesthetic Point of View: Selected Essays,* ed., Michael J. Wreen and Donald M. Callen (Ithaca, NY: Cornell University Press, 1982), p. 339.

9. Monroe C. Beardsley, "Aesthetic Experience Regained," *Journal of Aesthetics and Art Criticism* 28 (1969):3–11.

10. Beardsley, *The Aesthetic Point of View,* p. 81.

11. Ibid., pp. 288–289.

12. Monroe C. Beardsley, "Postscript 1980 — Some Old Problems in New Perspectives." Preface to *Aesthetics: Problems in the Philosophy of Criticism,* 2nd ed. (Indianapolis: Hackett, 1981), p. xix.

13. Ibid., p. xix.

14. Beardsley, *The Aesthetic Point of View,* pp. 309–312.

15. Ibid., p. 320.

16. Ibid., p. 106.

17. Monroe C. Beardsley, "On the Creation of Art," in *Aesthetic Inquiry: Essays on Art Criticism and the Philosophy of Art,* ed. Monroe C. Beardsley and Herbert M. Schueller (Belmont, CA: Dickenson, 1967), p. 178.

18. Ibid., p. 183.

19. Ibid., p. 187.

20. Ibid., p. 185.

21. Beardsley, *The Aesthetic Point of View,* p. 368.

22. Beardsley, "Postscript 1980," p. xxv.

23. Ibid.

24. Beardsley, *The Aesthetic Point of View,* pp. 369–370.

25. Ibid., p. 370.

26. Beardsley, *Aesthetics,* pp. 325–338.

27. Ibid., p. 334.

28. Ibid., p. 338.

29. Monroe C. Beardsley, "Understanding Music" in *On Criticizing Music: Five Philosophical Perspectives,* ed. Kingsley Price (Baltimore: Johns Hopkins University Press, 1981), p. 60.

30. Beardsley, *Aesthetics,* pp. 184–187.

31. Beardsley, "Understanding Music," p. 60.

32. Ibid., p. 70.

33. Ibid.

34. Ibid., p. 71.

35. Ibid.

36. Ibid., p. 72.

LEONARD BERNSTEIN
(1918–1990)

SOURCES

In addition to his work as a conductor, composer, pianist, and educator, Leonard Bernstein lectured extensively to the American public, particularly through the medium of television. Most of Bernstein's writings were drawn from the transcripts of his lectures: *The Joy of Music* (1959), *The Infinite Variety of Music* (1966), and *The Unanswered Question* (1976). He also published a collection of his works entitled *Findings* (1982). Although Bernstein expressed his viewpoints on the musical experience throughout all of his books, one of the most well known (and controversial) of these is *The Unanswered Question*. This book is based on six Charles Eliot Norton Lectures that Bernstein delivered at Harvard University in 1973.

GENERAL ORIENTATION TO MUSICAL EXPERIENCE

Leonard Bernstein's lectures and writings were directed primarily toward the general public. He was able to communicate with his audience from the perspective of the conductor, performer, and composer. Bernstein's discussions reflected his extensive musical knowledge, as well as his understanding of a broad range of subjects;

---

throughout his works, he drew on the writings of philosophers, aestheticians, psychologists, and poets.

In his first publication, *The Joy of Music,* Bernstein described how difficult it is to define the nature of the musical experience:

> We bumble. We imitate scientific method in our attempts to explain magic phenomena by fact, forces, mass, energy. But we simply can't explain human reaction to these phenomena. Science can "explain" thunderstorms, but can it "explain" the fear with which people react to them? And even if it can, in psychology's admittedly unsatisfactory terminology, how does science explain the *glory* we feel in a thunderstorm? . . . Only artists can explain magic; . . . the only way one can really say anything about music is to write music.
>
> Still, we go on trying to shed some light on the mystery. There is a human urge to clarify, rationalize, justify, analyze, limit, describe.[1]

Throughout his career, Leonard Bernstein worked toward understanding the elusive nature of the musical experience. He also stressed the importance of the role of music education in preparing the public "to receive the larger musical experience . . . to have the passion to probe ever more deeply."[2]

Bernstein's thinking on the musical experience was greatly influenced by the work of linguist Noam Chomsky. Chomsky has developed a hypothesis of an innate grammatical competence, a genetically endowed language faculty which is universal. He differentiates between the surface and deep structures of language and proposes that, at a deep level, all languages are based on the same structure. The literal or surface structure of the language is derived from deep structures through the use of *transformation rules,* and the relationships among the constituent parts are depicted through *immediate constituent tree* notation. Chomsky believes that the study of the structure of language reveals universal principles not only about language, but also about the workings of the human mind. (See *Language and Mind,* p. 288, for more on Chomsky's theories.)

In *The Unanswered Question* lectures, Bernstein applied Chomsky's linguistic theories of language to his own theories on the musical experience. He observed that music, like language, is a species-specific phenomenon, characteristic only of human beings. Similar to the idea of a universal grammar underlying human speech, Bernstein proposed that there is "a worldwide, inborn musical grammar."[3] In suggesting a more interdisciplinary approach to music, he asked, "Why not a study of musico-linguistics, just as there already exists a psycho-linguistics and socio-linguistics?"[4] Bernstein has been criticized for the ideas he presented, and his Norton Lectures have been the subject of a great deal of attention.

Many of Bernstein's previous writings reflected an underlying concern for the "Unanswered question" that he posed in his lectures at Harvard — "Whither music?"[5] Throughout his career, Bernstein grappled with the issues surrounding the direction of contemporary music and the use of avant-garde compositional techniques by composers such as John Cage and Arnold Schoenberg. In *The Joy of Music,* he raised the following three questions: (1) "Is this kind of music [serialism] denying a basic law of nature when it denies tonality?" (2) "Is the human ear equipped to take it all in?" and (3) "If the human ear can take it in, will the heart be moved?"[6]

In *The Infinite Variety of Music,* Bernstein arrived at the "inescapable conclusion" that "all forms that we have ever known — plain chant, motet, fugue, or sonata — have always been conceived in *tonality. . . .* This sense, I believe, is built into the human organism."[7] Furthermore, he noted: "As a conductor, I am fascinated by, and wide open to, every new sound-image that comes along; but as a composer I am committed to tonality. Here is a conflict, indeed, and my attempt to resolve it is, quite literally, my most profound musical experience."[8] In *The Unanswered Question* Bernstein brought a new perspective to his dilemma on contemporary music. Through his discovery of "the Chomsky connection," Bernstein reaffirmed his position in favor of tonality.

FEATURES OF MUSICAL EXPERIENCE

1. *The musical experience has an inherent meaning that is purely musical.*
Bernstein articulated the hazards in two approaches to helping people understand music — the music appreciation racket (Type A) and the overly technical discussion (Type B). He called Type A "the birds-bees-and-rivulets variety, which invokes anything at all under

the sun as long as it is extra-musical."[9] Although Bernstein found anecdotes, analogies, or figures of speech helpful, he used the referential devices only to make "the music clearer, more simply accessible, and not just to entertain or — much worse — to take the listener's mind *off* the music, as the Racket does."[10]

The Type B musical experience involves analysis:

> A laudably serious endeavor, but it is as dull as Type A is coy. It is the now-comes-the-theme-upside-down-in-the-second-oboe variety. A guaranteed soporific. What it does, ultimately, is to supply you with a road map of themes . . . but again it tells us nothing about music except those superficial geographical facts.[11]

Bernstein noted that musical analysis should be concerned with *musical* meaning — "if we are to try to 'explain' music, we must explain the *music*, not the whole array of appreciators' extra-musical notions which have grown like parasites around it."[12] The focus of the musical experience should always remain within the music itself:

> Call the opening of Beethoven's Fifth Symphony "Fate Knocking at the Door," or "The Morse Code Call to Victory," and you still have three G's and an E-flat. That's *all* you have. Through some freak in the human animal, these four notes, in their particular rhythmic pattern, have the power to produce a substantial effect on us.[13]

2. In the musical experience, the composer communicates with the listener.
Bernstein did not use the term "communicate" in the traditional sense:

> I wish there were a better word for *communication;* I mean by it the tenderness we feel when we recognize and share with another human being a deep, unnameable, elusive emotional shape or shade. That is really what a composer is saying in his music: *has this ever happened to you? Haven't you experienced this same tone, insight, shock, anxiety, release?* And when you react to ("like") a piece of music, you are simply replying to the composer, *yes.*[14]

In his communication with the listener, the composer is never literal and can never be factual. Bernstein emphasized that "you can't state facts with F sharps. You can't write music that is going to inform anybody about anything, and, in fact, you can't write music that is even going to describe anything unless I tell you what I want the music to be describing."[15]

What the composer is saying to the listener must be "emotional" or, more specifically, an emotion recollected. Bernstein wanted to dispel the notion that agitated music is written by an agitated composer, or despairing music comes from a desperate composer. Rather, he stressed that concentration and hard work ("not inspiration but perspiration"[16]) are required to work an idea into a complete form.

3. *The experience of musical creation arises from man's unconscious.*

In the process of creating a work of art, the composer needs to achieve "the trancelike, out-of-mind state for anything really important to emerge."[17] The act of creating can begin only when the composer's level of consciousness is lowered; artistic inspiration cannot result from a deliberate effort or from the "thinking, intellectualized, censoring, controlled part" of the brain.[18]

Once the composer has reached this unconscious state, the utmost that can be achieved is "a totality, a Gestalt, a work."[19] Once composers have the conception or a vision of the totality, all they have to do is "let it come and guide it along."[20] Bernstein then listed hierarchically the other possibilities that can emerge from a trance: a general climate, or atmosphere, without the formal structure found in the total vision; a theme, the basic idea or motive to be developed; a tune, which is less desirable because it cannot be developed; a harmonic progression or some other type of fragment of an idea or effect. The challenge for the creator is to remain conscious enough to be able to recall the ideas that have emerged during unconsciousness.[21]

Bernstein cited a number of nonmusical aspects that influence the artistic conception. Although music is an abstract art that operates independently of nonmusical matters, there are nonetheless factors that enter the mind during the trance — the audience, nationalism, prevailing trends, the critics, the society and social structure, other works of art, a specific performer, conductor, or orchestra, and finally, self-criticism. The composer must find a balance between the nonmusical and musical factors and prevent these external forces from interfering with the unconscious state.[22]

In essence, Bernstein believes that the creative process remains a mystery: "Please, God, leave us this one mystery, unsolved: why man creates. The minute that one is solved, I fear art will cease to be. . . . [Artists] write, they paint, they perform, produce, whatever, because life to them is inconceivable without doing so. . . . it is for that mad compulsion, that unmotivated persistence, that divine drive."[23]

4. *Like language, the musical experience can be studied through three areas: phonology, syntax, and semantics.*

Music phonology. Phonology is the study of the basic sound units of a language; "all languages share certain 'phonemes' in common, that is, minimal speech units that arise naturally from the physiological structure of our mouths, throats, and noses."[24] The field of inquiry devoted to exploring the common origin of human language is entitled *monogenesis.*

In his discussion of the adage that "music is heightened speech," Bernstein attributed the heightening to intensified emotion. The deepest universals shared by mankind are emotions or affects. "And in the sense that music may express those affective goings-on, then it must indeed be a universal language."[25]

In answering the questions of "where do the notes come from?" and "why just those notes?" Bernstein found an explanation in the "built-in, preordained universal known as the harmonic series."[26] He believed that "the innate musical-grammatical competence which we may all possess universally"[27] is based upon our ability to construe the overtone series. Just as different cultures of the world have constructed a large number of grammars or languages from the basic monogentic materials, various cultures have also constructed musical tongues from their common origins.[28] Bernstein hypothesized that "*all* music — whether folk, pop, symphonic, modal, tonal, atonal, polytonal, microtonal, well-tempered or ill-tempered, music from the distant past or the imminent future — all of it has a common origin in the universal phenomenon of the harmonic series."[29]

Musical syntax. Syntax is the study of the rules that govern the structure of language, how sounds are grouped into words and sentences. As Noam Chomsky began working with the existing concepts of grammatical analysis, he found them to be inadequate in explaining certain relationships. For example, the following sentences appear quite different, yet they all possess the same basic meaning: *The man hit the ball; The ball was hit by the man; It was the man who hit the ball; It was the ball that was hit by the man.* Chomsky gradually developed a theory of transformational grammar where he attempts to explain how the surface structures of sentences are derived from a deeper level of meaning. Chomsky postulates that this process is universal to all languages and all human beings; thus, through the study of syntax, he hopes to reveal insights into the fundamental workings of the human mind.

Bernstein discussed in greater detail several concepts of syntax which he later applied to music. *Transformation* is defined as "how the tiniest basic concepts, or units of information, buried in the depths of the mind, are selected, combined, connected, and refined, and make their way up from the 'neural net' to a mental surface where they are expressible."[30] Bernstein stressed that this is a *creative* process, "responsible for all the varieties of natural human speech, from a child's sentences to the most intricate word patterns of Henry James."[31]

According to the system of transformational grammar, several levels of language structure must be differentiated: the *surface structure* or the actual sentences that are produced, and the deeper structure, which is also called the *underlying string*.

Through various combinations of negative, interrogative, active, and passive transformation, a single underlying string can generate a number of different sentences. For example, an active transformation of the underlying string *Jack + Present tense + Love = Jill* would be *Jack loves Jill*. A negative transformation would be *Jack does not love Jill*; an interrogative transformation would be *Does Jack love Jill?*; a passive transformation would be *Jill is loved by Jack*; a passive plus interrogative transformation would be *Is Jill loved by Jack?*, and so on. Transformational grammar accounts for the ability of children to produce grammatical sentences that they have never heard before.

Bernstein also discussed the transformational process of *deletion*, using as an example the classic Chomsky sentence *Harry persuaded John to take up golf*. This sentence consists of two structural segments: *Harry persuaded John* and *John (to) take up golf*. Because the second *John* is unnecessary, it is deleted. Another example of transformation is *embedding*, which is illustrated through the sentence *John was glad that Harry persuaded him to take up golf.* This sentence consists of three different structural entities that are embedded into each other: (1) John was glad (that), (2) Harry persuaded John, (3) John (to) take up golf. A final example of transformation cited by Bernstein is *pronominalization,* which allows for the substitution of pronouns in place of repeating a name throughout a sentence, thus avoiding awkward sentences such as *John promised that John would do John's homework the minute John finished John's dinner.*

Bernstein then applied these principles to music, demonstrating at the piano how transformational rules such as deletion and embedding can be used in musical composition. (Refer to Bernstein's second chapter in *The Unanswered Question,* "Musical Syntax," for the specific musical examples used to demonstrate these techniques.)

Through the use of the first twenty-one bars from Mozart's Symphony in G Minor, Bernstein explored the relationships between the musical deep structure and the surface structure. The most basic components of music are the *chosen elements* (e.g., pitches, tonalities, meter). From these choices arise the *underlying strings* or the melodic motives and phrases, chordal progressions, rhythmic figures, etc., which are then recombined to create the *deep structure.* Deep structure, or *musical prose,* consists of the underlying strings and was defined by Bernstein as "the raw material waiting to be transformed into art."[32] This then becomes the surface structure or the music itself.

Bernstein noted the way in which Mozart created a sense of ambiguity in his music, how a composer deliberately takes our universal instinct of symmetry and plays with it through transformational processes such as deletion and embedding.[33] In a sense, Bernstein was discussing how art purposely violates the expectations of the perceiver, using the rules of transformational grammar to create a controlled ambiguity: "These ambiguities are beautiful. They are germane to all artistic creation. They enrich our aesthetic response, whether in music, poetry, painting or whatever, by providing more than one way of perceiving the aesthetic surface."[34]

Bernstein also pointed out that only music can present a type of ambiguity called *contrapuntal syntax.* This involves the perception of two different syntactic versions of the same idea simultaneously, made possible through the technique of counterpoint.

In his discussion of the analogies between language and art, Bernstein proposed the following:

LANGUAGE		MUSIC	
D.	Super-surface structure (poetry)	D.	Surface structure (music)
C.	Surface structure (prose)	C.	Deep structure ("prose")
B.	Underlying strings (deep structure)	B.	Underlying strings
A.	Chosen elements	A.	Chosen elements

For language to become art, Bernstein suggested that the linguistic surface structures must be transformed again into what he called "a new super-surface, an *aesthetic* surface,"[35] namely poetry. When prose becomes poetry, its structure more closely resembles the musical surface structure. Unlike language, which has both a communicative and an aesthetic function, music has an aesthetic function only. For that reason, musical surface structure is not equatable with linguistic surface structure, until the language is transformed to its super-surface structure.

Musical semantics. Semantics is the study of meaning, and Bernstein was primarily concerned with semantic ambiguity. For example, the sentence *the whole town was populated by old men and women* can be construed in different ways. When confronted with semantic ambiguity, e.g., *Juliet is the sun,* the human mind can either reject the sentence as illogical or find another level of meaning — a poetic level. "In other words, something in the mind intuits a *metaphorical* meaning; . . . metaphor is our key to understanding."[36] For music, there is no need to undergo this extra step in the transformational process, because "music *already exists in the poetic sense.* It's all art from the first note on."[37]

In his discussion of musical meaning, Bernstein repeated many of the ideas stated earlier in the paper on intrinsic and extrinsic meanings. He distinguished between musical meaning and expression:

> But when music "expresses" something to me, it is something I am feeling, and the same is true of you and of every listener. We feel passion, we feel glory, we feel mystery, we *feel something.* And here

we are in trouble; because we cannot report our precise feelings in scientific terms; we can report them only subjectively.[38]

According to Bernstein, everyone agrees that music does possess the power of expressivity, and human beings innately possess the capacity to respond to it. Although we are unsure of what music expresses, we do know how music expresses it: "In any sense in which music can be considered a language . . . it is a totally *metaphorical* language . . . because of its specific and far-reaching metaphorical powers — [music] can name the unnameable, and communicate the unknowable."[39] Bernstein proposed that all metaphors, verbal or musical, are derived through transformational processes, and with this he restated his hypothesis — "is it not conceivable that there exists an innate universal grammar of musical metaphor?"[40] Bernstein suggested that the answer is "an overwhelming yes."[41]

5. *The musical experience has been in a state of "crisis" in the twentieth century, as ambiguity has become "sheer vagueness."*

Bernstein posed the question: "But how ambiguous can you get before the clarity of musical meaning is lost altogether?"[42] He pointed in particular to the music of Arnold Schoenberg, whose musical "rules" were not based on innate awareness, on the intuition of tonal relationships: "They are like rules of an artificial language, and therefore must be learned."[43] But, according to Bernstein, a sense of tonality pervades some of Schoenberg's best works: "Even when it's not demonstrably present, it still haunts those works by its conspicuous absence."[44] He suggested that as long as the twelve tones used by Schoenberg are the same twelve tones that are derived from the natural harmonic series, one cannot destroy their inherent tonal relationships.[45] He proposed the following questions:

How does the wild thought strike you that *all* music is ultimately and basically tonal, even when it's nontonal?[46]

Is it not perhaps that the ambiguity [of Schoenberg] is simply too huge to be grasped, too self-negating to be perceived with our human ears, ears which are after all tuned to our innate predispositions, in spite of all conditionings or reinforcements? Let's put it another way: have we not finally stumbled on an ambiguity that cannot produce aesthetically positive results?[47]

Bernstein believed that contemporary music had reached a point of rediscovery and the reacceptance of tonality: "And I believe that no matter how serial, or stochastic, or otherwise intellectualized music may be, it can always qualify as poetry as long as it is rooted in the earth"[48] (for Bernstein, the source from which tonality springs)."

Judy Iwata Bundra

NOTES

1. Leonard Bernstein, *The Joy of Music* (New York: Simon and Schuster, 1959), p. 13.

2. Leonard Bernstein, *Findings* (New York: Simon and Schuster, 1982), p. 334.

3. Ibid., p. 7.

4. Ibid., p. 9.

5. Allan Keiler, "Bernstein's 'The Unanswered Question' and the Problem of Musical Competence," *Musical Quarterly* 64 (1978): 195–222.

6. Bernstein, *The Joy of Music*, p. 205.

7. Leonard Bernstein, *The Infinite Variety of Music* (New York: Simon and Schuster, 1966), p. 12.

8. Ibid., p. 142.

9. Bernstein, *The Joy of Music*, p. 14.

10. Ibid.

11. Ibid.

12. Ibid., p. 16.

13. Bernstein, *Findings*, p. 106.

14. Bernstein, *Infinite Variety*, p. 11.

15. Ibid., pp. 273–274.

16. Bernstein, *Infinite Variety*, pp. 274–275.

17. Ibid., p. 269.

18. Ibid.

19. Ibid.

20. Ibid.

21. Ibid., pp. 269–271.

22. Ibid., pp. 276–280.

23. Bernstein, *Findings*, p. 229.

24. Leonard Bernstein, *The Unanswered Question* (Cambridge, MA: Harvard University Press, 1976), p. 11.

25. Ibid., p. 23.

26. Ibid., p. 17.

27. Ibid., p. 29.

28. Ibid., p. 31.

29. Ibid., p. 33.

30. Ibid., p. 71.

31. Ibid., p. 70.

32. Ibid., p. 81.

33. Ibid., p. 105.

34. Ibid., p. 109.

35. Ibid., p. 79.

36. Ibid., p. 123.

37. Ibid., p. 128.

38. Ibid., p. 135.

39. Ibid., p. 139.

40. Ibid., p. 140.

41. Ibid., p. 141.

42. Ibid., p. 238.

43. Ibid., p. 283.

44. Ibid., p. 289.

45. Ibid.

46. Ibid., p. 291.

47. Ibid., p. 297.

48. Ibid., p. 424.

JOHN BLACKING
(1928–   )

SOURCES

John Blacking, musician and social anthropologist, has written about musical experience from a unique perspective. Because of his encounters with the peoples of Malaya, China, and India as well as experiences that occurred in the course of ethnomusicological field work among the Venda people of South Africa, he was forced to reassess his culture and cultural values. *How Musical Is Man?* (1973) serves as the focal question and point of departure for much of Blacking's thought on musical experience. He describes the text as "not a scholarly study," but as an attempt to reconcile his diverse experiences in music making. Other articles that focus on the musical experience include "The Study of Man as Music Maker" (1979), "Towards a Theory of Musical Competence" (1971), and "Can Musical Universals Be Heard?" (1975).

GENERAL ORIENTATION TO MUSICAL EXPERIENCE

In *How Musical Is Man?*, Blacking states that since musical behavior (like linguistic behavior) is species-specific to man, much can be learned about humanity through the study of music. As an anthropologist, Blacking holds that "music is a product of the behavior of human groups, whether formal or informal: it is humanly organized sound."[1] Music is organized into socially acceptable patterns. It cannot be analyzed apart from the society and culture of which it is a part. No musical style has "its own terms." Its terms "are the terms of its society and culture, and of the bodies of the human beings who listen to it, and create it, and perform it."[2]

Blacking again refers to extra-musical factors when considering the value and function of music. The worth of music is embedded in the human experiences that surround its creation as well as the functions and effects of the musical product in society. The chief function of music is "to involve people in shared experiences within the framework of their cultural experience."[3] Blacking believes that analyzing music in terms of social functions and cognitive processes does not diminish the importance of music.

Music confirms what is already present in society and culture, adding nothing new except patterns of sound. Therefore, any analysis of music must begin with an analysis of the social situation that generates the music. Blacking embraces the idea that artistic enjoyment is based essentially on a mental reaction to form. However, these forms are products of human minds whose habits of working are "a synthesis of given, universal systems of operation and acquired, cultural patterns of expression."[4] Through music, patterns of culture and society emerge in the shape of "humanly organized sound."[5]

While Blacking argues strongly that music cannot escape the "stamp" of the society in which it is composed, he believes that musical systems may still be compared. Our ability to be moved by the music of cultures to which we do not belong confirms the fact that music can transcend both time and culture. This is due to "the fact that at the level of deep structures in music there are elements that are common to the human psyche, although they may not appear in the surface structures."[6] Blacking asserts that the idea of "feeling in music" is one way in which deep structures have been explained. The most deeply felt performances of a pieces of music are those that approach the feeling of the composers when they began to capture their individual experiences in musical form. The right feeling may be captured by finding the right movement. By sharing a similar rhythmic stirring in the body, performer and composer may share "the most important thing about music, that which is in the human body and which is universal to all men."[7]

FEATURES OF MUSICAL EXPERIENCE

1. *The musical experience is dependent upon the development of listening skills.*

Blacking repeatedly asserts that listening is often ignored and underrated as an aspect of musical ability. He declares that "listening to music, like comprehending verbal language, is as much a creative act as making it."[8] A musical tradition flourishes only when performers and critical listeners interact.

Blacking acknowledges two types of listening experience. *External listening* refers to perception acquired in the course of social and cultural experience. *Inner listening,* a hypothetical process of hearing music in the head, is crucial to the discriminating performance of music. This phenomenon must take place before a musical performance can be authentically and sensitively rendered.[9] Blacking repeatedly stresses that in societies where music is not notated, accurate and informed listening is as important a measure of musical ability as is performance.

2. *The musical experience is reliant upon two specific kinds of musical competence.*

Blacking describes musical ability as a qualitative estimation of an individual's musical competence as a composer and/or performer, but most particularly as a listener. He describes two specific kinds of musical competence. *Particular musical competence* refers to the "innate or learned capacity to hear and create the patterns of sound which are recognized as music in the context of a particular cultural tradition."[10] *Universal musical competence* corresponds to the same capacities, but places them within the context of all cultural traditions.[11]

3. *The musical experience can be a powerful social encounter.*

All musical performance is guided by a system of rules for ordering sounds. These rules are agreed upon by a group of people and define the music of that culture. According to Blacking, the power of music is largely revealed in the social experience generated by its performance. Musical performance creates a "quasi-ritual association and concentration of human bodies in time and space."[12] While other activities may enable humans to experience a heightened awareness or altered state of consciousness, Blacking views musical performance as a more potent experience. This is due to the special relationship between people and bodily coordinations that are required for musical performance.

4. *The musical experience involves creativity that must be examined in terms of social, musical, and cognitive processes.*

Blacking describes the creation of music as "a sharing of inner feelings in a social context through extensions of body movement, in which certain species-specific capabilities are modified and extended through social and cultural experience."[13] The creative process will not always be found in a study of the surface structures of music, for many of the generative factors are not musical. Musical creativity is to be described and studied in terms of social, musical, and cognitive processes. Every composer has a "basic cognitive system that sets its stamp on his major works. . . . [This cognitive system] includes all cerebral activity involved in his motor coordination, feelings, and cultural experiences, as well as his social, intellectual, and musical activities."[14]

5. *The musical experience creates a world of virtual time.*

An essential quality of music is its power to create another world of virtual time. Through involvement in musical activities, humans create with their bodies "a special world of time distinct from the time cycles of natural seasons and of cultural events."[15]

Anne Reisner Armetta

NOTES

1. John Blacking, *How Musical Is Man?* (Seattle: University of Washington Press, 1973) p. 10.

2. Ibid., p. 25.

3. Ibid., p. 28.

4. Ibid., p. 73.

5. Ibid.

6. Ibid., p. 109.

7. Ibid., p. 111.

8. John Blacking, "The Study of Man as Music Maker," in *The Performing Arts,* ed. John Blacking and Joann Kealiinohomoku (The Hague: Mouton, 1979), p. 11.

9. John Blacking, "Towards a Theory of Musical Competence," in *Man: Anthropological Essays to O. F. Raum,* ed. E. J. DeJager (Cape Town, South Africa: C. Struik, 1971), pp. 23–24.

10. Ibid., p. 21.

11. Ibid.

12. John Blacking, "Can Musical Universals Be Heard?" *The Worlds of Music* 19 (1975), p. 16.

13. Blacking, "The Study of Man as Music Maker," p. 6.

14. Blacking, *How Musical Is Man?* p. 24.

15. Blacking, "Towards a Theory of Musical Competence," p. 25.

HARRY S. BROUDY
(1905–   )

SOURCES

Harry S. Broudy is professor emeritus of the philosophy of education at the University of Illinois. In 1972, Broudy wrote *Enlightened Cherishing: An Essay on Aesthetic Education* as part of the Kappa Delta Pi Lecture Series. Other writings representative of his work include *Paradox and Promise: Essays on American Life and Education* (1961), *Democracy and Excellence in American Secondary Education* (1964), *Exemplars of Teaching Method* (1965), *The Real World of the Public Schools* (1972), *Truth and Credibility: The Citizen's Dilemma* (1981), and *The Role of Imagery in Learning* (1987). In addition to these books, Broudy has written extensively for various education journals.

GENERAL ORIENTATION TO AESTHETIC EXPERIENCE

As a philosopher of education, Broudy has devoted much of his career to the examination of the aesthetic experience and its place in the educational process. He argues that, in the classroom, attention to the affective domain is needed to balance the predominant focus on the conceptual domains of learning. The aesthetic realm, given its concern with the beautiful, can not only provide a well-balanced education but can also enhance the quality of life for the student.[1]

The quotations in this chapter from Harry S. Broudy's *Enlightened Cherishing: An Essay on Aesthetic Education* are reprinted with permission of the University of Illinois Press.

Because there seemed to be no general consensus as to the meaning or use of the term *aesthetic education,* Broudy proposed the following five characteristics of aesthetic education as being those often associated with it, with more or less agreement by its advocates about each of the five:

1. An intent to educate in more than one of the arts and therewith a belief that the several arts have some common features that can be used to give structure to a program of aesthetic education.

2. A hope that aesthetic education will achieve a solid position (as a required subject) in the curriculum of the public schools, a status it has not achieved through existing programs in arts education.

3. A belief that aesthetic education is possible and desirable for the total school population and need not be restricted to pupils with special talent.

4. There is less agreement among the advocates of aesthetic education on the degree to which it should be linked with extra-aesthetic (moral, religious, political, economic, civic) values. The lack of agreement would extend to the use of aesthetic materials for facilitating the teaching of other subjects and the integration of aesthetic education with other fields of instruction.

5. The least agreement is to be found in the aesthetic and education theories by which the objectives of and approaches to aesthetic education are explicated and justified.[2]

When justifying arts education, Broudy is careful to base his arguments on the intrinsic value of the art form and not upon the contribution of the arts to other aspects of schooling. He states that aesthetic experience is as pervasive as cognitive and practical activities and that the skills of aesthetic perception, if properly cultivated, can change the quality of those experiences. Broudy admits that there are inherent difficulties that make it a challenge to approach the aesthetic experience. Chief among these is the fact that the connection between the work of the imagination and that of the intellect has been neglected. Indeed, by many it has been forgotten. It is precisely because of this link that Broudy so strongly postulates the need for arts education in the academic curriculum. Mere exposure to the arts (a common occurrence in our society) is not enough; aesthetic education must seek to raise the aesthetic consciousness of the student.[3]

Convinced that the aesthetic mode of experience is sufficiently distinctive to call for a special curriculum that should be required of all students and that the desired outcomes of such a curriculum cannot be achieved informally, Broudy outlines the goals of aesthetic education based on the peculiarities of the aesthetic experience. First among these goals is to improve the ability of the student to perceive aesthetic import in sensory images or patterns. Such perception finds human qualities (tension, conflict, balance, rhythm) that are characteristic of our life processes in sounds, gestures, colors, and shapes (where, common sense tells us, there should be no such human feelings). Broudy sees aesthetic education as bringing the learner to the point of perceiving (not necessarily performing), as the artist does in as many media as possible. Having accomplished this, appreciation, criticism, and performance are desirable additions to the abilities of the student. However, these must be preceded by perceptual habits if they are to be authentic.

It is not the goal of aesthetic education to provide a reliable guide to coping with the ordinary problems of life, nor is it designed as a source of knowledge about the ways in which things, persons, or institutions behave. Rather, a goal of aesthetic education is to engage a capacity of the human mind in an interesting, stimulating, and often liberating way. As inhabitants of a technological society that militates against the richness of sensory stimulation and the subtlety of artistic variation and nuance, we need to be excited by works of art that bring to us what John Dewey called a consummatory quality (that is, a basic unity resulting from conflict, climax, and resolution).[4] Otherwise, boredom and poverty of imagination and feeling will deprive us of zest, sympathy, and empathy.

For aesthetic education to have significance for us as a whole, it is necessary for those in the profession to make distinctions between the skills of *expression* and *impression* and between *serious art* and *popular art*. One goal of arts education is to assist the student in efforts of self-expression through artistic media. While the school should not be expected to produce professional artists (though it may help identify those who display an aptitude for such a career), the goal of freeing the individual for creative activity, uninhibited by stringent technical rules and standards, should remain paramount. Such teaching may reveal talent for a career in art, or it may develop resources for a lifelong hobby. But more generally, and perhaps more importantly, it may develop sensitivity to the manifold dimensions of the aesthetic experience. In order to make an image of feeling one must employ techniques that will give form to the sensory content, and this process of objectification of feeling is likely to result in a deepened understanding of the formal properties and technical peculiarities of the medium.[5]

The role of aesthetic education in the development of skills of impression is quite different, however. Whereas opportunities for creative activities are not systematically available outside the classroom, one need not enroll in school to be attentive to the appearance of things. Our senses are constantly besieged by stimuli. In fact, people of our society are inundated with heavy doses of popular and folk art that take no special training to perceive. For Broudy, the task of aesthetic education is to put the student in touch with serious art in order to enhance aesthetic consciousness:

> Indeed, we do not participate in a culture unless we share its aesthetic expressions. Those who could not resonate comfortably to the various degrees of hardness of rock music probably could not resonate to the young who vibrated with it. Today, when popular art serves a mass market, it is perforce designed to be assimilated without special training. For what then do we need the school in the skills of impression? To properly perceive the serious arts, of course.
>
> All I mean by serious art are objects that are produced with some concern for artistic merit and judged worthy of study by the critics, scholars, and artists of a given period. Serious art tends to be esoteric, complex, artificial, sophisticated and the talk about it equally so. It thus tends to elude the general public that is not privy to what counts in perceiving and judging it.[6]

Broudy also addresses the issue of selecting serious works of art for study in the classroom. The questions of which artistic creations merit the attention of the student and what authority is consulted in the making of such decisions are important to Broudy because he feels that art objects are value-laden and carry the potential of influencing the general conduct of the student. Aesthetic values may, indeed, influence nonaesthetic values. For Broudy, arts education is inextricably linked with value education.

The solution to these questions lies in the appeal to the "authority structure" of the discipline; that is, to those credentialed members of the discipline who carry on investigations in that field, who have been trained by credentialed members of that discipline, and who have been approved by their credentialed peers. Only the judgment of the connoisseur can be trusted in the matter of establishing standards in art. The practical outcome of this is that the mode of perception taught to students will be the same as that used by previous practitioners of the arts. Further, this credentialed authority structure will provide exemplars in each genre of art that are worthy of extended study.[7]

For Broudy, exemplars in art are those classics that are models from which principles of aesthetic quality may be extracted. Because these works may not align with the taste of the general public, a curriculum that is founded upon such works may be called elitist by some, even though the works are equally accessible by people of all races, creeds, colors, and economic strata. By Broudy's definition, exemplars are classics that (1) portray values of a particular period with unusual clarity, (2) mark a transition between periods, or (3) presage development of a future period.[8]

Exemplars can maintain their status as models only as long as their metaphorical dimensions are available to the general public. In recent years, Broudy has proposed a method for the viewing of visual arts that trains children in the classroom to locate and identify the aesthetic properties of the work of art. This method, known as *aesthetic scanning,* teaches children to make informed responses to aesthetic form by analyzing and discussing its sensory, formal, technical, and expressive properties.

The aesthetic scanning method of teaching has only two stipulations. First, the aesthetic property being discussed must appear phenomenologically in the work of art and, consequently, be accessible to all. Second, the scanner must be able to locate the observed property by describing or pointing to it. This technique for teaching the visual arts may be used with great success by teachers who have a limited art vocabulary and a scant knowledge about the work, its subject, its point of origin, and its medium. Broudy provides tables of initiating and continuing questions to assist classroom teachers in using this method, and he asks only that judgments about the work of art be restricted to the existence or nonexistence of a recognizable property in the work rather than the expressive meaning for the child observing it.[9]

Broudy would direct the attention of the student to those sensuous and formal properties and stylistic characteristics of serious art that would allow the learner to be engaged by and, subsequently, participate in the artistic medium. The object is not the accumulation of meaningless facts about art and artists, but the honing of perceptual skills that will allow for direct aesthetic experience:

> The role of art in aesthetic education is twofold. One is to objectify for perception those metaphors which the imagination of the artist creates. These help the pupil to objectify his own feelings and values. In doing so they expand his value domain, for they reveal life possibilities not available through direct experience. The second role of art is to purify the pupil's imagic store and thereby to make him more conscious of and less satisfied with the stereotyped image and the worn-out metaphor. In this sense it makes pupils more discriminating both about art and about life itself.[10]

FEATURES OF AESTHETIC EXPERIENCE

1. *The aesthetic experience results from sensory perception.*

Regardless of whether an aesthetic object is a natural phenomenon (such as a tree or flower) or a work of art, and regardless of the genre of that artistic creation, the aesthetic object will always be an image or a cluster of images. While the manifestation of the aesthetic image will vary according to the mode of expression, the aesthetic experience will always deal exclusively with imagery as opposed to facts, ideas, or theories. While an aesthetic image may be an image of an idea, it may also be an image of a feeling or a feeling about an idea. The aesthetic experience is, first of all, perceptual in nature in that it requires the recognition of the sensory properties of the aesthetic object.

These sensory properties are those elements that are essential to the aesthetic image. Because the image carries with it a particular value import, it cannot be changed without the consequent change of the aesthetic impact of the object itself. To modify any aspect of an aesthetic object is somehow to alter its sensory import. The aesthetic perception of an object requires that it be perceived as a particular individual entity and in its entirety. This requirement is unique to the aesthetic domain and bears great significance for the aesthetic educator because the ability to apprehend the fullness and richness of the sensory properties of objects is the first step in aesthetic education.[11]

2. *The aesthetic experience results from the formal properties of the aesthetic object.*

The aesthetic image is often powerful in its ability to engage the senses and convey its sensory properties. One way in which this happens is through the form of the aesthetic object; that is, through the arrangement of elements and images in a manner that is peculiar to a given aesthetic object. The form of the expressive image refers to its design or composition and is the result of conscious choices made by the artist. While it is difficult to determine why certain formal arrangements are pleasing to us, we perhaps respond sympathetically to them when they are encountered in an aesthetic object because these designs and rhythms are inherent in nature.

The fact that the artist makes conscious decisions regarding the ordering of artistic elements reflects the pervasive order of natural things, even though life may often seem chaotic and random.[12]

> The artist by selection throws into strong relief rhythms, variations of a theme, balances, and contrasts. He weaves a great variety into a unity, so that it seems as if nothing in it could have been omitted without destroying the whole work. Real life is not that orderly; the sounds of the street are not ordered as in a musical composition. There are perhaps many fine scenes in the world around us, but it takes the artist's eye to detect their pictorial possibilities.
>
> Sensory images or materials arranged for the greatest impact on perception constitute the formal properties of art. Form provides the unity in variety that captures and retains our interest, and to the degree that life fails to provide such unity, art is valued all the more for doing so.[13]

In order to explain why certain formal structures capture and hold our attention, Broudy turns to John Dewey's distinction between experiences and an experience as put forth in *Art as Experience.*

According to Dewey, an experience consists of selected events that are cumulative in their impact, thus creating a distinct beginning, development, climax, and resolution. Further, an experience is characterized by a quality that vividly pervades and unifies it.[14]

3. *The aesthetic experience includes the element of dramatic structure.*
Broudy would add to these stipulations the element of dramatic structure. Because human experience is not typically dramatic in nature, any experience that displays this property will, by virtue of this innate quality, seem inherently vivid and unified, requiring no further justification. Such an experience will have intrinsic value as an experience:[15]

> The search for significance, therefore, goes through the aesthetic route as well as the scientific one. A form of life that has dramatic structure does not guarantee its ultimate goodness for others or even for oneself. Some dramas are tragedies, and some turn out to be obscene comedies, but it is human to prefer that risk to the safety of insignificance. The aesthetically satisfying experience is the opposite of the drab, meaningless, formless, pointless passage of time.[16]

While Broudy is aware that many (perhaps all) aestheticians might have trouble including dramatic structure in aesthetic form, and while he concedes that some artistic creations are devoid of plot, suspense, and climax, he feels that some opposition and resolution must be present, even in a minute proportion, in order to avoid triviality and command some degree of attention from the observer. Sensitivity to this dramatic structure of aesthetic images distinguishes the aesthetically developed person from the undeveloped. This sensitivity lies at the center of the aesthetic experience and is the primary concern of the aesthetic educator.[17]

4. *The aesthetic experience results from the expressiveness of the aesthetic image.*
Broudy defines the expressiveness of the aesthetic image as its value import. He distinguishes two features of expressivity. One is its metaphorical nature; the other is its presentational nature. Expressiveness is simultaneously indirect and direct. The term *metaphor* as used by Broudy refers to the ability of the aesthetic image to present itself as

actually being a particular quality of human experience rather than saying that it is *like* something else. To clarify this matter, Broudy refers to Susanne Langer's distinction between signs and symbols.[18]

The practical demands of the adult life that are so important to daily existence result in a world that is less and less expressive and in people who are less and less sensitive to aesthetic metaphor. The lack of vividness and drama renders life uninteresting and lacking in richness, significance, and opportunities for human valuation. By contrast, the artist is the source of originality and freshness who "draws upon the memory bank of the race" in order to create fresh and apt metaphors. Whatever the artistic medium, the aesthetic creation brings expressiveness to an otherwise mundane existence:

> Accordingly, in aesthetic education we are speaking about the cultivation of the pupil's receptivity to expressiveness via metaphor. This expressiveness is achieved by giving form to a sensory content, creating a surface on which meaning and value import are presented directly for imaginative perception. If works of art have any "messages" — and many a formalist denies that they do — it is because there are similarities between all sorts of objects and ideas. Through these resemblances we discover something important about what to love and what to hate, what to cherish and what to disdain. We learn something about ourselves when we imagine what a rock would feel if it had a mind and soul.[19]

It seems as though it is impossible for Broudy to contemplate the aesthetic experience apart from his own concern for the existential condition of humanity. Seeing the world as largely devoid of artistic expression and the human race as tragically ignorant of the inner workings of expressive form, the fundamental impetus of his career has been to bring students to the realm of artistic achievement and to assist them in perceiving more sensitively and profoundly the aesthetic import of art. That the world is largely devoid of aesthetic sensitivity is, according to Broudy, accounted for by the dominance of our need to perceive practically and intellectually as well as by the unimaginative nature of the artifacts that make up our modern environment. Such pervasive poverty in aesthetic achievement and appreciation is the proper concern of the educational institution and is the most serious problem facing the professional arts educator. The nurturing of

aesthetic sensitivity and the subsequent enjoyment of artistic achievement in a society dominated by utilitarianism is the route by which
humanity can plumb the depths of its own soul:

> Just as it is dangerous to entrust the life of the nation and the world
> to citizens ignorant of good science and technology, so is it danger-
> ous to entrust it to men and women whose feelings and values are
> uncultivated and undisciplined. This is the overriding reason for
> the cultivation of the young in the aesthetic dimension of experi-
> ence. For a good society there must be enlightened cherishing.[20]

Jeffrey E. Wright

NOTES

1. Harry S. Broudy, "Quality Education in the Arts." Unpublished manuscript, pp. 1–2.

2. Harry S. Broudy, "Some Reactions to a Concept of Aesthetic Education," *Journal of Aesthetic Education* (July/October 1976), pp. 29–30.

3. Harry S. Broudy, "Arts Education: Necessary or Just Nice?" *Phi Delta Kappan* (January 1979), pp. 347–348.

4. John Dewey, *Art as Experience* (New York: Capricorn Books, 1958), pp. 35, 37, 41, 56.

5. Harry S. Broudy, "Arts in Education," address delivered to the Annual Confer-ence of the Pennsylvania Music Educator's Association, Pittsburgh, Pennsylvania, January 3, 1974, pp. 1–7.

6. Ibid., p. 8.

7. Harry S. Broudy, *Enlightened Cherishing: An Essay on Aesthetic Education* (Urbana: University of Illinois Press, 1972), pp. 94–104.

8. Harry S. Broudy, *The Role of Imagery in Learning* (Los Angeles: Getty Center for Education in the Arts, 1987), pp. 37–42.

9. Gloria J. Hewett and Jean C. Rush, "Finding Buried Treasure," *Art Education* (January 1987), pp. 41–42.

10. Broudy, *Enlightened Cherishing,* p. 44.

11. Ibid., pp. 29–30.

12. Ibid., pp. 30–31.

13. Ibid., p. 32.

14. Dewey, *Art as Experience,* pp. 35–57.

15. Ibid., pp. 33–35.

16. Ibid., p. 35.

17. Ibid., p. 36.

18. Susanne K. Langer, *Philosophy in a New Key: A Study in the Symbolism of Reason, Rite, and Art* (New York: Mentor Books, 1956), p. 117.

19. Broudy, *Enlightened Cherishing*, pp. 38–44.

20. Ibid., pp. 113–114.

JOHN CAGE
(1912–   )

SOURCES

For several decades, John Cage has been identified with the avant-garde in the United States, gaining recognition as composer, writer, and philosopher. Among his extensive list of essays and lectures, three collections seem most pertinent to his understanding and description of the musical experience. They are *Silence* (1961), *A Year From Monday* (1967), and *Empty Words* (1979). In addition, "A John Cage Reader" (1982) was published as a tribute to Cage on his seventieth birthday.

GENERAL ORIENTATION TO MUSICAL EXPERIENCE

Unlike other writers included in this study, Cage does not directly address the musical experience. Instead, he expresses what he believes is necessary if the musical experience is to take place in the most uninhibited way. With an extensive background in composition, philosophy, and visual art, Cage has become a controversial spokesperson regarding the musical experience. Throughout his career, he has noted that "music — as an activity separated from the rest of life — doesn't enter (his) mind."[1] Cage accepts the ideas set forth by Ananda K. Coomaraswamy in *The Transformation of Nature in Art* (1935), in

The quotations in this chapter from *Silence,* © 1961 by John Cage, Wesleyan University Press, are reprinted with permission of the University Press of New England.

which he states that the function of art is to imitate nature in its manner of operation.[2] Cage is not interested in creating order (music) out of chaos (sound). Rather, he is interested in observing what life has to offer and accepting it:

> And what is the purpose of . . . music? [It is] an affirmation of life, not to bring order out of chaos nor to suggest improvements in creation, but simply a way of waking up to the very life we're living, which is so excellent once one gets one's mind and one's desires out of the way and lets it act of its own accord.[3]

Describing an experience he had while visiting an anechoic chamber at Harvard University, Cage remembered hearing two sounds — one high and one low. An engineer explained the phenomenon to him. The high sound was caused by the operation of his nervous system, and the low sound resulted from the circulation of his blood. This led Cage to realize: "Until I die there will be sounds. And they will continue following my death. One need not fear about the future of music."[4] From this point on, sound and silence (unintended sounds) appeared to him to be the elements of music most analogous to life.

Cage speaks of musical habits or traditions. These include scales, modes, theories of counterpoint and harmony, and the study of timbres (both singly and in combination). Cage refers to these habits as limited sound-producing mechanisms that do not allow for the vast possibilities of such materials as magnetic tape and other contemporary devices for sound production.[5] Regarding the habit of harmony, Cage writes:

> When Schoenberg asked me whether I would devote my life to music, I said, "Of course." After I had been studying with him for two years, Schoenberg said, "In order to write music, you must have a feeling for harmony." I explained to him that I had no feeling for harmony. He then said that I would always encounter an obstacle, that it would be as though I came to a wall through which I could not pass. I said, "In that case I will devote my life to beating my head against that wall."[6]

Since that time, Cage has given up attempts to control sound in order to discover means that allow sounds to be themselves. Sound for the sake of sound (rather than for theories or elements of sentimental human expression) has been his goal. "And sounds, when allowed to be themselves, do not require that those who hear them do so unfeelingly. The opposite is what is meant by response ability."[7]

The feelingful nature of sounds, unique in and of themselves and not tied to any musical line or harmony, has occupied Cage both philosophically and compositionally for his entire career. With regard to the question of "feelings," Cage wonders if these, like emotions, may arise spontaneously from within, or whether they might resemble the likes and dislikes that arise from sense perceptions. He maintains that we must learn to be more "convivial":

> Though the doors will always remain open for the musical expression of personal feelings, what will more and more come through is the expression of the pleasures of conviviality . . . and beyond that a nonintentional expressivity, a being together of sounds and people, . . . a walk . . . in the woods of music, or in the world itself.[8]

> New music: new listening. Not an attempt to understand something that is being said, for, if something were being said, the sounds would be given the shapes of words. Just an attention to the activity of sounds.[9]

All of this attention to sound has led many to question whether or not Cage is actually involved in music. He responds, "If one feels protective about the word music, protect it and find another word for all the rest that enters through the ears."[10] Cage further states, "We are not, in . . . music, saying something. . . . If we were saying something we would use words. We are doing something."[11] Finally, he writes that "our common answer to every criticism must be to continue working and listening, making music with its materials, . . . disregarding the cumbersome, top-heavy structure of musical prohibition."[12] Cage expresses his "Credo" in *Silence:*

> I believe that the use of noise to make music will continue and increase until we reach a music produced through the aid of

electrical instruments which will make available for musical purposes any and all sounds that can be heard. Photoelectric, film, and
mechanical mediums for the synthetic production of music will be
explored.

Whereas, in the past, the point of disagreement has been between dissonance and consonance, it will be, in the immediate
future, between noise and so-called musical sounds. The present
methods of writing music, principally those which employ harmony and its reference to particular steps in the field of sound, will
be inadequate for the composer, who will be faced with the entire
field of sound. New methods will be discovered, bearing a definite
relation to Schoenberg's twelve-tone system and present methods
of writing percussion music and any other methods which are free
from the concept of a fundamental tone.

The principle of form will be our only constant connection
with the past. Although the great form of the future will not be as
it was in the past, at one time the fugue and at another the sonata,
it will be related to these as they are to each other: through the
principle of organization or man's common ability to think.[13]

For Cage, *musical structure* refers to its divisibility into successive
phrases or longer sections. *Form* is the content and continuity of music.
Method is the means of controlling the continuity from note to note.
The *material* of music is sound and silence. Integrating all of these
components is composing.[14] In his music, nothing takes place except
sound — planned (notated) or unplanned (silence or "absence of
intention").[15] Rather than melody, Cage argues for the expressiveness
of the unique individual sound (silence): "I write in order to hear;
never do I hear and then write what I hear."[16]

As an advocate of noise, Cage has affected the musical world at
large. There is no longer the same discrimination against noise that
existed prior to his work. In addition, he observes that what was once
considered poor intonation is currently called microtonality. The
musical concepts of melody, rhythm, and harmony have been greatly
expanded so that "anything goes, but not everything is attempted."[17]
Cage implies that there is infinitely more that can be done in the
development of a creative musical experience. He believes that the
possibilities of contemporary technology available to each of us have

been ignored. Now, as throughout all of history, attention is largely focused on the past:

> That one sees that the human race is one person . . . enables him to see that originality is necessary, for there is no need for eye to do what hand so well does. . . . The past and the present are to be observed and each person makes what he alone must make, bringing for the whole of human society into existence a historical fact, and then, on and on, in continuum and discontinuum.[18]

In order to alter our ways of perceiving, we must develop attitudes that are nonexclusive, that include what we know with what we can not yet imagine. According to his former student and fellow composer, Christian Wolff:

> What have generally been most influential in his music . . . are the explorations, and inducements to exploration, in sound production, to include in a variety of aspects the presence of noise or complexly pitched and irregularly, aperiodically and fluidly rhythmed sound; the element of theater; and the reestablishment of the sense of an American identity in the experimental music tradition.[19]

In summary, two specific statements seem to encapsulate Cage's orientation to the musical experience. First is his conviction that music is analogous to life. Second is the belief that one's musical habits can (and often do) thwart the discovery of expressive musical materials.

FEATURES OF MUSICAL EXPERIENCE

1. *The musical experience is dependent upon open-mindedness.*
Musical open-mindedness has to do with much of what has been called avant-garde music in the twentieth century, that is, the musical innovations made by contemporary composers. According to Cage, it is best exemplified in the works of such composers as Charles Edward Ives, Carl Ruggles, Henry Dixon Cowell, and Edgard Varèse:

> Cowell used to tell the story about Ruggles and the Florida class in harmony. The problem of modulating from one key to another

"very distant" one was discussed. After an hour, the instructor asked Ruggles how he . . . would solve the problem. Ruggles said: I wouldn't make a problem out of it; I'd just go from one to the other without any transition.[20]

In addition, the technological advances of this century such as the tape recorder, synthesizers, sound systems, magnetic tape, and computers have made new musical explorations possible. Cage finds it quite curious that, given such wonderful technological means for creativity, our schools continue to fix their minds on historical means of creating music.

Ethnomusicology has also opened new vistas for exploring the possibilities of music. Previously disparate cultures and musical traditions are now thriving together. It is possible, in fact quite easy, to hear ancient music from India, Africa, or China as well as contemporary types of electronic music. A pluralistic society by its very nature promotes a wealth of musical experiences. Young people, senior citizens, and physically or mentally handicapped individuals can open new avenues into the musical experience and broaden our understanding of musical possibilities. "If one of us doesn't have an idea that will open the minds of the rest of us, another will."[21]

Finally, interruptions caused by modern developments (such as the telephone) open up a world outside of ourselves. "Music's ancient purpose — to sober and quiet the mind . . . is now to be practiced in relation to the Mind of which through technological extension we all are part, a Mind, these days, confused, disturbed, and split."[22]

2. *The musical experience is dependent on the adoption of a less hierarchical and more democratic relationship among composers, performers, and listeners.*

For several reasons, the distinctions among composers, performers, and listeners are growing less distinct. *Indeterminacy* in many compositions has served to blur these distinctions by allowing performers to cooperate in musical creation. Composers of such pieces have trusted the individual creative perceptions of the listeners and the musicians.

Technological advancements have also blurred these distinctions. It is increasingly possible for any individual to fill any and all of the roles of composer, performer, and listener. In effect, this could remove music from its social role. The decreasing need for notation due to technology and the interpenetration of different musical paradigms (such as jazz, raga, and tala) has further blurred the differences between composers, performers, and listeners. Cage suggests that "the feelings that people have for one another, fear, guilt, and greed associated with hierarchical societies are giving way to mutual confidence, a sense of common well-being, and a desire to share with another whatever one person happens to have or to do."[23] He sees that this is already occurring within the musical community with the development of music without notation, rehearsals without a conductor, and aleatoric music.

3. *The musical experience is dependent upon the encounter of musical difficulties.*

The final notion that Cage discusses is *work*. He emphasizes that musical experience must find itself through overcoming difficulties, doing the impossible, keeping abreast of the latest musical and techno-logical developments, thereby inspiring further musical discoveries. Something so rewarding as musical experience demands strenuous dedication to the task of exploring, listening, creating, analyzing, and inventing. There are no shortcuts. There can be no time limit. There is no substitute. Cage states: "People frequently ask me what my definition of music is. This is it. It is work. This is my conclusion."[24]

Scott R. Johnson

NOTES

1. John Cage, *Empty Words* (Middletown, CT: Wesleyan University Press, 1979), p. 177.

2. John Cage, *A Year From Monday* (Middletown, CT: Wesleyan University Press, 1967), p. 31.

3. John Cage, *Silence* (Middletown, CT: Wesleyan University Press, 1961), p. 12.

4. Ibid., p. 8.

5. Ibid., p. 9.

6. Ibid., p. 261.

7. Ibid., p. 10.

8. Cage, *Empty Words*, p. 179.

9. Cage, *Silence,* p. 10

10. Ibid., p. 190.

11. Ibid., p. 94.

12. Ibid., p. 87.

13. Ibid., p. 3.

14. Ibid., p. 62.

15. Cage, *A Year From Monday,* p. 31.

16. Cage, *Silence,* p. 169.

17. Cage, *Empty Words,* p. 178.

18. Cage, *Silence,* p. 75.

19. Christian Wolff, "Under the Influence," in *Triquarterly* 54 "A John Cage Reader," (Spring 1982) ed. Reginald Gibbons, p. 146.

20. Cage, *Empty Words,* p. 180.

21. Ibid., p. 182.

22. Ibid., p. 181.

23. Ibid., p. 182.

24. Ibid., p. 186.

THOMAS CLIFTON
(1935–1978)

SOURCES

Thomas Clifton's writings apply the principles of phenomenological analysis to musical experience. The most systematic application may be found in Clifton's text *Music as Heard: A Study in Applied Phenomenology* (1983). The primary purpose of this work is to "contribute to the effort of reuniting music theory with musical experience."[1] This text represents the first full-scale phenomenological study of the aesthetics of music. Published five years after his untimely death, *Music as Heard* is Clifton's only book.

Essays devoted to the exploration of musical experience from a phenomenological perspective include, "Music and the A Priori" (1973), "Music as Constituted Object" (1976), "The Poetics of Musical Silence" (1976), and the review by Clifton of Alfred Pike's book entitled, *A Phenomenological Analysis of Musical Experience and Other Related Essays* (1970). In an essay entitled "Some Comparisons between Intuitive and Scientific Descriptions of Music" (1975), Clifton criticizes modern music theorists' preoccupation with cataloging musical information and developing complex analytical techniques. He suggests that musical understanding should rely more on intuition as a basis for musical analysis.

The quotations in this chapter from Thomas Clifton's *Music as Heard,* © 1983 by Yale University Press, are reprinted with permission.

GENERAL ORIENTATION TO MUSICAL EXPERIENCE

Phenomenology is the study of pure appearances. It is a means of knowing more about those fields in which the human contribution is an inseparable part of the subject matter. Although the application of the phenomenological method to musical experience is as yet undeveloped, Clifton's work represents an important beginning. Because the art of music is inseparably bound to the texture and dynamics of human experience, Clifton's phenomenological view of music as "the outcome of a collaboration between a person and real or imagined sounds" provides a humanistic, perceiver-oriented approach to musical aesthetics.[2]

Music from a phenomenological perspective is not an object separate from the perceiver, but an experience dependent on the perceiver: "Music is what I am when I experience it."[3] Clifton's view of musical experience calls for a closer relationship between the object and the subject. Borrowing from Martin Buber's terminology, Clifton refers to musical experience as an "I-Thou" relationship. This view is similar to Michael Polanyi's, that "as human beings we see things from a centre lying within ourselves."[4] For Clifton, "there is no music without the presence of a music-ing self."[5] The idea that personal involvement distinguishes music from nonmusic is a theme developed throughout the book.[6]

Clifton's phenomenological look at musical experience is guided by the philosophies of Edmund Husserl and Martin Heidegger, the two founders of phenomenological reduction (which means to suspend, to put out of play any presuppositions). Phenomenology is a controlled method of investigation requiring *epoche,* or what phenomenologists refer to as *purposeful naivete.* Epoche establishes a *phenomenological attitude,* or the perspective from which the nature of experience itself is to be understood.

Phenomenology is a descriptive method of philosophical investigation that aims to take note of, describe, and analyze (not explain) anything about an experience that can be noted. Husserl developed a methodology of analytic steps, requiring a naive view in order to make new discoveries possible. Phenomenological investigation goes beyond the notation of facts to the description of all fulfillable possibilities.

Clifton's work is based on the phenomenological model that all experience has a specific shape. The name for this shape of experience is intentionality. The phenomenological model may be described in the following way: within experience there is that which is experienced and there is the act of experiencing. For every object of experience there is an act of consciousness that apprehends that object, and for every act there is an intended correlate.

For the purposes of understanding Clifton's method of inquiry, it is necessary to remember that music is "not a fact or thing in the world, but a meaning constituted by human beings."[7] A phenomenological description concentrates not on facts, but upon essences, and attempts to uncover what there is about an object and its experience which is essential (or necessary) if the object and its experience is to be recognized at all.[8]

The subjective experience of the observer is a necessary component of phenomenological description. Yet according to Clifton's interpretation, phenomenology affords "a way of uttering meaningful statements which are objective in the sense that they attempt to describe the musical object adequately, and subjective in the sense that they issue from a subject to whom an object has some meaning."[9] For Clifton, the description of musical experience is an act of communication with oneself. The act of description helps transform latent knowledge into explicit knowledge useful in learning about the world: "Insofar as music is of the world, it teaches me about the world."[10]

Clifton's view on the nature of music contrasts with that of the empiricists. Although he does not deny the value of empirical methods, he feels that the nonempirical status of music is covered up with research on the empirical sounds that are its *medium,* the empirical techniques that are its *means,* and the empirical marks (the notation) that are its *signs:* "The sounds, the techniques, and the notation are all vastly important aspects of music, but *they are not music itself.*"[11]

Clifton's description of musical experience pays close attention to feeling. He says "feeling, like space and time, is a necessary constituent of the musical experience rather than a psychological by-product of the listener."[12] In *Music as Heard,* the difference between sound and music (music and nonmusic) is decided by human acts including the act of feeling. Whereas traditional aesthetics views musical objects as symbols or metaphors separate from the "art–ing" subject, Clifton views what are usually regarded as the sonorous traits of musical objects as shapes of human experience. He defines music as an ordered arrangement of sounds and silences whose meaning is presentative rather than denotative: "Music is the actualization of the possibility of any sound whatever to present to some human being a meaning which he experiences with his body."[13] (The term body in this text refers to a combination of mind, feelings, senses, and will.) Clifton's definition involves the listener in the question of whether a collection of sounds is or is not music. It says nothing about standards the object is supposed to meet. The order of a work is constituted by the experiencing person, who according to Clifton is "just as likely to experience it in a collection of natural sounds, as in . . . a finely wrought fugue."[14]

Clifton's applications of phenomenology to musical experience include definitions of basic concepts of music theory — pitch, interval, harmony, and tonality. This is done phenomenologically, using familiar terms and concepts as a reference point but expanding the traditional definitions to reflect the "essence" or possibilities of these musical concepts. Regarding pitch, for example, we experience music *through* the pitch rather than experiencing the pitch itself. We hear the musical activity of the pitch. Likewise, tonality is not the materialization of a system in which a certain pitch functions as a center around which other musical elements arrange themselves. It is instead a habit, an aptitude acquired by the body, a bodily movement, a sensuous experience, and a feeling — which combine in the intuitive givenness of tonality.[15]

Clifton's criteria for musically valid descriptions of the phenomenological kind are (1) that "one must be aware of the actual music;" (2) that the description be restricted to the composition itself rather than including facts about the composition, or "bare acoustical data;" (3) that the object of the description be "not the materials of a composition . . . or the medium (the sound as such) . . . [but rather] the sense of the sounds: the meaning act, as well as the object of the act;" (4) that "the description must be rendered with precision . . . , systematically relevant, and interesting;" and (5) that "the truth of descriptive statements does not depend on whether something exists empirically or not."[16]

FEATURES OF MUSICAL EXPERIENCE

1. *Musical experience includes the essence of time.*
Clifton regards time as "the experience of human consciousness in contact with change."[17] Like Susanne Langer, Clifton distinguishes musical time from clock time. He differs from Langer in that time is not an absolute medium, but an "experience . . . which is in constant flux."[18] Clifton notes that there is a confusion about "whether the composition is in time, or whether time is in it."[19] In an application of Husserl's ideas about time to musical perception, Clifton discusses time in terms of *horizon* (the "field of presence" of an experienced event), *retention* (remembering the event), and *protention* (the term for a future we anticipate, and not merely await). Taking into account the Gestalt character of temporal experience, Clifton speaks of time as horizon: "The horizon refers to the temporal edge of a single field, which itself may enclose a multitude of events interpreted . . . as belonging to this field."[20]

Clifton's description of musical time is an elaboration of Langer's concept of *virtual time.* He distinguishes between musical time and what is referred to as world time or chronological time. There is a distinction between the time a piece takes and the time a piece presents or evokes. Time is something "in" the music; time is presented or evoked by the music; and time is also designated by the music.

Clifton concludes that the content of any temporal horizon is determined by the object and that "the object is its horizon."[21] The musical object (as content) is equivalent to the horizon (as boundary), which is equivalent to the span itself (as field of presence), and all of these things, finally, are indistinguishable from actual clock time.

2. *Musical experience includes the "essence" of musical space.*
Clifton's concept of musical space is influenced by Merleau-Ponty's *Phenomenology of Perception.* Readers are encouraged to think of space and spatial relations not as properties of objects, but as fields of action for a subject: "Texture — or space is what we experience when we hear duration, registers, intensities, and tone qualities."[22]

Clifton argues that music is not a purely auditory experience: it must be understood rather as synaesthetic perception and thus a bodily engagement with sound. Spatial relations are therefore not physical properties of objects, but fields of action in which a perceiver participates. Musical space is space as lived, not environmental space. Space in musical perception exhibits characteristics of closeness and directionality.[23]

The simplest form of musical space is musical line. Musical line reveals both thinness and thickness. Line can be complex texturally to include at least six parameters: contour, width, distance, timbre, rhythmic level, and, potentially, text.[24]

The notion of *surface* as a type of texture is another form of musical space. Undifferentiated surface occurs under three conditions: the absence of movement, the absence of any contrast in dynamics, and the absence of timbral complexity. Clifton also describes surfaces with low relief where there is more active change in the conditions, and the surfaces with high relief where the changes are more pronounced.[25]

Visual depth is differentiated from musical depth. In visual experience, depth is a relation between magnitude and distance. In musical space, a melodic line or gesture can sound either close at hand or far away and still retain its size. An object in musical space heard "in front of" some other object will still be heard with the same magnitude as when it is heard "behind" another object. There are several aspects of musical depth that Clifton discusses, including the notion of *distance* — music that appears to be far away or very close. The notion of *penetration* is another aspect of musical depth, such as the element of silence that can penetrate volume without interruption.[26]

Clifton talks about the experience of instantaneous shifts in perspective, where the movement suddenly appears from another point of view, as *faceting*. Faceting involves the shifts, changes, or exchanges of musical space (one chord to another; sound to silence).[27]

3. *Musical experience includes the element of play.*

The element of play constitutes an essence of musical experience. Clifton distinguishes four various forms of play. Finding ritual a parallel of play (and play parallel to music), Clifton defines *ritual* as the experience of being absorbed in an activity whose continuation is desired.[28]

Ludic (ritual) play provides a necessary context or setting for the motivations of musical meaning. The aim of ritual is to permit an experience of achievement or accomplishment. Music is connected with ritual: both involve directed action rather than mere movement.

The characteristics of ritual can be seen as the constituent elements of play, which are the essences of musical experience: (1) the absorption in an activity for its own sake, (2) the designation of a special place in which the activity is to be played out, (3) the recombination and sublimation of certain "real-life" activities, and (4) the specification of certain bodily motions regarded as necessary to the successful perform-ance of the play activity.[29]

Aleatoric play refers to a certain method of composition. Clifton considers the relationship of aleatoric music to its actual experience. About avant-garde music Clifton says:

> We listen to aleatoric music and indeterminate music in essentially the same way we listen to any other kind of music — purely in terms of the musical experience, it is a matter of supreme indiffer-ence to me how a composer went about his task. Let him engage in whatever irrational practice imaginable; if the result is a musical experience, then the result is not irrational.[30]

Agonic play is the activity of friendly competition or engaging in a contest. Clifton suggests that music itself contains agonic elements of a certain kind. The music wins or triumphs because it has succeeded in defining space or time, and claiming it as its own. This is the essence of tonal music.[31]

Comic play is not a necessary constituent of every piece of music, yet Clifton regards the comic as a material and experienceable essence of musical experience to the extent that its experience is of an imme-diate and irreducible phenomenon. The comic, as an aspect of play, teaches us something about the world around us.[32]

4. Musical experience includes the element of feeling.

The answer to Clifton's question as to the nature of musical experience may be found in the following thesis: music involves a reciprocal relation — a "collaboration" between the sounds and the listener. "This collaboration cannot be achieved without the necessary constitutive activities of feeling and understanding."[33] Feeling is a foundational constituent of musical experience.

Based on what Husserl calls *intention,* the experience of music is contingent on a belief that there is an object (music) and that *I* am the one experiencing it. For musical experience to occur, people must believe that they are experiencing music. Clifton expands the idea of belief to a broader notion of *possession*. Possession is a more active kind of experience whereby "our beliefs are continuously revised, reconsidered, canceled, or reinforced."[34]

Belief is a form of feeling and, as Polanyi writes, "To avoid believing one must stop thinking."[35] In experiencing music we affirm a belief in its existence. When we attend to something in which we believe, the act of commitment is involved. In this sense we possess the moment that makes meaning possible — we own it; it is ours. At this moment, the structure of musical experience is possible because the idea and the meaning are joined. When this happens the materials begin to have meaning to us.

Possession involves *willing*. It is not a mechanical act and, in fact, the person is not a mere spectator of events impinging upon him or her. The person, in willing, determines the value of the thoughts, feelings, and emotions that might otherwise be unorganized confusion. The will organizes these and brings them to order.[36]

The constituents of possession are described as (1) acts of belief, which underlie all cognitive and affective acts; (2) freedom, which provides the possibility for either possessing or not possessing; (3) caring, a fundamental feeling stemming from an attitude of concern for the object of possession; and (4) willing, which urges the continuity of the possessed object and the act of possession.[37]

From the perspective of aesthetics, the concept of possession may be understood as a coming together, or as a closure between the experiencer and the music being experienced. Clifton calls this "the institution of a felt harmony."[38] A harmoniousness is experienced between the acts of feeling, willing, and thinking, and the object of these acts: "The act and object are meaningful to the extent that both contribute to a single structure and rhythm of experience that blends receiving and doing, anticipating and absorbing, plunging in and taking in."[39] Such a structure does not consist of just seeing or hearing, or even seeing and hearing plus emotion; rather, "the essence of aesthetic experience necessarily involves the movement of emotion and feelings in the acts of seeing and hearing."[40]

Possession denotes the act of giving phenomenal existence (music) to an empirical sign (sound). The act of possessing, or giving expression, brings the meaning into being. *Being* in a musical space means that I am in contact with it; I dwell in it. Clifton agrees with Merleau-Ponty, who says that "music has meaning because it is ours, and not that it is ours because it has meaning."[41] This view erases the boundary between the self and the music. The meaning of musical experience is in the perceiver's active participation and involvement in music. Participating in music through the act of expression (possession = willing, thinking, feeling) causes the attention to shift from ourselves to the object of concern (music).

"Music is what I am when I experience it."[42] This is the essence of Clifton's thesis. In this sense musical experience is personal. It belongs to those intentionally involved in the music; it belongs to those who willingly participate in the music; and it belongs to those whose feelings make music meaningful. Feeling constitutes the human being. Persons are individuated by feeling, and so is music.

Westerners are cautioned not to confuse the signs of music (notation, scores, materials) with what is signified by the music. The study of music cannot be made by passive observation or casual encounters. Musical experience is dependent on the ability to identify the world of music and refer to it — to participate and be involved in the musical activity of time, space, play, and feeling.

Doreen B. Rao

NOTES

1. Thomas Clifton, *Music as Heard: A Study in Applied Phenomenology* (New Haven: Yale University Press, 1983), p. 296.
2. Thomas Clifton, "Some Comparisons Between Intuitive and Scientific Descriptions of Music," *Journal of Music Theory* 19 (Spring 1975), p. 74.
3. Clifton, *Music as Heard*, p. 297.
4. Michael Polanyi, *Personal Knowledge* (Chicago: University of Chicago Press, 1958), p. 3.
5. Clifton, *Music as Heard*, p. 281.
6. Ibid., p. 3.
7. Ibid., p. 5.
8. Ibid., p. 9.
9. Ibid., pp. viii–ix.

10. Ibid., p. 6.

11. Ibid., pp. 36–37.

12. Ibid., p. 14.

13. Ibid., p. 1.

14. Ibid., p. 4.

15. Ibid., p. 35.

16. Ibid., pp. 38–41.

17. Ibid., p. 56.

18. Ibid., p. 55.

19. Ibid., p. 51.

20. Ibid., p. 57.

21. Ibid., p. 58.

22. Ibid., p. 69.

23. Ibid., pp. 65–68; 140–142.

24. Ibid., pp. 143–155.

26. Ibid., pp. 178–202.

27. Ibid., pp. 202–204.

28. Ibid., p. 205.

29. Ibid., pp. 205–236.

30. Ibid., p. 228.

31. Ibid., pp. 236–256.

32. Ibid., p. 228.

33. Ibid., p. 74.

34. Ibid., p. 275.

35. Michael Polanyi, *Personal Knowledge,* p. 314 (quoted in Clifton, *Music as Heard,* p. 275).

36. Clifton, *Music as Heard,* p. 276.

37. Ibid., pp. 276–277.

38. Ibid., p. 286.

39. Ibid.

40. Ibid., p. 287.

41. Ibid., p. 290.

42. Ibid., p. 297.

AARON COPLAND
(1900–1990)

SOURCES

Aaron Copland enjoyed a long and prestigious career as composer, conductor, and writer. While he is known primarily for his laudable achievements as a composer and for his distinctive compositional style, Copland also has made valuable contributions to the literature on the musical experience. The book providing the most insight into Copland's thoughts regarding the musical experience is *Music and Imagination* (1952). Other sources of information used here include *The New Music* (1968), *Copland on Music* (1944), and *What to Listen for in Music* (1939).

GENERAL ORIENTATION TO MUSICAL EXPERIENCE

In his writings on music, Copland makes clear that he is not functioning on the level of knowledge normally associated with matters of learning and scholarship. Rather, he is speaking "on the plane of intuitional perception" and of "immediate or sensitive knowledge."[1] As a composer, he feels he can provide insight into the understanding of music because he is involved in creating it.

"That music gives pleasure is axiomatic. . . . [But] the source of that pleasure, our musical instinct, is not at all elementary; it is, in fact, one of the prime puzzles of consciousness."[2] Though Copland makes a strong case for the development of listening skills, he recognizes that music affects all of us, simple-minded or sophisticated, with a sense of immediacy and that "music attracts all of us, in the first instance, on the primordial level of sheer rhythmic and sonic appeal."[3] By comparing music with poetry, Copland illustrates this idea of immediacy with the words of Wystan Auden: "A verbal art like poetry is reflective; it stops to think. Music is immediate; it goes on to become. . . . [Because of its elusive quality, its never-ending flow, music is in a] continual state of becoming."[4]

Our understanding of music is based on our ability to listen (to hear what actually goes on in a piece of music) and to use the imagination freely. "Music provides the broadest possible vista for the imagination since it is the freest, the most abstract, the least fettered of all the arts: no story content, no pictorial representation, no regularity of meter, no strict limitation of frame need hamper the intuitive functioning of the imaginative mind."[5]

The imagination, however, cannot be fully utilized without the accompanying skill of intelligent listening. Though the lay listener is aware of musical flow, of the magnetic forward pull of music, "to the enlightened listener this time-filling, forward drive has fullest meaning only when accompanied by some conception as to where it is heading, what musical-psychological elements are helping to move it to its destination, and what formal architectural satisfaction will have been achieved on its arriving there."[6]

Meaning in music is closely related to meaning in life, although "words . . . can never hope to encompass the intangible greatness of music."[7] From Susanne Langer, Copland borrows the idea that music has vital import and that it exists as a "living form." Musical meaning is closely tied to the reason for musical creation — the need to express one's feelings about life. If these feelings are perceived by the listener (even though they may lie beyond verbal description), then it can be said that the import of the music was understood.

FEATURES OF MUSICAL EXPERIENCE

1. *The musical experience requires the development of listening skills.*
Listening is a talent possessed in varying degrees by all people. Like any talent, it is capable of being developed, but it is subject to the following provisions: (1) "the ability to open oneself up to the

musical experience," and (2) "the ability to evaluate critically that experience."[8]

This type of critical evaluation implies additional abilities or "gifts" on the part of the listener. The first of these is the ability to "see all around the structural framework of an extended piece of music."[9] One must be able to relate what is heard to what has gone before and what is about to come. "In other words, music is an art that exists in points of time."[10]

One must also have an awareness of music history in order to distinguish stylistic differences in music. This awareness helps the listener know which properties to look for and focus on in the music. Finally, potentially intelligent listeners must be able to recognize a melody when they hear one. Copland emphasizes the vital function of melody in music when he likens it to that of story in fiction.

Music can be listened to on three planes. The "simplest way . . . is to listen for the sheer pleasure of the musical sound itself. That is the sensuous plane."[11] Though Copland agrees that this kind of listening can be enjoyable, he feels that many people abuse this plane of listening. Music listening should be active listening. This means that there is more to be considered than music's purely sensuous appeal.

The second plane is the expressive level. Here we deal with the thorny question of musical meaning. Music has meaning, to be sure, but it is just as certain that this meaning cannot be stated in words. Copland strongly discourages a referentialistic approach to the determination of musical meaning (though he does not use this term). He states that it is more important to be able to feel the expressive quality of a piece of music and to be aware that each hearing may produce varying responses in the listener.[12]

The third plane is the sheerly musical. "Besides the pleasurable sound of music and the expressive feeling that it gives off, music does exist in terms of the notes themselves and of their manipulation."[13] Most listeners are not conscious enough of this plane, while professional musicians are sometimes too concerned with the "musical facts," so to speak. This raises the question: does the professional musician, with all of his or her training, have the advantage over the lay listener?

Copland feels that the musically trained or gifted individual has a greater awareness of what happens in the music, comparing this person to the minister who has direct contact with the "Source."[14] Professional musicians approach music with a better balance. They are neither too carried away by it nor too limited in their enthusiasm for a single type of music. On the other hand, the "sensitive amateur" comes to music without the prejudices or preconceptions of the professional and can often, because of a greater instinct in judgment, be the "surer guide to the true quality of a piece of music."[15] Ideal listeners combine the training of the professional with the innocence of the intuitive amateur. They display a balance of the subjective and the objective in their attitudes; they are both inside and outside the music at the same time; they are able to keep "psychical distance," as Edward Bullough has termed it.[16]

Listening is a talent that can and must be developed if one is to build a better understanding of music. Copland writes:

> No composer believes that there are any short cuts to better appreciation of music. The only thing that one can do for the listener is to point out what actually exists in the music itself and reasonably to explain the wherefore and the why of the matter. The listener must do the rest.[17]

2. *The musical experience is characterized by a continual need for self-expression (artistic creation).*

Two central questions regarding the creation of music are raised and answered by Copland, the first being "why create?" Copland believes that people have a need for self-expression, a "basic need to make evident one's deepest feelings about life."[18] "One part of everything he is and knows is implicit in each composer's single work, and it is that central fact of his being that he hopes he has communicated."[19]

In *What to Listen for in Music,* Copland discusses the process of musical creation in a straightforward manner. For the composer, the creation of a musical product is as natural a function as eating or sleeping. The composer starts with a musical idea, decides on the medium to be used, adds complementary ideas, elongates, and welds them together in a form that exhibits flow and continuity. What about the composer's inspiration in this process? Copland writes, "Inspiration is often only a by-product," an idea "tacked on at the end" [of the creative process].[20]

In later writings, Copland discusses the creation/inspiration issue more fully. He feels all composers "derive their impulse from a similar drive" in which both emotion and objective manipulation of notes are involved.[21] The inspiration for the piece comes at the moment of possession of the germinal idea. "Inspiration may be a form of super-consciousness or perhaps of subconsciousness, . . . but I am sure that it is the antithesis of self-consciousness."[22] One half of the mind dictates while the other half takes it down. Inspiration may also take the form of a "spontaneous expression of emotional release." Here, the creative impulse takes over and blots out consciousness. Both types of inspiration are brief, exhausting, and rare. They are the "kind we wait for every day." The less divine afflatus that makes it possible to compose each day — to induce inspiration, as it were — is "a species of creative intuitions in which the critical faculty is much more involved."[23]

In further discussion of musical creation, Copland states that there is too much emphasis placed on the idea of craftsmanship in composing. The composer's technique is, on the lowest level, a mastery of musical language. On a higher level, a composer is a "musical thinker, a creator of values," values that are "primarily aesthetic, hence psychological, but hence, as an inevitable consequence, ultimately of the deepest human importance."[24]

The second question regarding the creation of music is "Why is our job never done?" or "Why do we continually create?" Copland states that "each added work brings with it an element of self-discovery."[25] "Like life itself, music never ends, for it can always be re-created. Thus the greatest moments of the human spirit may be deduced from the greatest moments in music."[26]

3. *The musical experience involves the understanding of musical meaning (its import) and a response to the spiritual nature inherent in great music.*

The problem of determining meaning in music troubles only the literary mind; music lovers are not disturbed by this mystery. In fact, they are intrigued by it. "Whatever the semanticists of music may uncover, composers will blithely continue to articulate 'subtle complexes of feeling that language cannot even name, let alone set forth.' "[27]

For Copland, the concern is not whether listeners are deriving pleasure from his music, nor is it with the precision of technical execution. What matters is whether or not listeners are "understanding the import of the music."[28] He compares himself to the playwright who wants the significance of a scene to come across to the theater audience.[29] When one listens to music, one listens to the voice of the composer and connects with the personality of the composer.[30] This is not to say, however, that there is but one way to interpret any given piece. Copland likes to feel that his music can be "read" several different ways (as long as these interpretations are within the limits of stylistic truth) and further states that the finest interpreters can help the composer discover more about the character of his or her work.[31]

When listening to music, one can hear tension and release, swelling and subsiding, length and speed, without the aid of any special "training." Awareness of these phenomena stems from the fact that they reflect our physical life. For Copland, the process of music and the process of life will always be closely conjoined. "So long as the human spirit thrives on this planet, music in some living form will accompany and sustain it and give it expressive meaning."[32]

Copland touches on the spiritual aspect of music when he writes, "Is one a better person — morally — for having heard a great work of art?" He feels this is doubtful:

> What happens is that a masterwork awakens in us reactions of a spiritual order that are already in us, only waiting to be aroused. . . . His [Beethoven's] music cannot persuade; it makes evident. It does not shape conduct; it is itself the exemplification of a particular way of looking at life. A concert is not a sermon. It is a performance — a reincarnation of a series of ideas implicit in the work of art.[33]

Finally, in regard to musical meaning and the place music holds in our life, Copland says: "The art of music, without specific subject matter and with little specific meaning, is nevertheless a balm for the human spirit — not a refuge or escape from the realities of existence, but a haven wherein one makes contact with the essence of human experience."[34]

Ramona Quinn Wis

NOTES

1. Aaron Copland, *Music and Imagination* (Cambridge, MA: Harvard University Press, 1952), p. 3.

2. Aaron Copland, *Copland on Music* (New York: W. W. Norton, 1944), p. 24.

3. Ibid., p. 27.

4. Wystan H. Auden, "Some Reflections on Opera as a Medium," *Partisan Review* (January/February 1952), p. 11 (quoted in Copland, *Music and Imagination*, p. 2).

5. Copland, *Music and Imagination*, p. 7.

6. Copland, *Copland on Music*, p. 28.

7. Ibid., p. 38.

8. Copland, *Music and Imagination*, p. 8.

9. Ibid., p. 15.

10. Aaron Copland, *What to Listen for in Music* (New York: McGraw-Hill, 1939), p. 16.

11. Ibid., p. 18.

12. Ibid., p. 27.

13. Ibid.

14. Copland, *Music and Imagination*, p. 9.

15. Ibid.

16. Edward Bullough, " 'Pyschical Distance' as a Factor in Art and as an Aesthetic Principle," *British Journal of Psychology* V (1912), Part II, p. 91 (quoted in Copland, *Music and Imagination*, p. 10).

17. Copland, *What to Listen for in Music*, p. 17.

18. Copland, *Music and Imagination*, p. 41.

19. Ibid., p. 16.

20. Copland, *What to Listen for in Music*, p. 25.

21. Copland, *Music and Imagination*, p. 12.

22. Ibid., p. 43.

23. Ibid.

24. Ibid., p. 44.

25. Ibid., p. 41.

26. Copland, *Copland on Music*, p. 63.

27. Copland, *Music and Imagination*, p. 13 (internal quote from Susanne K. Langer, *Philosophy in a New Key: A Study in the Symbolism of Reason, Rite, and Art* [New York: Mentor Books, 1956], p. 180).

28. Ibid., p. 11.

29. Copland, *What to Listen for in Music*, p. 18.

30. Ibid., p. 265.
31. Copland, *Music and Imagination,* p. 17.
32. Copland, *Copland on Music,* p. 72.
33. Copland *Music and Imagination,* p. 17.
34. Copland, *Copland on Music,* p. 51.

NELSON GOODMAN
(1906–   )

SOURCES

The influential philosopher Nelson Goodman viewed music and all the arts as various types of symbol systems. His conception of these symbol systems and the kind of experience they are able to provide is given fullest treatment in *Languages of Art* (1976). Additional ideas on this topic can be found in *Ways of Worldmaking* (1978) and *Of Mind and Other Matters* (1984).

GENERAL ORIENTATION TO MUSICAL EXPERIENCE

Historically, philosophy has seen several major shifts in focus. Philosophers first concerned themselves with identifying the structure of the world. Immanuel Kant exchanged this focus for an attempt to identify the structure of the mind. Modern philosophy has replaced interest in the structure of the mind with an attempt to identify the structure of concepts and, even more recently, has expanded this study to include the structure of the several symbol systems of the sciences, philosophy, the arts, and everyday discourse.

Goodman specifically attempts to identify the characteristic ways in which artistic symbols differ from symbol systems in other fields in respect to their function and types of organization. Therefore, his conception of the aesthetic experience is based on claims made about the nature of the aesthetic symbol. Howard Gardner summarizes succinctly this approach to works of art:

Goodman's artistic creator is the individual with sufficient under-standing of the properties and functions of certain symbol systems to allow him to create works that function in an aesthetically effective manner — works that are replete, expressive, susceptible to multiple readings and the like. By the same token, the artistic perceiver, whether audience member, critic or connoisseur, must be sensitive to the properties of symbols that convey artistic mean-ing — to repleteness, expressivity, density, and plurisignificance.[1]

Goodman explains that the scope of his theorizing does not coincide very closely with what is ordinarily taken to be the field of aesthetics. His objective is an approach to a general theory of symbols. The procedure he uses is to analyze the variety of relationships that exist between symbols and their referents. According to this perspec-tive, each art manipulates its own characteristic symbol system that is defined as a "symbol scheme correlated with a field of reference."[2]

To assist him in his analysis of symbol systems, Goodman formu-lates an ideal model of notationality. Five criteria are theoretically necessary for any notational system to function effectively:

1. *Syntactic disjointness.* One mark in an alphabet may not belong to more than one character.

2. *Syntactic finite differentiation.* It must be possible to distinguish each mark from all other marks: *a*'s must be distinguishable from *d*'s.

3. *Semantic unambiguity.* It must be possible to tell whether an object complies with an allotted character.

4. *Semantic disjointness.* No two characters may have any compliant in common.

5. *Semantic finite differentiation.* It must be possible to distinguish among the compliants so that wrong categorizations are not made.[3]

These criteria distinguish a notational system from a nonnotational system. They are categorically required and are not mere recommenda-tions for good and useful notation. They also provide a useful yardstick for the purpose of analyzing, comparing, and contrasting symbol systems in art, science, and life in general. According to these criteria, natural languages do not qualify as notational systems. They meet the syntactic requirements but do not meet the semantic ones. That is to say, they are full of ambiguity, and the compliance requirements are violated when one object, a wheelbarrow, complies with "metal object," "wheeled vehicle," "gardening aid," etc. Art forms and sculpture violate all the features of notationality listed previously.

In *Languages of Art* Goodman argues that the symbolization scheme used in musical scores in general meets the requirement of a truly notational system. Most characters of a musical score are syntactically disjoint and differentiated.[4] Semantically, it is flawed by some redundancy: the same sound event complies with the characters C-sharp, D-flat, and E-triple-flat, but redundancy is not altogether fatal for a notational system.[5] If the series of whole note, half note, quarter note, eighth note, etc., were to be continued without end, the requirement of finite differentiation would be violated. But since in practice there is a tacit tradition to set the limit at five flags, or the 1/128 note, this preserves differentiation.[6] Semantic unambiguity seems to be threatened by the use of figured-bass versus specific notation. Goodman gets around this by calling them two notational subsystems; the one in use must be adhered to if identification of a work from performance to performance is to be ensured.[7] A painter's sketch does not define the final painting like the score does a performance. The painter rather uses a system without either syntactic or semantic differentiation. The sketch does not function as a character in a language at all:

> We have seen that a musical score is in a notation and defines a work; that a sketch or picture is not in a notation but is itself a work; and that a literary script is both in a notation and is itself a work. Thus in the different arts the work is differently localized. In painting, the work is an individual object; and in etching, a class of objects. In music, the work is the class of performances compliant with a character [a score]. In literature, the work is the character itself.[8]

Discussing the relationship of a building to its plans, Goodman concludes that "architecture is a mixed and transitional case"[9] between music and the graphic arts.

Goodman argues that the traditional question "What is art?" has ended so often in frustration and confusion, it would appear that it is the question that is wrong. He replaces it with the question "When is art?" His answer is based on considerations of symbolic function. When a painting or a piece of music functions as an aesthetic symbol for the creator or observer, it is art. If a Rembrandt is being used to replace a broken window, it may cease to function as a work of art.[10]

A work of art can symbolize in three important and different ways: (1) if a painting *represents* an object, the painting refers to or denotes the object; (2) if a painting *expresses* a quality, the painting metaphorically possesses that quality; or (3) if a painting *exemplifies* a property, the painting shows forth certain patterns of shape, color, or texture.[11] Put into musical terms, a piece of music can (1) represent a sound in the natural environment, (2) metaphorically express the quality of pomp and circumstance, or (3) exemplify the property of thematic repetition with variation. One of these three ways of symbolizing must be present in a work if it is to function as a work of art: "Art without representation, or expression, or exemplification, — yes; without all three — no."[12]

Other symbol systems may make use of representation, expression, or exemplification. The presence of any of these three ways of symbolizing does not in itself distinguish an art symbol from other symbols. For example, a graph may represent the ups and downs of the stock market over a given period. A letter of apology may express someone's sincere regret for an oversight, and a tailor's swatch exemplifies the bolt of material from which it was cut in certain respects (its color but not its size). None of these things are considered works of art. Goodman supplies further criteria that help to distinguish aesthetic from other symbols; these will be presented in the following section.

Goodman concedes that if all symbol systems have their own kind of merit, this pluralism entails our living with versions of the world that conflict. That "truths conflict reminds us that truth cannot be the only consideration in choosing among statements or versions."[13] It is often necessary to judge whether a statement is true, whether a description or representation is right, and this is done on the basis of fit. Attempting to show how works of art that present worlds through exemplification can be judged, he asks, "When is a sample right?" It must be a fair sample.[14]

Despite the difficulty of determining fairness, such judgments are frequently made. Observers exposed to exemplified forms, feelings, affinities, and contrasts in works of art often recognize that the artist has created an authentic version of reality:

> Briefly, then, truth of statements and rightness of descriptions, representations, exemplifications, expressions — of design, drawing, diction, rhythm — is primarily a matter of fit: fit to what is referred to in one way or another, or to other renderings, or to modes and manners of organization . . . And knowing or understanding is seen as ranging beyond the acquiring of true beliefs to the discovering and devising of fit of all sorts.[15]

FEATURES OF MUSICAL EXPERIENCE

1. *The musical experience requires an aesthetic symbol that can be distinguished by five important symptoms: syntactic density, semantic density, relative repleteness, exemplification, and multiple and complex reference.*

These five symptoms are not necessary conditions for aesthetic functioning. They are criterial attributes that are likely to be in the foreground when a symbol is functioning aesthetically, and likely to be minimized or absent in cases where it is not. Each attribute will now be described in greater detail.

Syntactic density. Goodman describes this feature in terms of the sensitivity of the graduations used. Syntactic density is found when the finest differences in certain respects constitute a difference between symbols.[16] An ungraduated mercury thermometer calls for sensitive reading of the information displayed. In contrast, an electronic instrument giving digital read-outs is not offering syntactically dense information. An artistic example would be that of a song in which the most subtle differences between repetitions of a melodic line may convey important expressive distinctions.

Semantic density. This time it is those things to which symbols refer that are distinguished by the finest differences in certain respects.[17] For example, human body temperature is subject to extremely fine and subtle fluctuations that may be critical for a specific medical diagnosis. If the fluctuations of temperature were not semantically dense, there would be no need for a syntactically dense thermometer. In language, the meanings of words overlap each other in many subtle ways. Gardner gives the example of three synonyms: it is impossible to say where the mental state of *intentionally* or *deliberately* ends and *on purpose* begins.[18] A work such as *La Mer* by Claude Debussy, which attempts to portray the ocean's subtle changes in lighting and mood throughout the course of a single day, would be an unambiguous musical example of semantic density.

Relative repleteness. In this instance, comparatively many aspects of a symbol are significant. Goodman provides the example of a drawing of a mountain by Katsushika Hokusai, where every feature of shape, line, thickness, etc., counts, in contrast with the same line as a chart of daily stock market averages. In the latter, the constitutive elements of the diagram are expressly and narrowly restricted: "The only relevant features of the diagram are the ordinate and abscissa of each of the points the center of the line passes through."[19] In the case of the sketch, any thickening or thinning of the line, change of color, or contrast with the background is full of significance. In music, small changes in one or more of the elements making up a phrase can convey a quite definite and intended change in feeling tone.

Exemplification. Goodman suggests that exemplification is a major symbolic function for the arts.[20] He argues that it is the most striking feature distinguishing literary from nonliterary texts. In this case a symbol, whether or not it denotes, symbolizes by serving as a sample of certain properties that it literally possesses. To provide a musical example, a theme can be described as literally exemplifying speed and metaphorically exemplifying gracefulness. (If Goodman would agree to a modification and extension of this idea, he could be congratulated on raising an important point. Liberated from a certain trivialization made necessary by the attachment of a verbal concept such as *gracefulness,* it could be claimed that the theme metaphorically exemplifies qualitative correspondences between its own properties and human experience of affective life.)

Multiple and complex reference. Here the symbol carries a number of overlapping and difficult-to-separate meanings, each of which contributes to the effect of the whole work. Goodman describes this feature in the following terms:

Scientific and practical discourse, verbal or pictorial, normally aims at singularity and directness, avoiding ambiguity and complicated routes of reference. But in the arts, multiple and complex reference of all sorts — from the simple ambiguity of denotation to reference through one or more straight or tortuous chains transversing several levels — is common and is often a powerful instrument. Though not a universal or exclusive feature, it is a symptom of the aesthetic.[21]

Most philosophers of art have subscribed to a view that sees the meanings of art as extending beyond the relationships of the actual elements of the medium. John Dewey suggested that, in every work of art, an imaginative quality dominates because "meaning and values that are wider and deeper than the particular here and now in which they are anchored are realized by way of *expressions*."[22] However, it is important to understand that Goodman is not advocating that attention be directed away from the art object to any of these multiple referents. Study of the symbol itself is the only means an observer has to grasp any of these complexities.

2. *In the aesthetic experience feelings function cognitively.*

Goodman's conception of cognition is a broad one, and he felt it necessary to articulate his conception of it in detail: "Rather, knowing is conceived as developing concepts and patterns, as establishing habits, and as revising or replacing the concepts and altering or breaking the habits in the face of new problems, needs, or insights. Reconception, reorganization, [and] invention are seen to be as important in all kinds of knowing as they are in the arts."[23]

For the cognitivist, cognition includes learning, knowing, gaining insight and understanding, by all available means. Developing sensory discrimination is as cognitive as inventing complex numerical concepts or proving theorems. Mastering a motor skill involves making subtle kinesthetic distinctions and connections. Coming to understand a painting or a symphony in an unfamiliar style, to recognize the work of an artist or a school, to see or hear in new ways, is as cognitive an achievement as learning to read or write or add. Even the emotions function cognitively: in organizing a world, felt contrasts and kinships, both subtle and salient, are no less important than those seen or heard or inferred.[24]

From a variety of statements Goodman makes about the way feelings function cognitively in relation to a work of art, two important features can be identified: feelings are one means of making crucial discriminations, and they are also a means of classifying and organizing the complexities of the perceptual field.

Feelings as the basis of discriminations. For Goodman, feelings as well as the senses are a means of discerning what properties an artistic work has and expresses: "Emotional numbness disables here as definitely if not as completely as blindness or deafness."[25] Feelings are not only used to explore the emotional content of the work, but many of the perceptual factors as well. This claim for a cognitive use of feeling does not deprive the aesthetic experience of emotions, but rather endows the understanding with them.

Goodman claims that we do not discern stylistic affinities and differences by a process of rational analysis, "but by sensations, perceptions, feeling, emotions, sharpened in practice like the eye of a gemologist or the fingers of an inspector of machine parts."[26] Goodman does not want to desensitize the aesthetic experience; he wants to sensitize cognition: "Emotions function cognitively not as separate items but in combination with one another and with other means of knowing. Perception, conception, and feeling intermingle and interact; and an alloy often resists analysis into emotive and nonemotive components."[27]

Feeling as the basis of classification/organization. Goodman recognizes that the cognitive use of emotions is not unique to encounters with works of art. This feature is neither present in every aesthetic experience nor absent in every nonaesthetic one:

> In daily life, classification of things by feeling is often more vital than classification by other properties: we are more likely to be better off if we are skilled in fearing, wanting, braving, or distrusting the right things, animate or inanimate, than if we perceive only their shapes, sizes, weights, etc. And the importance of discernment by feeling does not vanish when the motivation becomes theoretic rather than practical.[28]

The cognitive use of the emotions involves "discriminating and relating them in order to gauge and grasp the work and integrate it with the rest of our experience and the world."[29] Classifications by means of feeling can range from simple divisions between dissonance and consonance to more complex ones: selecting and appreciating elements on the basis of their contribution to establishing a desired quality or mood. Although Goodman does not add this feature (the cognitive use of feeling) to his list of "symptoms of the aesthetic" (probably because it is a human response and not a feature of the symbol), it is obvious that he considers this mode of relating to the art work an important aspect of the aesthetic experience.

W. Ann Stokes

NOTES

1. Howard Gardner, *Art, Mind, and Brain* (New York: Basic Books, 1982), p. 61.
2. Nelson Goodman, *Languages of Art,* 2nd ed. (Indianapolis: Hackett, 1976), p. 143.
3. Ibid., pp. 133, 135, 148, 151, 152.
4. Ibid., p. 181.
5. Ibid.
6. Ibid., p. 183.
7. Ibid., p. 184.
8. Ibid., p. 210.
9. Ibid., p. 221
10. Nelson Goodman, *Ways of Worldmaking* (Indianapolis: Hackett, 1978), p. 67.
11. Ibid., p. 32.
12. Ibid., p. 66.
13. Ibid., p. 120.
14. Ibid., p. 134.
15. Ibid., p. 138.
16. Goodman, *Languages of Art,* p. 252.
17. Ibid.
18. Gardner, *Art, Mind, and Brain,* p. 60.
19. Goodman, *Languages of Art,* p. 229.
20. Ibid., pp. 52–53.

21. Nelson Goodman, *Of Mind and Other Matters* (Cambridge, MA: Harvard University Press, 1984), pp. 136–137.

22. John Dewey, *Art as Experience* (New York: Paragon Books, G. P. Putnam's Sons, 1934, 1979), p. 273.

23. Goodman, *Of Mind and Other Matters*, p. 19.

24. Ibid., p. 147.

25. Goodman, *Languages of Art*, p. 248.

26. Goodman, *Of Mind and Other Matters*, p. 8.

27. Goodman, *Languages of Art*, p. 249.

28. Ibid., p. 251.

29. Ibid., p. 248.

PAUL HINDEMITH
(1895–1963)

SOURCES

Paul Hindemith, a prolific composer in the neo-classical tradition, wrote several books on musical subjects. These include *The Craft of Musical Composition* (1945), *A Concentrated Course in Traditional Harmony* (1943), *Elementary Training for Musicians* (1949), *A Concentrated Course in Traditional Harmony II: A Course for Advanced Students* (1953), and *Johann Sebastian Bach: Heritage and Obligation* (1952). The primary source of information in this essay on Hindemith's conceptions of the musical experience is his book *A Composer's World: Horizons and Limitations* (1952).

GENERAL ORIENTATION TO MUSICAL EXPERIENCE

In establishing his philosophical approach to the musical experience, Hindemith addresses the qualities of a work that determine its value. He dismisses the eternal body of music, the sound properties themselves, and the frail and unstable conditions of human life. None of these offer sufficient stability to underpin the enduring value of music and its experience. He argues, however, that such enduring values in music do exist:

The quotations in this chapter are reprinted by permission of the publisher, from *A Composer's World: Horizons and Limitations* by Paul Hindemith, Cambridge, MA: Harvard University Press, Copyright © 1952 by the President and Fellows of Harvard College.

If we want to recognize and understand such values, we must perceive music not as a mere succession of reasonably arranged acoustical facts; we must extricate it from the sphere of amorphous sound, we must in some way participate, beyond the mere sensual perception of music, in its realization as sound; we must transform our musical impressions into a meaningful possession of our own. . . . These values, not being tied to the instability of sound or to any other external quality of musical creations, are domiciled in the more esoteric realms of our musical nature. We have to turn to the immaterial, the spiritual aspects of music in order to find them.[1]

Hindemith turns to ancient writers to formulate the tenets of this spiritual approach to music. From Saint Augustine's *De musica,* Hindemith borrows a five-part analysis of music perception:

1. The physical fact of sound.
2. The faculty of hearing.
3. The ability to imagine music without the actual sound stimulus.
4. The ability to remember previous musical experiences.
5. The ability to intellectually examine and judge musical shape and grade.[2]

The process of musical perception must then continue with one additional step:

Musical order, as recognized and evaluated by our mind, is not an end in itself. It is an image of a higher order which we are permitted to perceive if we proceed one step further to the sixth degree on our scale of musical assimilation: if we put our enjoyment of such knowledge . . . into the side of the balance that tends towards the order of the heavens and towards the unification of our soul with the divine principle.[3]

Hindemith then turns to Boethius's *De institutione musica* to balance the role of the perceiver with the power of the perception. According to Boethius, as a part of human nature, music has power to "improve or debase our character."[4] Music becomes active and the perceiver becomes passive in this view. The study of music itself, therefore, becomes the central focus of music experience. Three types of music are considered: (1) *Musica humana,* which unifies reasoning with corporeal existence, (2) *Musica instrumentalis,* as executed by human voice or musical instrument, and (3) *Musica mundana,* which governs the universe, providing ultimate order to existence.

In contrast to the Augustinian notion in which our mind absorbs music and transforms it into moral strength, the Boethian precept argues for the "power of the music, its ethos, brought into action upon our mind."[5] Hindemith argues for the unification of these two extremes into a single act of will power. The balance of his discussion on the musical experience is founded on these guiding tenets.

FEATURES OF MUSICAL EXPERIENCE

1. *The musical experience requires a receptive mind.*

"Music, whatever sound and structure it may assume, remains meaningless noise unless it touches a receiving mind. But the mere fact that it is heard is not enough: the receiving mind must be active in a certain way if a transmutation from a mere acoustical perception into a genuine musical experience is to be accomplished."[6] Hearing does not imply only the receiving of acoustical events. It includes all of the musical "impressions" from acoustical stimuli to recall, to imaginings, to anticipated events, to impulses. Hindemith speaks of an "inner ringing and singing," which is at its most vague and undefined levels. It is from this that the phenomenon of composition arises. Likewise, for the listener, this "ringing and singing"[7] allows for the mental construction of parallel, mirrored musical images from the musical stimuli: "Listening to music or imagining music is based on previous audibly-musical or imaginary-musical experiences."[8]

Hindemith had this to say about music education:

> Everyone who wants to listen understandingly to musical structures builds up within his mind his own technique — the musical specialist as well as the unsophisticated recipient. The difference between their actions is one of degree rather than of quality. Courses in music appreciation, like other equally well-meant but silly educational devices which intend to help the man of little

experience, will add just as little in his accumulation of analytical knowledge beyond the crudest outlines as any instruction in fiddle playing can tell the pupil what his subtlest muscular adjustments at any given moment ought to be.[9]

2. *Since the musical experience requires listening (this anticipating and construction of parallel images), and because the full range of listeners will, at any given moment, bring only limited energy and ability to the task, certain limits seem inherent in the meaningful ordering of sound.*

Therefore, we may conclude that there is

in principle never anything new in the general order, shape, and mutual relationship of musical successions. We may even go so far as to say that basically nothing new can ever be introduced in such successions, if we do not want to see the participant in music degraded to a dull, apathetic receptacle, an absorbent sponge reaching the point of saturation without showing any sign of reaction.[10]

Given this assumption, the implications for the composer are quite different from what might commonly be assumed. The building materials of composition cannot be far removed from certain structural, harmonic, and melodic prototypes. Hindemith also suggests limits of the musical experience for the listener: "The continual accumulation of experiences in a listener's mind should not be over-rated. Once he reaches a certain point of versatility in his power of musical coconstruction, no further progress seems to be possible."[11]

3. *The musical experience (the relationship of music to feeling) is not based on programmatic or onomatopoetic devices, nor is it symptomatic of the emotional state of the composer at the time of composition.*

Hindemith makes the argument that if music is to remind us of extra-musical events from nature, it does so less well than the original sound source. Further, if the original sound sources were the emotive tie, they would carry the same emotive import as art. Hindemith suggests that this is not the case.[12]

As to the emotional state of the composer, Hindemith observes that the composer usually works at a composition for extended periods of time and that it would not be possible, much less mentally healthy, for him to attempt to sustain a single mood or set of moods for such prolonged intervals. Further, mood shifts in music occur much more quickly and with much greater contrast than occur in the emotional life of a normal person.[13]

4. *The musical experience does not require that music be a language of emotion.*

While the verbal expressions of language have precise definitions upon which those who understand the language agree, there is no such counterpart in the domain of musical elements. Even if one were to attempt to offer definitions, it would be difficult to find two composers who could agree on what made up a single discrete musical element, much less its definition.[14]

5. *While musical experience involves responses to music, "the reactions music evokes are not feelings, but they are the images, memories of feelings."*[15]

Hindemith likens the musical experience to that of dreams:

Dreams, memories, musical reaction — all three are made of the same stuff. We cannot have musical reactions of any considerable intensity if we do not have dreams of some intensity, for musical reactions build up, like dreams, a phantasmagoric structure of feelings that hits us with the full impact of real feeling. Furthermore we cannot have any musical reactions of emotional significance, unless we have once had real feelings the memory of which is revived by the musical impression.[16]

This is the reason musics of other cultures are often misunderstood by the untrained ear. When we make no connection of these musical stimuli with our own feelingful memories, we "resort to hilarity," finding the music amusing or odd.[17]

6. *The musical experience links music to emotive images.*

The basic factor that links music to emotive images "may be expressed by the equation: actual motion on the one side equals feeling of motion on the other side."[18] This must be so in that the youngest children respond to music even though they do not have a storage of emotional experiences that relate to the musical stimuli. Hindemith suggests that children are able to relate to these musical events at the most fundamental and "primordial" level — by relating to motion, a feeling they all share from the womb.[19]

Hindemith supports this tenet further by citing the ancient argument of the emotional relationship of musical tempo to that of heart rate. According to this notion, tempi that match the pulse at rest suggest a state of repose. Tempi that exceed this heart rate create a feeling of excitation. To Hindemith, this pace or "motion" of music is at the most fundamental level of musical experience, preceding the construction of mental structures alluded to earlier.[20]

7. *The musical experience includes the central ingredients of musical time, musical space, and musical vision.*

Musical time, in contrast to meter, has irregularity in duration as "the essential condition, irregularity which possibly is heightened to incommensurability. This is musical time expressed in forms of rhythm."[21] Rhythm may be understood to include musical form in this context.

Musical space describes the "undeniable . . . successions of tones (that) bring about effects of spatial feelings which in their obviousness are convincing even to the entirely untrained mind. Since neither the loudness nor the color of tones can produce or influence this effect, it must be the pitch relation among tones that is the reason for it."[22]

Musical vision describes the process of musical inspiration as a single moment in which the composer grasps the details of a future work. "If we cannot, in the flash of a single moment, see a composition in its absolute entirety, with every pertinent detail in its proper place, we are not genuine creators."[23]

John W. Richmond

NOTES

1. Paul Hindemith, *A Composer's World: Horizons and Limitations* (Cambridge: Harvard University Press, 1952).

2. Saint Augustine, Bishop of Hippo, *Musik: De musica libri sex,* Sprache von Carl Johann Perl (Paderborn: F. Schoningh, 1962).

3. Ibid., p. 4.

4. Boethius, *De Institutione Musica,* trans. Calvin Bower, ed. Claude Palisca (New Haven: Yale University Press, 1989), p. 1.

5. Ibid., p. 11.

6. Ibid., p. 14.

7. Ibid., p. 15.

8. Ibid., p. 17.

9. Ibid.

10. Ibid., p. 20.

11. Ibid.

12. Ibid., pp. 28–32.

13. Ibid., pp. 32–33.

14. Ibid., p. 34.

15. Ibid., p. 38.

16. Ibid., p. 39.

17. Ibid., p. 40.

18. Ibid., p. 42.

19. Ibid., p. 18.

20. Ibid., pp. 42–43.

21. Ibid., p. 50.

22. Ibid., p. 52.

23. Ibid., p. 61.

SUSANNE K. LANGER
(1895–1985)

SOURCES

Susanne K. Langer, noted aesthetician and author, wrote three books that are basic to this essay. *Feeling and Form* (1953) is Langer's central book, and it describes the general import and significance of the musical experience. This volume can be considered an extension of an earlier work, *Philosophy in a New Key* (1956), in which she developed her original theory of symbolism based on the musical experience. *Problems of Art* (1957) contains ten short lectures focusing on that which is created, expressed, and experienced in works of art.

GENERAL ORIENTATION TO MUSICAL EXPERIENCE

Langer's writings present music according to the following axioms: (1) music makes perceptible for experience the forms of human feeling; (2) the import of music is nondiscursive; and (3) music's characteristic symbolic function is not self-expression but logical expression.

For Langer, the tonal structure in music bears a close logical similarity to the forms of human feeling. Feeling, as Langer describes it, is a more comprehensive concept than emotion. Her broad use of the word *feeling* is meant to include the entire range of our awareness as vital living organisms. Music, according to Langer, while not being able to symbolize individual feelings, does "bear a close logical similarity to the forms of human feeling."[1] This unique power of music and all of the arts enables us to extend the quality of our subjective lives through the creative and disciplined shaping of perceived artistic materials.

In *Problems of Art,* Langer speaks of how her comprehensive theory of art has evolved in an effort to solve the problem of "meaning" in musical aesthetics. While it is commonly agreed that music consists of tones conveyed in certain rhythmic and harmonic relations, the aesthetic difficulty arises from the question as to whether or not music conveys other elements such as ideas, emotions, and representations.

Eduard Hanslick, voicing the formalist position, asserts that "the essence of music is sound and motion."[2] Music means itself, and each composition contains its own peculiar set of significant meaningful elements. To the formalist, the aesthetic meanings of music are unique, intellectual, and confined to the formal analysis of the score. Opposing this view are the referentialists, who maintain that music is primarily a language capable of communicating specific emotions, ideas, and even philosophies of life. To them, meaning exists outside of the musical work.

To Langer, what is logically expressed from the experience of music is not meaning in the traditional sense, but what she calls *vital import,* a "wordlessly presented conception of what life feels like."[3] She includes the word *vital* because a successful work of art is an expressive form analogous to the dynamism of subjective experience. And it is by virtue of its dynamic structure that art can express the forms of vital experience that language is particularly unfit to convey. Thus, Langer says that the import (or meaning) of music is inseparable from the expressive form of the work being perceived. From this it follows that music's import is a function of its internal content and never exclusively its referential content. By contrast, a genuine symbol such as a word has meaning when it refers to or designates something apart from itself. This type of symbol is closed or consummated because it refers to an agreed-upon conception.[4]

Langer believes that feelings cannot be articulated in a meaningful way through the consummated symbolic mode of language.[5] But she holds that, by means of presentational symbolism, the forms of feeling can be made articulate. Langer believes that music lacks denotation but has connotation and can inform us of the very nature and pattern of feelings. Music as a presentational form displays a semantic aspect. In that context, music is a logical form of expression that articulates the forms of feeling for the perceiver's objective contemplation.[6]

FEATURES OF MUSICAL EXPERIENCE

1. *Musical experience is a tonal analogue of emotive life.*

To Langer, music is essentially nonrepresentational and thus becomes the prime example of art as expressive form. "An expressive form is any perceptible or imaginable whole that exhibits relationships of parts, or points, or even qualities or aspects within the whole, so that it may be taken to represent some other whole whose elements have analogous relations."[7] Music upholds this definition due to its ability to present forms that are analogous to, or reminiscent of, the forms of feeling. Thus, we can learn what certain aspects of our subjective lives are like through experiences with music. Because our affective lives are so unexplainable through discursive means, a different, more precise way of formulating this subjective part of our lives is required. Music articulates these forms that are expressive of our emotive lives:

> The tonal structures we call "music" bear a close logical similarity to the forms of human feeling — forms of growth and attenuation, flowing and stowing, conflict and resolution, speed, arrest, terrific excitement, calm, or subtle activation and dreamy lapses — not joy and sorrow perhaps, but the poignancy of either and both — the greatness and brevity and eternal passing of everything vitally felt. Such is the pattern, or logical form, of sentience; and the pattern of music is that same form worked out in pure, measured sound and silence. Music is a tonal analogue of emotive life.[8]

Though Langer rarely makes statements that apply her theories of art to aesthetic education, the following passage points to the social and personal benefits of art as the education of feeling:

> Art penetrates deep into personal life because in giving form to the world, it articulates human nature: sensibility, energy, passion, and mortality. More than anything else in experience, the arts mold our actual life of feeling. . . .

Artistic training is, therefore, the education of feeling, as our usual schooling in factual subjects and logical skills such as mathematical "figuring" or simple argumentation . . . is the education of thought. Few people realize that the real education of emotion is not the "conditioning" effected by social approval and disapproval, but the tacit, personal, illuminating contact with symbols of feeling.[9]

2. Musical experience is a logical expression of feeling as embodied in the unconsummated, nondiscursive symbolic content of the music itself.
Langer argues that the popular romantic theory of self-expression does not adequately explain the nature of musical experience. According to that view, the composer or performer presents his or her own feelings by way of the musical work. All that is created and expressed is symptomatic of the artist's present emotional state. Langer argues against this by pointing out that an artist working on a tragedy need not be in personal despair. Such a state of mind would, in fact, be an obstacle to a work's logical expression. She makes use of an effective analogy when she states that "a screaming baby gives his feeling far more release than any musician, but we don't go into a concert hall to hear a baby scream."[10] To further her argument, she points out that interpreters of a work would be faced with the impossible task of determining the exact shades of emotional expression originally intended by the composer. This would prohibit a musical composition from being interpreted in more than one way — the original way in which the composer felt it should go.[11]

Yet, Langer does agree that the strength of the self-expression theory lies in its affirmation of the role of feeling in relation to music and in its support of music without any assigned connotation. In pairing the vague concept *expression* with music's symbolic function, Langer states that "a complex symbol . . . is an articulate form. Its characteristic symbolic function is what I call logical expression. It expresses relations; and it may "mean" — connote or denote — any complex of elements that is of the same articulate form as the symbol, the form which the symbol 'expresses.' "[12]

This notion of logical expression supports Langer's claim that no particular feeling or emotion can be assigned as the content of a particular musical work. Whereas discursive forms may point to a particular feeling, the role of music is to "formulate the life of feeling"[13] and present it directly to perception for objective under-standing. As such, music's import as an unconsummated symbol is ambivalent. Almost a true symbol, music has all the symbol's attributes except one: assigned connotation. Music is symbolic of subjective reality, but its import is never fixed:[14] "The real power of music lies in the fact that it can be true to the life of feeling in a way that language cannot; for its significant forms have that *ambivalence* of content which words cannot have."[15]

3. *The musical experience makes time audible and its form and continuity sensible.*

The primary illusion of music, created whenever its tonal ele-ments form a musical impression, is virtual time: "The semblance of this vital, experiential time is the primary illusion of music."[16] A human being's immediate sense of passage, the semblance of his or her subjective time, is analogous to the virtual time in music. Within the tensions and resolutions of this lived time there may be many strands of experience moving along together, diverging, opposing one an-other, so that subjective time comes to have a quality unlike the single dimension of time measured by the clock. This lived time can be measured by the quality and the volume of the tensions and resolutions experienced by the individual. Because it is not possible to attend to all the strands of lived time, the result is memories of only certain experiences and certain times. But our immediate sense of passage serves as the model of the virtual time of music:

> There we have its image, completely articulated and pure; every kind of tension transformed into musical tension, every qualitative content into musical quality, every extraneous factor replaced by musical elements. The primary illusion of music is the sonorous image of passage, abstracted from actuality to become free and plastic and entirely perceptible.[17]

If music is time made audible, then the listener should not strive to hear actual movement such as the physical motions caused by sound's vibrations. Also, the listener need not be overly concerned with the materials of music. One should not be occupied with detect-ing the structure, naming the chords, devices, or instruments used, because such perception is not a prerequisite for musical intuition.

What should be perceived is the virtual movement that exists only for the ear. The listener hears "the elements of music . . . meaning forms of sound"[18] that progress through a definite tonal range even though no tangible things are moving from one place to another. Langer insists that no special training or knowledge is necessary to recognize these global musical forms which articulate the forms of emotive life. She believes all human beings can gain access to emotive life through the expressive form of music. Musical perception is not an elitist enterprise. However, Langer also believes that an appreciation of the power of music in the education of human feeling could be enhanced by a more detailed knowledge of what the musician is making, to what end, and by what means.[19]

The secondary illusion of music is space. Perhaps the most noticeable source of spatialization in music can be perceived from its harmony. Certain harmonies and sonorities can produce the illusion of great open spaces while others present apparently confined spaces. This illusory space in music is always secondary to the illusion of time. It is the same "virtual space" found in the plastic arts that creates the illusion of depth. With regard to music, Langer states that "it is really an attribute of musical time, an appearance that serves to develop the temporal realm in more than one dimension."[20]

4. *The musical experience stems from an occurrent art form that grows from its initial inception to its complete presentation.*

From the initial moment a musical work is conceived until the time of its performance, it undergoes certain distinguishable stages of growth. "The first stage is the process of conception that takes place entirely in the composer's mind."[21] After putting aside "a loose fantasy" of wandering sounds, the composer eventually is presented with the Gestalt or commanding form which will be developed into a composition. Once the idea is recognized, the composer creatively interacts with the "embryonic musical work" in order to more completely refine its articulate character. During this stage of the process, the commanding form continually guides the artist as the composition's expressive possibilities are developed. If the composer is proficient at his craft, Langer believes that "his mind is trained and predisposed to see every option in relation to others, and to the whole."[22] She goes on to say:

Under the influence of the total "Idea," the musician *composes* every part of his piece. The principles of articulating music are so various that each composer finds his own idiom, even within the tradition he happens to inherit. The Idea as it occurs to him already suggests his own way of composing; and in that process lies the individuation of the piece.[23]

The argument as to whether or not a musical work is complete once the composer has heard the entire piece in his or her inner ear is addressed by Langer in the following way:

The composer's piece is an incomplete work, but it is a perfectly definite piece carried to a perfectly definite stage. . . . Performance is the completion of a musical work, a logical continuation of the imagination, carrying the creation through from thought to physical expression.[24]

5. *The musical experience is primarily obtained by listening.*

According to Langer, musicians listen to their own ideas before they perform or compose. They possess a certain power of inner hearing that serves as the foundation of their musical thinking. In relation to performance, she calls this ability *kinetic hearing*. The process is described in the clearest of terms when she states, "The mind hears, the hand follows, as faithfully as the voice itself obeys the inward ear."[25]

Langer makes a distinction between two kinds of musical hearing. Physical or actual hearing depends on the production of sound from some outside stimulus. It is essentially our mind's "actual sensory perception of sound."[26] Intelligent listeners must attentively focus on the immediacy of the musical experience at hand. Careless listeners only give superficial attention to the sounds their ears receive. They are prone to mental distractions that cause them to miss, to a greater or lesser degree, the elements of the musical experience. The more listeners are able to conceptually perceive the immediacy of the musical experience, the greater will be the awareness of its "commanding form."[27]

Inward or mental hearing is "a work of the mind, that begins with conceptions of form and ends with their complete presentation in imagined sense experience."[28] For example, during the silent reading of music, one's "inward hearing usually stops short of just that determinateness of quality and duration that characterizes actual sensation."[29] Listeners rarely "hear" a written note at absolute pitch. Dynamic levels are only perceived in the imagination at the points of greatest contrast within a work. "Moreover, the real length of tones is not always heard though it is somehow understood; in reading a slow movement one tends to read faster than the performance would pass in actual time."[30]

Langer states that inward musical hearing is a talent, "a special intelligence of the ear, and like all talents it develops through exercise."[31] But she is careful to point out that the first premise of listening to music is not conceptual, but sonorous. The primary activity of musical hearing "is not as many people assume, the ability to distinguish the separate elements in a composition and recognize its devices, but to experience the primary illusion, to feel the consistent movement and recognize at once the commanding form which makes this piece an inviolable whole."[32]

Thus, while conceptualization, analysis, and evaluation have their place in the understanding of a musical composition, they should be preceded and followed by the experience of the total work as an expressive form.

6. *In the musical experience, performance and composition are equally creative means of realizing expressive form.*

To Langer, "real performance is as creative an act as composition."[33] A performer who is unaware of the music's commanding form will respond manually to the printed page much as a typist copying uncomprehended material. As the culmination of the musical act, performance must carry through musical ideas from thought to physical manifestation.

Langer feels that a basic requisite of the natural, virtuoso performer is the power of utterance. She distinguishes between artistic utterance and simple emotional expression: "Artistic utterance always strives to create as complete and transparent a symbol as possible, whereas personal utterance, under the stress of actual emotion, usually contents itself with half-articulated symbols, just enough to explain the symptoms of inward pressure."[34] Ideally, the musician should express him- or herself on the deepest level that has nothing to do with moods and anxieties but with "the element of *ardor for the import conveyed.* This, of course, is actual feeling; it is not something symbolized by the music, but something that makes the symbol effective; it is the contagious excitement of the artist over the vital content of the work."[35] During performance it cannot be planned but must appear spontaneously or not at all. Without it the music will lack warmth; "it is the quality of impassioned utterance."[36]

Langer distinguishes between vocal and instrumental utterance. Instrumentalists, though they can be highly flexible and accurate in their tone production, aspire to the quality of utterance characteristic of the voice. On the other hand, a vocal performance is powerful if it approaches the speed, range, and flexibility of which instruments are capable. For either one, a truly musical performance requires that one concentrate personal feeling on the import of the music. Then such feeling becomes the drive, the aesthetic emotion, that motivates the performer's work. All of these energies and aesthetic emotions are then given to the service of the music itself.[37]

Langer does not believe that a musician has to have previously experienced the range of feelings being portrayed, but he or she should be able to imagine them. Both the instrumentalist and vocalist must be able to imagine what their muscles will feel like as they produce certain tones heard in their inner ear.[38] This kinetic hearing[39] is the final step before the actual sound is produced. Without this "muscular imagination" to aid performers in preparing their physical equipment, they will play badly or not at all. In addition to a muscular imagination, performers need what Langer calls a *sonorous imagination* or *conceptual imagination.* This type of inner hearing is related to muscular imagination in that it conceives the kind and quality of tone the commanding form of the piece requires. Ideally, the natural gifts of sonorous and muscular imagination should work together inside the minds of performers to help them produce the transparent image of expressive form. If this occurs, then the artist will be able to imagine what the feelings of a piece would be like without ever having experienced these feelings personally. But, performers should be aware of their imaginal limitations, for Langer also stresses the need for each artist to have a "proper repertoire" that can be convincingly presented to the audience.[40]

7. *In musical experience, aesthetic responsiveness can be developed to enhance intuitive and natural responses.*

To Langer, the fundamental response to music is a reaction to its primary illusion, virtual time. This involves, on the part of perceivers, the ability to recognize the distinction between musical elements and materials. Listeners who focus too closely on the technical aspects of a work's construction will be limiting their potential for aesthetic response to the music. Even though Langer argues that responsiveness is a "natural gift," she seems to say that it can be developed:

> That [responsiveness] is primarily a natural gift, related to creative talent . . . where if it exists in any measure it may be heightened by experience or reduced by adverse agencies. Since it is intuitive, it cannot be taught; but the free exercise of artistic intuition often depends on clearing the mind of intellectual prejudices and false conceptions that inhibit people's natural responsiveness.[41]

8. *In evaluating musical experience, one should attend to the expressive qualities inherent in each work rather than to rigid standards of good taste or beauty.*

Langer does not believe that a theory of art can provide criteria for judging a work's degree of expressiveness or standard of beauty. She holds that works of art are "not usually comparable" and should be judged solely on their expressiveness.[42] What is artistically good is whatever articulates and presents feeling to our understanding. It is the responsibility of the perceiver to intuitively react to and appreciate the aesthetic qualities of a work. Judgments can be made following this initial experience, "guided by the virtual results, the artist's success or failure, which is intuitively known or not at all."[43] At this point "the critic must see the commanding form of the . . . work, because that is the measure of right and wrong."[44]

Ian M. Alvarez

NOTES

1. Susanne K. Langer, *Feeling and Form* (New York: Charles Scribner's Sons, 1953), p. 27.

2. Eduard Hanslick, *The Beautiful in Music*, trans. G. Cohen (New York: Da Capo Press, 1974), p. 57 (originally published 1885).

3. Susanne K. Langer, *Problems of Art* (New York: Charles Scribner's Sons, 1957), pp. 59–60.

4. Ibid., p. 20.

5. Ibid., p. 24.

6. Susanne K. Langer, *Philosophy in a New Key: A Study in the Symbolism of Reason, Rite, and Art* (New York: Mentor Books, 1956), p. 218.

7. Langer, *Problems of Art*, p. 20.

8. Langer, *Feeling and Form*, p. 27.

9. Ibid., p. 401.

10. Langer, *Problems of Art*, p. 25.

11. Langer, *Philosophy in a New Key*, pp. 216–217.

12. Langer, *Feeling and Form*, pp. 30–31.

13. Ibid., p. 126.

14. Ibid., pp. 31–32.

15. Langer, *Philosophy in a New Key*, p. 197.

16. Langer, *Feeling and Form*, p. 109.

17. Ibid., p. 113.

18. Ibid., p. 109.

19. Ibid., p. 119.

20. Ibid., p. 117.

21. Ibid., p. 121.

22. Ibid., p. 122.

23. Ibid., p. 123.

24. Ibid., p. 138.

25. Ibid., p. 145.

26. Ibid.

27. Ibid., p. 147.

28. Ibid., p. 137.

29. Ibid.

30. Ibid.

31. Ibid.
32. Ibid., p. 147.
33. Ibid., p. 139.
34. Ibid.
35. Ibid., p. 141.
36. Ibid.
37. Ibid., p. 145.
38. Ibid., p. 144.
39. Ibid., p. 145.
40. Ibid., p. 146.
41. Ibid., p. 396.
42. Ibid., p. 406.
43. Ibid., p. 407.
44. Ibid.

FRED LERDAHL *and* RAY JACKENDOFF
(1943–   ) (1945–   )

SOURCES

Fred Lerdahl is professor of music theory and composition at the University of Michigan, and Ray Jackendoff is professor of linguistics at Brandeis University. The book in which they present their most developed ideas, *A Generative Theory of Tonal Music* (1983), is the third book in the *MIT Press Series on Cognitive Theory and Mental Representation*. Several articles preceding and following the book contain less rigorous presentations of the same ideas. These articles include "Discovery Procedures vs. Rules of Musical Grammar in a Generative Music Theory" (1980), "Generative Music Theory and Its Relation to Psychology" (1985), "Toward a Formal Theory of Tonal Music" (1977), and "On the Theory of Grouping and Meter" (1981). Their book is the primary source of information used in this essay.

GENERAL ORIENTATION TO MUSICAL EXPERIENCE

The goal of *A Generative Theory of Tonal Music* is to devise a theory of music that formally describes the "musical intuitions of a listener who is experienced in a musical idiom."[1] This theory describes musical organization in terms of a set of hypothetical mental constructs:

The present study will justify the view that a piece of music is a mentally constructed entity, of which scores and performances are partial representations by which the piece is transmitted. . . . Seen in this way, music theory takes a place among traditional areas of cognitive psychology such as theories of vision and language.[2]

By the "musical intuitions of the experienced listener," the authors are not describing a conscious grasp of musical structures (such as fugue or deceptive cadence), but rather

> the largely unconscious knowledge (the "musical intuition") that the listener brings to his hearing — a knowledge that enables him to organize and make coherent the surface patterns of pitch, attack, duration, intensity, timbre, and so forth. Such a listener is able to identify a previously unknown piece as an example of the idiom, to recognize elements of a piece as typical or anomalous, to identify a performer's error as possibly producing an "ungrammatical" configuration, to recognize various kinds of structural repetitions and variations, and, generally, to comprehend a piece within the idiom.[3]

The authors' theory of music tries to create an explicitly formal musical grammar that can characterize the type of organizations (musical intuitions) described above. Their theory of musical grammar describes the connection between the presentation of music and the listener's mental structuring of that music.

The "experienced listener" is meant as an idealization. While it is rare that two people hear a piece of music in exactly the same way, it is thought that there is one way to hear the piece that is the most natural. The present theory describes the "most natural hearing," but it can also allow for situations in which there are alternate interpretations.

Another unique component of Lerdahl and Jackendoff's theory is that it is concerned with the final state of a listener's understanding rather than the listener's real time mental process: "In our view it would be fruitless to theorize about mental processing before understanding the organization to which the processing leads."[4] This is their methodological choice.

The authors also deal with the question of how much of an experienced listener's knowledge is learned and how much is due to innate musical capacity or general cognitive capacity:

A formal theory of musical idioms will make possible substantive hypotheses about those aspects of musical understanding that are innate; the innate aspects will reveal themselves as "universal" principles of musical grammar. . . . A theory of a sufficiently intricate musical idiom will be a rich source of hypotheses about psychological musical universals.[5]

These universals of musical grammars are "the principles available to all experienced listeners for organizing the musical surfaces they hear, no matter what idiom they are experienced in."[6]

Finally, they summarize their intentions as follows:

In this book we develop a music theory along the lines suggested by these general considerations. Specifically, we present a substantial fragment of a theory of classical Western tonal music (henceforth "tonal music"), worked out with an eye toward an eventual theory of musical cognitive capacity. Our general empirical criteria for success of the theory are how adequately it describes musical intuition, what it enables us to say of interest about particular pieces of music, what it enables us to say about the nature of tonal music and of music in general, and how well it dovetails with broader issues of cognitive theory. In addition, we impose formal criteria common to any theoretical enterprise, requiring internal coherence and simplicity of the formal model relative to the complexity of the phenomena it accounts for. In short, we conceive of our theory as being in principle testable by usual scientific standards: that is, subject to verification or falsification on various sorts of empirical grounds.[7]

A very strong influence on the theory is the study of language by the school of generative-transformational grammar (whose chief advocate is Noam Chomsky).[8] This generative linguistic theory is an attempt "to characterize what a human being knows when he knows how to speak a language, enabling him to understand and create an indefinitely large number of sentences, most of which he has never heard before."[9] The formal system of rules (the grammar) describes (generates) the possible sentences of a language.

The depth of psychological understanding of language resulting from Chomsky's work has been significant. Lerdahl and Jackendoff believe that such a process of formalizing unconscious psychological processes also can add to the understanding of musical experience. They feel, however, that although music and linguistics have parallels, the situation in the two fields is not identical. The parallels between music and language lie in the fact that both have elements that interact with each other. (In music these elements include rhythm and pitch organization, dynamic and timbral differentiation, and motivic-thematic processes, while in language the elements are known as nouns, verbs, prepositions, verb phrases, etc.) But in no way do the authors give any discursive or referential "meaning" to music, as compared with linguistic meaning.

The use of the term *generate* does not mean to produce (as an electrical generator produces electricity) but to describe (as in the mathematical sense — "to describe a usually infinite set by formal means"). In music, this means the theory is not meant to show what pieces are possible, but rather to give a "structural description" for any tonal piece, which is the structure that experienced listeners infer when they hear a piece:

> Linguistic theory is not simply concerned with the analysis of a set of sentences; rather it considers itself a branch of psychology, concerned with making empirically verifiable claims about one complex aspect of human life: language. Similarly, our ultimate goal is an understanding of musical cognition, a psychological phenomenon.[10]

Lerdahl and Jackendoff's theory deals with aspects of music that are hierarchical in a way that exploits the dominant and subordinate relationships of the different levels of the hierarchy. There are four components of music that the theory treats in this hierarchical fashion: grouping structure, metrical structure, time-span reduction, and prolongational reduction.[11]

Within each of the four components in the theory, there are two types of rules that describe the listener's hearing of a piece. *Wellformedness rules* specify the possible structural descriptions. *Preference rules* "designate out of the possible structural descriptions those that correspond to the experienced listener's hearing of any particular piece."[12] Well-formedness rules are very similar to the rules of grammar

in language, but there is no such linguistic counterpart for the preference rules. The latter are not needed in linguistics because of the
meaning of the words in a sentence. However, they are needed in
music to express preferences among interpretations.[13]

The parameters of music subjected to the theory are largely the
"syntactical" parameters (pitch and rhythm). In dealing with the "statistical" parameters, Lerdahl and Jackendoff state:

> Other dimensions of musical structure — notably timbre, dynam-
> ics, and motivic-thematic processes — are not hierarchical in
> nature, and are not treated directly in the theory as it now stands.
> Yet these dimensions play an important role in the theory in that
> they make crucial contributions to the principles that establish the
> hierarchical structure for a piece. The theory thus takes into ac-
> count the influence of nonhierarchical dimensions, even though it
> does not formalize them.[14]

FEATURES OF MUSICAL EXPERIENCE

1. *The musical experience is affected by the experienced listener's ability
to apply grouping structure to a piece of music.*

This grouping structure expresses a hierarchical segmentation of a
piece into motives, phrases, and sections. The process of grouping is
common in many areas of human cognition. People tend to organize
elements of a sequence of events into "chunks." "The ease or difficulty
with which someone performs this operation depends on how well the
intrinsic organization of the input matches his internal, unconscious
principles for constructing groupings."[15] When the idealized experienced listener listens to music, the musical units are apparent, and it is
obvious which units fit together and which do not. The authors
describe grouping structure as "the most basic component of musical
understanding."[16]

2. *The musical experience is affected by the experienced listener's ability
to apply metrical structure to a piece of music.*

This metrical structuring expresses the intuition that the events of
a piece are related to a regular alternation of strong and weak beats at
a number of hierarchical levels. Metrical structuring revolves around
the concepts of accent and beat. Phenomenal and structural accents are

found in the surface of the music (the former by a high note, long note, harmonic change, dynamic change, etc.; the latter by a point of harmonic gravity, especially a final cadence), and metrical accents are found in any beat that is relatively strong in its metrical context. Beats are points in time (with no duration) that are very strongly governed by hierarchical relationships.[17]

3. *The musical experience is affected by the experienced listener's ability to apply time-span reductions to a piece of music.*

In regard to the two types of reduction in their theory, the authors state: "The listener attempts to organize all the pitch-events of a piece into a single coherent structure, such that they are heard in a hierarchy of relative importance."[18] As an example of this, Lerdahl and Jackendoff point to the version of a popular song that is played in "stop time" to accompany a tap dancer. Despite the fact that only a few notes of the song are played, the listener accepts it as a complete version of the song. Their notion of a reduction hypothesis is modified by asking three questions that, when answered, add three variables to the construction of the reduction: (1) what are the criteria of structural importance? (2) what relationships may be obtained between the more or less structural events? and (3) what musical intuitions are conveyed by the reduction as a result of questions 1 and 2?

These time-span reductions assign a hierarchy of "structural importance" to the pitches of a piece with respect to their position in grouping and metrical structure. This component of the theory uses grouping and metrical structure to create a visual representation of music the authors call a "time-span tree." On the local level there are four types of branching that a time-span tree may contain: (1) the downbeat may dominate the afterbeat, (2) the afterbeat may dominate the downbeat, (3) the downbeat may dominate the upbeat, and (4) the upbeat may dominate the downbeat. These four branchings can be found in all hierarchical levels.[19]

4. *The musical experience is affected by the experienced listener's ability to apply prolongational reductions to a piece of music.*

These prolongational reductions assign a hierarchy to the pitches that express harmonic and melodic tension and relaxation, continuity, and progression. In the grouping, metrical, and time-span components of the theory there is nothing that expresses the sense of tension and relaxation involved in the ongoing process of music. With the prolongational reduction one is able to speak of "points of relative tension and repose and the way the music progresses from one to the other."[20]

David L. Nelson

NOTES

1. Fred Lerdahl and Ray Jackendoff, *A Generative Theory of Tonal Music* (Cambridge, MA: MIT Press, 1983), p. 3.

2. Ibid.

3. Ibid., p. 3.

4. Ibid.

5. Ibid., p. 4.

6. Ibid., p. 278.

7. Ibid. pp. 4–5.

8. Relevant works by Chomsky are listed in the bibliography.

9. Ibid., p. 5.

10. Ibid., p. 6.

11. Ibid., pp. 13–26.

12. Ibid., p. 9.

13. Ibid., pp. 10–13.

14. Ibid., p. 9.

15. Ibid., p. 13.

16. Ibid.

17. Fred Lerdahl and Ray Jackendoff, "On the Theory of Grouping and Meter," *The Musical Quarterly* 67 (1981), pp. 485–493.

18. Lerdahl and Jackendoff, *A Generative Theory*, p. 106.

19. Ibid., pp. 106–111.

20. Ibid., p. 179.

ABRAHAM MASLOW
(1908-1970)

SOURCES

Abraham Maslow, the father of humanistic or "third force" psychology, developed his theories as a reaction to what he believed were inadequacies in both the behavioristic and Freudian psychologies. Maslow's concept of *peak experience* is the one most relevant to the study of musical experience. Although he never directed his studies toward musical peak experiences, he did discuss implications of the peak experience as they relate to music and education.

References that are key to the understanding of Maslow's research on and development of the idea of the peak experience include *Toward a Psychology of Being* (1962), *Religions, Values, and Peak Experiences* (1964), *Motivation and Personality* (1970), and *The Farther Reaches of Human Nature* (1971). In 1961 Maslow delivered a public lecture entitled "Lessons from the Peak Experiences," which summarized his research on the subject at the time. In 1967 Maslow spoke at the Music Educators National Conference (MENC) Tanglewood Symposium on the topic "Music, Education, and Peak Experiences." Both lectures subsequently were reprinted in professional journals.

GENERAL ORIENTATION TO "PEAK EXPERIENCE"

In developing his theory of psychology, Maslow conducted extensive interviews with and observations of what he described as healthy people — "the best specimens of mankind."[1] One of the things he discovered was that many of these individuals reported having what he originally described as a variety of mystic experience:

> These were moments of pure, positive happiness when all doubts, all fears, all inhibitions, all tensions, all weaknesses, were left behind. Now self-consciousness was lost. All separateness and distance from the world disappeared as they felt one with the world, fused with it, really belonging in it and to it, instead of being outside looking in.[2]

Maslow later discarded the use of the term *mystic experience* when it became evident that these experiences could occur as a result of a number of different "triggers." He described them as being natural rather than supernatural, and he later discovered that they were not limited to particular individuals but appeared to occur in psychologically sick people as well as healthy people:

> These experiences mostly had nothing to do with religion — at least in the ordinary supernatural sense. They came from great moments of love and sex, from great esthetic moments (particularly of music), from bursts of creativeness and the creative furor (the great inspiration), from great moments of insight and discovery, from women giving natural birth to babies — or just from loving them, from moments of fusion with nature (in a forest, on a seashore, mountains, etc.), from certain athletic experiences, e.g., skindiving, from dancing, etc.[3]

Maslow described peak experience as being transitory, a moment of self-actualization or psychological health. It is evident from his writing that he did not view peak experiences obtained through music as different from those obtained through other vehicles or events. He believed that the subjective experience is always similar, but that the stimuli may differ: "I feel more sure of this after reading in the literatures of mystic experiences, cosmic consciousness, oceanic experiences, esthetic experiences, creative experiences, parental experiences, sexual experiences, and insight experiences. They all overlap, they approach similarity, even identity."[4]

FEATURES OF PEAK EXPERIENCE

1. *Peak experiences come unexpectedly.*
Maslow suggested that it isn't possible to search for peak experiences; they just happen. However, he did believe that experiences in the past can affect the likelihood of their occurrence.[5]

2. *The peak experience is most accessible when there is a receptive frame of mind.*
This frame of mind, according to Maslow, requires a kind of passivity, trust, or surrender. He likened it to the Taoistic attitude of letting things happen, or noninterference: "You have to be able to give up pride, will, dominance, being at the wheel, being in charge."[6]

3. *The peak experience is characterized by mutual feedback between the peak and the peaker.*
According to Maslow, there is a kind of "mutual and parallel feedback or reverberation between the characteristics of the perceiver and of the perceived world so that they tend to influence each other. . . . The perceiver has to be worthy of the percept."[7]

In addition to these more general concepts concerning the features of the peak experience, Maslow listed nineteen characteristics of cognition found in peak experiences. This list represents the entire scope of possibilities in a generalized peak experience:

1. The object tends to be seen as a whole.

2. The percept is exclusively and fully attended to.

3. The world is seen as independent of human strivings in general. Cognition is noncomparing, nonjudging.

4. Repeated *B*-Cognizing (Being-Cognition) seems to make the perception richer.

5. Perception is relatively ego-transcending; it tends to be organized around the object rather than the ego.

6. The peak experience is felt as a self-validating, self-justifying moment that carries its own intrinsic value with it. This is a universal characteristic.

7. There is a characteristic disorientation in time and space.

8. The peak experience is experienced only as good and desirable, never as evil or undesirable.

9. Peak experiences are more relative and less absolute from the point of placement in time and space and historical referents.

10. B-Cognition is much more passive and receptive than active.

11. The emotional reaction in the peak experience has a special flavor of wonder, awe, reverence, and surrender before the experience as before something great.

12. In some peak experiences, one small part of the world is seen as if it were for the moment all of the world.

13. The perception of the unique nature of the object is characteristic of *all* peak experiences.

14. Dichotomies, polarities, and conflicts may be fused, transcended, or resolved.

15. The person at the peak is godlike in the complete, loving, uncondemning, compassionate, and perhaps bemused acceptance of the world.

16. Perception in the peak moment tends strongly to be idiographic and nonclassificatory.

17. There is complete though momentary loss of fear, anxiety, inhibition, defense, and control.

18. As the essential Being of the world is perceived by the person, so also does he concurrently come closer to his own being.

19. A certain childishness may accompany maturity.[8]

Not all of these characteristics, however, would necessarily be found in a single peak experience. A more complete discussion of these characteristics can be found in Maslow's *Toward a Psychology of Being*.

MASLOW ON MUSIC, EDUCATION, AND PEAK EXPERIENCE

In a speech delivered at the 1967 MENC Tanglewood Symposium, Maslow discussed peak experience and its relationship to some of the arts and education. This is the only time that he spoke at any length about peak experience and music. The following summarizes his comments related to music as they were reprinted in *A Documentary Report of the Tanglewood Symposium.*

According to Maslow, music and sex are the two easiest means of reaching peak experience. In his own research he found that peak experience in music occurred only as a result of listening to what he termed "the great classics":

> I have not found a peak experience from John Cage or from an Andy Warhol movie, from abstract expressionistic kind of painting, or the like. I just haven't. The peak experience that has reported great joy, the ecstasy, the visions of another world, or another level of living, have come from classical music — the great classics.[9]

Maslow goes on to say that music "melts over and fuses into" dancing and rhythm.[10] This includes a love for, and awareness of, the body. All of these are described as being good paths to growth toward full-humanness and self-actualization. Maslow believes this to be the goal of education. He feels that music and the arts can help attain that goal. He labels this teaching of full-humanness (learning to grow, learning the difference between good and bad, and between desirable and undesirable) as intrinsic education:

> In this realm of intrinsic learning, intrinsic teaching, and intrinsic education I think that the arts, especially the ones that I have mentioned (music, dancing), are so close to this identity, this biological core, rather than think of these courses as a sort of whipped cream or luxury cream, they must become basic experiences in education. I mean that this kind of education can be a glimpse into the infinite, into ultimate values.[11]

Penelope Smith Woodward

NOTES

1. Abraham Maslow, "Lessons from the Peak Experiences," *Journal of Humanistic Psychology* 2 (Spring 1962), p. 9.

2. Ibid.

3. Ibid., p. 10.

4. Ibid.

5. Ibid., pp. 9–10.

6. Ibid., p. 13.

7. Ibid., pp. 13–14.

8. Abraham Maslow, *Toward a Psychology of Being* (Princeton, NJ: Van Nostrand, 1962), Chapter 6.

9. Abraham Maslow, "Music, Education, and Peak Experience," in *A Documentary Report of the Tanglewood Symposium,* ed. Robert Choate (Reston, VA: MENC, 1968), p. 73.

10. Ibid.

11. Ibid.

LEONARD B. MEYER
(1918–   )

SOURCES

Emotion and Meaning in Music (1956) represents Leonard B. Meyer's major contribution to our understanding of the nature and value of the musical experience. *Music, the Arts, and Ideas: Patterns and Predictions in Twentieth-Century Culture* (1967), though essentially a study of musical modernism, examines central themes of musical meaning and musical affective experience. In *Explaining Music: Essays and Explorations* (1973), Meyer further amends his notions of expectation. Taken together, these three books provide a model of the psychological experience of musical phenomena from the listener's perspective. While *Emotion and Meaning in Music* remains Meyer's primary study of the musical experience and his most influential book, three recent works modify his earliest concepts of musical experience: "Toward a Theory of Style" (1979), "Exploring Limits: Creation, Archetypes and Change" (1980), and "Innovation, Choice, and the History of Music" (1983).

GENERAL ORIENTATION TO MUSICAL EXPERIENCE

Two propositions underpin Meyer's study of musical experience: (1) music is meaningful, and (2) the meaning of music is communicated to both participants and listeners.[1]

For Meyer, the source of musical meaning is found intra-musically through the comprehension of musical relationships.[2] Although he acknowledges the importance of referential musical meaning, Meyer is primarily concerned with explaining how an abstract nonreferential pattern of sounds can have meaning for and be experienced as emotion by a listener who understands a given musical work. More precisely, he is concerned with explaining the intellectual satisfaction a *formalist* derives from musical experience, the affective response experienced by the *absolute expressionist,* and the relationship between these basic categories of musical experience.[3]

Implicit in Meyer's values and concerns is a populist orientation toward the nature and value of musical experience. His model is dominated by a concern for explaining musical meaning in contexts that elitist studies usually pass over. It pivots on (1) the learned responses of a listener familiar with an established musical style — rather than on a composer's intentions or strategies, on the isolated musical stimulus, or on scores in the abstract;[4] (2) a universal psychological mechanism that explains a wide range of affective and intellectual responses;[5] (3) a wide range of musical styles; and (4) fundamental laws of human perception and cognition.[6] Most notably, perhaps, Meyer's theory attempts to link a theory of musical understanding to a theory of musical value. This linkage is important to a full explanation of musical experience because the value of a work can only be realized and assessed by the listener to the extent that the listener experiences the work with understanding.

Although the absolutist view of musical import was widely accepted in the 1950s, *Emotion and Meaning in Music* demonstrates an unusual willingness to confront the problems presented by referential musical experience, as well as an unusual ability to resolve the then-current philosophical dichotomies through the application of concepts from a wide range of disciplines. Drawing from psychological theory, Meyer expands concepts that were still largely misunderstood by many authorities at the time and applies them to a variety of musical examples to demonstrate his central theses. From John Dewey and the post-Freudian psychoanalyst David Rapaport, Meyer takes the "conflict theory of emotion" (or "psychoanalytic theory of affect") as the basis for his concept of the arousal of musical meaning. Traditional models of the psychology of music (exemplified by Hermann von Helmholtz, Wilhelm Wundt and Karl Stumpf) are disputed, and the mechanisms of affective-intellectual engagement are elaborated with reference to the conflict theory as well as principles of Gestalt psychology borrowed from Kurt Koffka and Max Wertheimer. Meyer draws upon the writings of a variety of music theorists, musicologists, critics, and ethnomusicologists to support the musical analyses he employs to illustrate the efficacy of his psychological explanations. Finally, his invocation of information theory to link his theory of musical understanding to musical value depends upon concepts from logic, probability, clinical psychology, communication theory, cybernetics, anthropology, and philosophy.

FEATURES OF MUSICAL EXPERIENCE

1. *Musical experience (a) shares the conditions of all affective experience and (b) is differentiated from ordinary experience.*
Meyer's absolutist account of musical experience is grounded on the proposition that the nature of musical affective experience and the conditions of musical affective experience are the same as affective experience in general. Regardless of the nature of the stimulus situation, Meyer believes that "emotion or affect is aroused when a tendency to respond is arrested or inhibited."[7] To Meyer, the inhibition of a tendency or an expectation (musical or otherwise) is a necessary and sufficient condition for the arousal of affect. In short, although affective experience may be differentiated by a given stimulus situation, affect itself is undifferentiated.

Having established the congruency between musical affective experience and nonmusical affective experience, Meyer makes a crucial distinction. He points out that, whereas musical tendencies to respond are activated and inhibited by the same stimulus, and whereas the tensions created by the inhibition of those musical tendencies are resolved by this same musical stimulus, the activation, inhibition, and resolution of tendencies in ordinary events usually lack such common linkage.[8] Thus, there is no meaningful relationship between the onset of a tendency and the resolution or disappearance of tension in ordinary events.

2. *Musical experience, whether intellectual or affective, is aroused when a tendency to respond is inhibited.*

A tendency is actually an automatic response pattern — a chain of expectations.[9] These expectations may take the form of objective (self-conscious) concepts or tacit awarenesses; they may be general or specific; they may be formally or informally acquired. Since some musical consequents of given antecedents are more probable than others, expectations are activated in a listener by the progress of the musical stimuli. Each unexpected musical consequent creates tension in the listener.[10] This tension is experienced as affect if the listener's original expectations were tacit or unconscious. An objective conceptualization (or conscious) awareness of musical tendencies and their inhibitions is a function of a listener's attitude. Such awareness leads to a rationalization of response, or an "intellectual" experience of the music.[11] Thus, it can be seen that the same processes that give rise to musical affective experience also give rise to the objectification of embodied musical meaning. Musical meaning, whether affective or intellectual, arises when a tendency to respond is inhibited. This explanation effects a reconciliation between absolute formalism and absolute expressionism. It also underlines the fact that meaningful musical experience depends crucially on a listener's musical expectations.

3. *Musical experience is meaningful.*

Something is meaningful if and only if it points to, indicates, or implies something beyond itself. A stimulus has *designative meaning* if it points to an event different in kind from itself. A stimulus has *embodied meaning* if it implies an event of the same kind as itself. It follows from this that "embodied musical meaning is a product of expectation."[12] That is, a musical event has meaning for a listener if and only if it points to or arouses a listener's expectations for another musical event. To Meyer, "to mean" is "to expect."[13] Thus, a listener with no experience in a given musical style — a listener with no musical expectations — is unlikely to have a meaningful experience of any work in that particular style. Conversely, the meaning of a musical passage for an experienced listener is the expectation that it produces for a weighted set of musically probable events — not just a single, fully definite musical event. This is so because an experienced listener would rarely anticipate only one way for a musical passage to continue. In fact, to a large extent, listeners' experiences are equivalent to their internalized set of musical expectations (probabilities or hypotheses) relative to the musical passages they hear.[14] This mental set — including the listener's modes of learning and perception — partakes of universal mental tendencies[15] (the principles of which are associated with the Gestalt school of psychology) including (1) a desire for completeness and stability; (2) a desire for continuation; (3) a need to regularize; and (4) an expectation of growth, change, or novelty.

Meyer notes that the sounds experienced listeners expect are the "hypothetical meaning" of the sounds they actually hear.[16] As the listener's expectations are confirmed, denied, or amended during the course of a work's unfolding, the listener may experience at least two other stages or types of embodied musical meaning: *evident meaning* and *determinate meaning*.[17] Evident meaning occurs to a listener in retrospect when a listener gleans the causal relationship between a musical antecedent and its consequent upon completion of the consequent. Determinate meaning is the larger form of evident meaning: it occurs in the retrospective consideration and interpretation of all the musical relationships in a piece of music.

4. *Musical experience is informative.*

In *Music, the Arts, and Ideas*, Meyer suggests that "the psycho-stylistic conditions which give rise to musical meaning, whether affective or intellectual, are the same as those which communicate information."[18] Meyer's concept of "information" can be summarized quite succinctly: information is the inverse of probability. The most probable event produces the least information; the most unlikely event produces the most information. Thus, Meyer's theory of musical meaning can be modified to this: musical meaning arises when a listener, uncertain of the music's progress, objectively or tacitly estimates the probabilities of the music's continuation. When less probable events occur, the music is experienced as meaningful.[19]

Meyer's application of information theory to musical experience further suggests that music is a process that produces a chain of elements according to certain probabilities in which the probabilities depend on the previous elements.[20] In summary, Meyer believes that music is as meaningful as it is informative. Whatever increases the amount of information communicated by music also increases its value. These concepts form the basis of Meyer's theory of musical value.

5. *Musical experience that is meaningful and informative is also valuable.* Meyer suggests that musical value is proportional to musical meaning and, therefore, to musical information.[21] Because a piece of music is meaningful if and only if it creates an expectation for its continuation, a work that creates no such expectations has no meaning and therefore no value. If a work reaches the most probable consequents directly, it has little or no meaning and value. If it attains its goal only after irrelevant diversions, or if it does not attain its goal, it forfeits its potential for meaning and value. Overall, embodied musical meaning, musical affective experience, intellectual musical experience, musical information, and musical value are all a function of the inhibition of musical tendencies and the resultant inhibition of the experienced listener's tendencies to respond.[22]

According to Meyer's early writings, a listener's response to the syntactic dimensions of a work is more important than his or her response to designative meanings and sensuous musical dimensions. Furthermore, these aspects are considered to be of minor importance in evaluating music for three reasons: (1) determining sensuous appeal is a purely subjective process; (2) syntactic musical relationships are essential to all but the most primitive works; and (3) the superior of two works of equal sensuous power can only be determined by reference to the syntactic organization of each.[23]

Continuing with this discussion, Meyer adds three important insights on musical value and musical greatness. First, he acknowledges that a syntactically simple work may arouse profound response. However, Meyer suggests that such response is actually a function of the extra-musical significance such a piece has for the listener, not its syntax.[24] Second, Meyer acknowledges that a syntactically simple work may have greater value than a complex work due to the economy of means involved in producing the musical information. That is, if a simple work produces the same amount of information as a complex work, the simple work has the greater syntactic value by virtue of its economic disposition of musical materials.[25] Third, Meyer believes that although a syntactic theory may be appropriate for assessing musical value, musical greatness can only be determined by considering the interaction between a work's syntactic structure and the profundity of its associative or extra-musical content (aspects of human existence like "[man's] awareness of his own insignificance and impotence in the face of the magnitude and power of creation"[26]). When both dimensions (syntactic and associative) are superior; "we attain a new level of consciousness, of individualization."[27]

6. *Musical experience includes an appreciation of syntactic and statistical parameters.*

Although Meyer's recent writings are principally concerned with the nature of musical style and the relationship of style development to cultural history, several concepts presented in these contexts alter his original formulations. For example, Meyer observes that the syntactic (or primary) and statistical (or secondary) parameters of music are distinguished by their material means.

The musical elements of syntactic parameters (such as melody and harmony) "can be segmented into discrete, nonuniform entities so that similarities and differences between them are definable, constant and proportional."[28]

However, statistical parameters (exactly equivalent rhythmic patterns; constant modes of timbral, textural, or rhythmic activity; dynamic gradations) "cannot be segmented into perceptually discrete entities."[29] The latter tend to be perceived and considered in terms of amounts: louder, softer; brighter, darker; thicker, thinner; more drive, less drive. Statistical musical elements therefore tend to support rather than define and shape music; they may signal points of closure or they may cease, but they cannot, by themselves, create closure.

Nevertheless, these statistical parameters "often play important roles — reinforcing or undermining the processes generated by the primary parameters" in styles where "syntactic constraints" are essential.[30] They establish their own "processive relationships" because, once initiated, these modes of musical activity — constancy, gradual change, regular alternation — imply their own continuation, and "such implication is understood as being processive."[31]

Meyer adds that musical parameters need not simply be categorized as syntactic or statistical, "but within each group some parameters may be more important than others in shaping or qualifying the structure and process of music in a particular style."[32] Musical styles can thus be defined to a considerable degree by the dominance or absence of parameters and/or their particular musical constituents.

Finally, in a discussion of the important role played by statistical parameters in nineteenth-century Romantic style, Meyer hints at their affective power:

> It is necessary to recognize that the secondary parameters are, perhaps paradoxically, a more natural means for shaping musical processes and articulating musical forms than are the primary ones. . . . This is because the physical patterning of the sound continuum — of pitch frequency, concord and discord, dynamic intensity, rate of impulse, instrumental timbre, and so on — *shapes states of tension and repose in an almost unmediated, direct way.*[33] [Emphasis added.]

In summary, Meyer's recent articles offer several amendments to his early thesis. First, Meyer reconceptualizes the sensuous dimension of music in terms of statistical musical parameters. Second, he acknowledges that statistical parameters can shape states of tension and release. Third, Meyer suggests that the evaluation of music must include considerations of the "relational richness" between these parameters and among their constituents.[34]

7. *Musical experience can lead to individualization.*

Meyer's belief in the ability of musical experience to advance personal psychological development is evidenced in at least two references. In his account of musical value in *Music, the Arts, and Ideas,* Meyer defends his exclusive focus on musical syntax by suggesting that, unlike associative and sensuous musical responses, the syntactic musical response enables the listener to achieve self-awareness and a sense of individuality because it involves the listener in the consideration of various probabilities and the retrospective understanding of the relationship among musical events.[35] This sense of individuality is enhanced to the degree that immediate gratification is withheld by the music.

In a more recent source, Meyer makes the same connection in broader terms:

> Music is a metaphor not primarily because . . . it depicts feelings and ideas connected with particular events in the extra-musical world, but because music is a model, an archetype, of all experience — experience in which making inferences and predictions,

sensing ambiguities, feeling uncertainties, and revising opinions are the most basic facts there are in a world of probability.[36]

David J. Elliott

NOTES

1. Leonard B. Meyer, *Emotion and Meaning in Music* (Chicago: University of Chicago Press, 1956), p. 1.

2. Ibid., p. 4.

3. Ibid.

4. Ibid., p. 30.

5. Ibid., p. 13.

6. Ibid., p. 30

7. Ibid., p. 14.

8. Ibid., p. 23.

9. Ibid., p. 24.

10. Ibid., p. 27.

11. Ibid., p. 31.

12. Ibid., p. 35.

13. Ibid.

14. Ibid., p. 77.

15. Ibid., p. 91.

16. Ibid., p. 37.

17. Ibid., pp. 37–38.

18. Leonard B. Meyer, *Music, the Arts, and Ideas: Patterns and Predictions in Twentieth-Century Culture* (Chicago: University of Chicago Press, 1967), p. 5.

19. Ibid., p. 27.

20. Ibid., p. 15.

21. Ibid., p. 21.

22. Ibid., p. 9.

23. Ibid., pp. 34–37.

24. Ibid., p. 37.

25. Ibid.

26. Ibid., p. 38.

27. Ibid.

28. Leonard B. Meyer, "Toward a Theory of Style," in *The Concept of Style,* ed. B. Lang (Philadelphia: University of Pennsylvania Press, 1979), p. 18.

29. Ibid.

30. Ibid., p. 20.

31. Ibid., p. 19.

32. Ibid., p. 22.

33. Leonard B. Meyer, "Exploring Limits: Creation, Archetypes, and Style Change," *Daedalus* 109 (1980), p. 194.

34. Leonard B. Meyer, "Grammatical Simplicity and Relational Richness: The Trio of Mozart's G Minor Symphony," *Critical Inquiry* 2 (1976), p. 694.

35. Meyer, *Music, The Arts, and Ideas,* p. 35.

36. Leonard B. Meyer, "Review of: Donald N. Ferguson, *Music as Metaphor,*" (Minneapolis: University of Minnesota Press, 1960) in *Journal of the American Musicological Society* 15 (1962), p. 236.

JAMES MURSELL
(1893–1963)

SOURCES

James Mursell was an eminent music educator as well as a philosopher and scholar. The last twenty-four years of his career, until his retirement in 1959, were spent at the Teachers College of Columbia University where he chaired the departments of Education and Music Education. Mursell wrote twenty-three books and numerous articles on music education. Six of his books describe the musical experience in depth: *Principles of Musical Education* (1927), *Human Values in Music Education* (1934), *The Psychology of Music* (1937), *Music in American Schools* (1943), *Education for Musical Growth* (1948), and *Music Education: Principles and Programs* (1956). Two addresses presented at the Eastern Music Educators Wartime Institute in Rochester, New York, on March 20–23, 1943, offer further insight; these were reprinted in the April and May/June 1943 issues of the *Music Educators Journal*.

GENERAL ORIENTATION TO MUSICAL EXPERIENCE

Mursell viewed musical experience as inherently positive, enhancing the quality of human life. He thought of it as appealing, vital, significant, and enjoyable. These effects could be lost, however, if a natural emphasis on expression and joy of discovery was replaced by pointless drill or analysis. In general, music's natural tendency is to bring a lifetime of enjoyment to all kinds of people. According to

Mursell, the essence of musical experience could be explained in terms of musical feeling:

> When we listen to and enter into music we are carried away into a world of feeling. The music possesses us, flows through us, and sweeps us along with it. So it is that music has been called the language of emotions, though this is a misleading phrase. But certainly musical feeling is the supreme outcome of musical culture.[1]

Mursell held that feeling was objectified in musical design just as beauty was embodied in musical ideas, and that musical feeling could be represented by expressive devices that reflect life struggles. These expressive devices create musical expectations that may be either satisfied or frustrated.

Expressive devices in music are neither arbitrary nor extrinsic. The ordering of tones, dynamic shadings, tempi, and tempo variations help listeners feel fairly specific moods. However, like human emotions, musical feelings are ineffable and dependent on the conditions that arouse them. Moreover, a piece of music may present several moods at once. In this case, the unique experiences of each listener will determine which moods will capture his or her attention. Since the emotions presented in music are not literal, they differ from the objective emotions experienced in daily life.

Mursell believed that emotions are actually felt and that they can be described in tactile terms, just as musical phrases could be described in terms of physical motion. Some people react kinesthetically to music. Unlike the visual arts, music occurs in time, and its temporal nature controls the timing of responses to it.[2] Listeners respond to musical sounds and so experience the emotional effects of the music. There are two approaches to music that inhibit the enjoyment of musical feeling. The first is an inability or refusal to consider the tonal effects of the music that elicit feeling. The second is an overemphasis on the analysis of the music to the neglect of the music as an expressive entity. Mursell saw both of these approaches to music as being unsatisfying and inadequate.[3]

Mursell also held that some musical experiences can be enhanced by extra-musical associations. He felt that such references sometimes assist in acquiring a proper mood to experience the music. At the same time, he viewed these associations as a possible hindrance to the musical experience. He thought it best if they are viewed as optional means for approaching music rather than primary ones. Extra-musical images and associations are never the meaning of music, but are simply aids to feeling it more fully.[4] Some referentialist claims are clearly invalid. Music cannot induce specific actions, evil or saintly. If music affects morals in any way, it does so only because of social conditioning. Jazz is not inherently demoralizing or sexual, he felt (although it may be boring); a Franck symphony does not preach a sermon; minor keys are not "sad." When pieces of music are perceived in these ways, the perceptions result entirely from the human processing involved:[5]

> Music paints no picture, tells no story, stands for no system of articulate concepts. It does not directly symbolize anything at all beyond itself. It is design in sound. Often, it seems to be just itself, and nothing else, and to have no other meaning whatsoever. Yet this is not precisely true. The great creative artist, let us say, has some profoundly moving experience. In his music he does not, and indeed cannot, tell us of its detail. He does not paint for us the sunset, recall the love affair, tell the story of a tragic loss. But he takes the emotional essence of that experience and crystallizes it in tone. Of all the sensory media, tone is most closely connected with emotion. This is a psychological fact. Thus music is the most purely and typically emotional of all the arts. Here we find its essence. This must be our chief clue to its proper educational treatment, for it is the central secret of its human appeal and its power in the lives of men. Education in and through music must mean, first of all, participation in noble and humanizing emotion.[6]

It is legitimate to ask what music "means." The meaning of music, though ineffable, is profound. Music conveys emotional meanings rather than intellectual ones in a way no other medium can duplicate. One must take a proper attitude toward a piece of music in order to grasp its precise meanings. Such an attitude facilitates active involvement in the music, which is a prerequisite to musical experience.

Musical experience must also be holistic: "Music offers opportunity for an experience almost unique — an experience in which bodily movement and mental and emotional apprehension are integrated."[7]

When the body is freed, the mind is opened, and music is presented in its entirety (or at least in large sections), people can understand its meaning, mood, and detail. This concept of the whole can be upset easily when technical or interpretive problems are addressed in isolation. Such problems should be considered in context and only after the essence of a piece of music has been felt through the performance of the entire piece (or at least a major section of it).[8]

Musical experience also depends for its full effect on musical intelligence, some aspects of which can be taught and developed:

> The fact is that musical feeling should be intelligent feeling. It is not something arbitrary, ill-disciplined, and wild that we contribute to our own good will and pleasure. It is a total response to a fully understood and appreciated situation. The sort of musical feeling experienced by some people is like the emotion of a Zulu who finds himself in the jam of a strike mob, and is wildly excited by the pressure and rush of people about him, but, because he has no adequate understanding of the meaning of events, can have no adequate emotional response to them.
>
> So, to arrive at a definition of musical feeling, we may say that essentially it is a discriminating, but appreciative and emotional response to the beauty of the musical structure. And that structure produces emotion in us by directly stimulating appeal to the organism, in which it sets up a deep resonance.[9]

When music is heard, the listener perceives relationships in tones, expressive shadings, and (ultimately) forms that are processed by way of musical memory and imagination. This mental process requires that one attend to music, recognize its elements, and discriminate among them.[10] Musical intelligence should not be confused, however, with knowledge about music.[11] Knowledge about music's technical aspects is needed to fully perceive it, but must be lowered to a subconscious level during active experience with the music. Otherwise, the experience becomes analytical rather than musical.

The mental processes that distinguish the formal elements of music can be taught. Musicians who have been trained in this way gain the most from musical experience because they bring to it considerable knowledge about musical detail and formal aspects that aids their musical understanding. Such expertise in musical perception is not abstract; it involves precise elements.[12] Though subconscious (except, perhaps, in unusual roles that require selective attention such as that of the music critic or performer), this ability to perceive musical detail is critical to understanding music.[13]

Such ability is in part native and in part acquired (taught). The ear hears pitches; this is a native ability. Then the brain discriminates the pitches.[14] This is native to a degree, but education is required for its full development.[15] Recognition of intervals, harmonies, melodies, and timbres involves mental processes that can be developed to the limits of students' mental capabilities. Auditory imaging involves some native ability but, again, needs education for its full development. Professional music students need ear training, which is really "mind training."[16] "In all cases it may be truly said that we hear with our minds rather than with our ears."[17]

The issue is not whether musical intelligence can be developed, but to what degree it should be. It is not to a student's advantage to be expected to reach unreasonable musical heights. Virtuosity is not a good goal for just any child, especially one lacking in native musicality. Nonetheless, even monotones should be encouraged to experience music. Many are quite musical; they can love, enjoy, and be fulfilled by musical experience. Music can give all children opportunities for achievement and activity. None should be deprived of these opportunities.[18]

Finally, musical experience involves not only musical aspects but also social ones, which are especially important in educational settings. This view appears in Mursell's earliest writings and becomes more prominent in later works. Vital musical experience is good for all people, including children. Music embodies the whole purpose of education and of life itself.

Valid musical experience is a means to education's major goal: to help people become human. Musical experience gives people interests for the present and future, leisure, and self-discipline. If properly presented, it lets them experience adventure and helps them dare to think creatively. It can help them discover talents. Furthermore, group aims are attained through musical participation. Democratic goals of free association and cooperation are met as music is preserved through musical activity.[19] When music is properly presented in school settings, its benefits will also transfer to homes, churches, and communities.[20]

Some of these views may not seem directly related to musical experience. However, Mursell thought them important because musical experience is something that happens to people. The increasing prominence of social goals is the most apparent change in his writings over the course of his career. He added a revealing comment, though, in his second Wartime Institute address. While social outcomes are too important to be ignored, he said, particularly during periods in our history when the people who must support music education think them important, "never fear but that artistic outcomes will be added unto you likewise."[21]

FEATURES OF MUSICAL EXPERIENCE

1. *Musical experience can occur through the act of composing.*
Musical composition starts with a musical idea that is shaped to bring out its meaning.[22] Meaning is present from the beginning but becomes more clearly defined and more sharply realized through the creative process.[23] During this process the composer is driven to discover the technical resources needed to express the music's feelings. Composers need enough resources to freely imagine musical sounds; they must be able to think in the musical medium before they can embody musical ideas. This ability results from drill and discipline, which are necessary prerequisites to musical experience through composition. (Training does not make creative genius but does facilitate it.) Composers must study the techniques of past composers, counterpoint, and music theory, although often, as Robert Schumann put it, "What sounds beautiful makes a mock of all rules."[24] In the end, composers move beyond their studies to discover themselves through their own creation of music.[25]

The mechanics of composing are handled differently by different composers, but the purpose is always the same: to mold tones into shapes with embodied musical meaning. Ideally, a piece is heard in the mind and "tinkered with" there through the generation of many tone forms. A mood develops — actively, not theoretically — and the piece determines its own order. In a gestation period it grows organically, taking on its own "life." In all of this, the main focus must be musical.[26]

2. *Musical experience can occur through the act of listening.*

"Listening should by no means be considered mere passive reception — not even when the main consideration is the evocation of a mood. The successful listener enters into the music, possesses it, is possessed by it, and so is inspired and enabled to make it for himself."[27] Listening is an active process involving selective physical and aesthetic responses. The goal of good listening is to share musical feeling. This is accomplished when musicality and musical intelligence are used to discriminate and understand the significance of musical details. Educated listeners attend to the right things; effective listening requires education.

Listeners decide how to mentally process the musical stimuli received through their ears. They should listen both for subjective factors (applicable moods, associations, visual images, and symbolism) and objective factors (tone color, melody, harmony, rhythm, and form). To force the use of subjective factors could result in absurd reactions, but even absurd reactions are better than no feelings at all. It is useless, said Mursell, to say people should not use subjective factors. It is a fact that people use them. However, objective factors allow perceptive listeners to feel music more precisely through anticipation and surprise. The ability to perceive objective factors increases with education.[28]

There are three types of listeners. *Intellectual listeners* hear technical factors and analyze rather than feel the music. Pure *motor listeners* feel only rhythm and volume of sound. This may be a weakness, but at least it is a start. *Emotional listeners* arbitrarily assign moods and feelings that often have nothing to do with the music; they need discipline. Though each of these types in its pure form describes a faulty method of listening, effective listening may incorporate and transform all three.[29]

3. *Musical experience can occur through the act of performing.*

Performers actively employ aural perception, imagination, musical intelligence, musical feeling, and physical feeling to provide a link between composers and audiences.[30] Good tone quality, attention to melody, harmony, dynamics, tempo, and rubato, technical facility and accuracy, and the ability to read a musical score are all means to musical experience.[31] These means give music a proper sense of form and clarify expression by eliminating distractions. Technique involves hearing, imaging, controlling, and responding emotionally. However valuable it might be, technique should never be venerated for its own sake.[32]

Performers interpret music.[33] They realize a composer's intentions through their own insightful decisions based on logical relationships presented by the score, especially with regard to dynamics, tempi, and timbres. To interpret successfully, they must balance discipline with self-expression. This should be a natural outgrowth of technical study and self-criticism directed toward a musical purpose.

Two principle modes of performance are available. Singing is ideal because the voice is directly part of the body and its kinesthetic feelings. Instrumental music tends to be fragmented. However, some people prefer it since it allows for exciting accuracy and wide varieties of tones and ranges. This performance mode is especially good for discipline and social values. Whatever the means of access to musical experience, the experience needs to be active.[34]

4. *Musical experience depends upon musical intelligence.*

The existence of musical experience implies an intellectual aspect. Musical sounds have meaning for musically intelligent people who experience them. For listeners who have not developed musical intelligence, however, sounds may be meaningless. Unmusical listeners feel something when they hear music, but they would likely feel more if they were musically educated.

Mursell described with some specificity what musically intelligent listeners perceive. The basic elements are timbre (differentiated by overtones) and pitch, both of which are organized in listeners' minds through relational structures. The central nervous system "hears" vibration ratios and the ear corrects as necessary. Then, how the sounds are processed depends upon a listener's background. Through fusion, a listener's mind can organize two sounds into one. Aural perceptions of fusion, consonance, dissonance, and beat result in musical experience. Noises are perceived as extraneous to the music. Listeners are aware of noises and the sound of breathing, but do not process them as part of the music. Unfamiliar sounds from a musical score may also be heard as noise.[35]

Melody (based on scale, tonality, and harmony) is the primary musical element. A melody can go as far afield as listeners' minds can perceive. Listeners expect melodies to contain both unity and subtle variations. A melody may not have a key center, but it must have a tonality or it lacks meaning.[36]

Harmony is an important addition to melody, but one that is not well understood. Mursell wrote that traditional rules of harmony are unsound.[37] For instance, a "chord" is really a qualitative experiment, and from a phenomenal viewpoint each chord has its own color, even if it has only two notes. Many chord types are possible, and they need not all resolve.[38] Furthermore, tonality does not need to define a key; it only needs to be understood when aurally perceived.[39] Some traditional rules work because of explainable effects on the central nervous system. For example, parallel fifths and octaves should be avoided in contrapuntal textures because they create unclear fusions.[40] These matters, and trends of tonality and resolution, are matters of opinion and listener experience. Great composers "used their ears and followed the dictates of aural perception."[41] They did not try to follow theoretical rules.

Traditional notions of consonance and dissonance are also unsound. In fact, the term *dissonance* is relative and, acoustically, an illogical label. Consonance and dissonance do relate to pleasantness and unpleasantness, respectively, but human judgments (which can be cultivated) define the relationship of the sounds. While traditional conventions dictate that dissonances must be resolved, this really depends upon the listener's perceptions.[42]

5. *Musical experience involves a primitive physical appeal that is dependent on musical elements, particularly rhythm.*

Musical sounds cause a sensuous effect in the mid-brain that both humans and lower animals can experience. This primitive appeal of musical experience is a response to the orderings of musical tones. Distinct tones in series can arouse powerful emotions, causing physical changes in listeners. Such effects are not limited to specific genres or musical structures.[43] Physical changes may involve rates of pulse and breathing (though not in time with the music), blood pressure, digestive processes, and an increase in muscle tonicity and sensory keenness. The effects may be heightened when music is heard at social events such as ceremonies. Training does not reduce the physical effects of music; it only enhances them.[44]

In his earliest writings, Mursell noted that music's physical effects transcend the auditory: "Rhythm as such is not an auditory experience at all; and our experience of rhythm depends, not on what we hear, but on the feel of muscular play and activity in response to what we hear."[45] Performers and listeners move with music, affected by its "strange and magical effect."[46] They breathe with phrases. Their large muscles move with large rhythmic divisions, and smaller muscles move with smaller ones. "To give a concrete instance," Mursell wrote, "the writer regularly feels the ponderous rhythm of the opening measures of the second movement of Schumann's C-Major Fantasy in terms of a swing of the whole body, while he feels the beat of the Minute Waltz as a sort of rapid chattering of the teeth."[47] The *takt* (beat and beat groupings) is a force that attracts the attention of a listener's body in a subjective process explainable through laws of psychology. Even complex rhythmic devices such as syncopation cannot overcome this force.

Rhythm is not the same thing as absolute time.[48] Since the perception of rhythm is what matters, the tempo of a piece must differ with varying situations (such as performance halls with different decay times) to be psychologically correct. Also, preset muscle choices must be taken into account when tempi are set.[49] If music is performed too fast, listeners feel discomfort as their muscles respond at the fast rate; if it is too slow, their systems are dragged down.

In 1927, Mursell believed that rhythm in music must literally be felt in order to be experienced.[50] By 1937 he had expanded his views. He then saw rhythm as an abstraction through which elements are organized into wholes of perception and response. It requires a feeling of accent (not always intense) and a perception of regularity (not necessarily mechanistic). Instinctive reaction helps a listener feel beauty, simplicity, or proportion, but this is less important than intelligent perception. In a bridge between earlier and later thinking, Mursell stated that "the ultimate foundation of rhythm is to be found in mental activity."[51] Listeners perceive rhythmic patterns in sensory media (even media that seem nonrhythmic) and invent structures if needed.

Despite the role of the mind, rhythm is literally felt in the muscles of the listener. Observed physical reactions to rhythm can be explained through motor theory. Because voluntary muscles are controlled by the brain, it is quite feasible that they actually move according to musical features perceived by trained listeners. However, the earlier notion that involuntary muscles move with small divisions of musical time is here dismissed as an "unproven hypothesis."[52]

By 1943 Mursell's ideas were refined further: "Rhythm is a moving, onward flow, and must be taught, learned, and apprehended as such."[53] The listener perceives tempo and mentally organizes the flow. Rhythm essentially involves beat but also involves durations, stresses, and subtle metric relationships. Expression demands flexibility because time follows rhythm, not vice versa. Although rhythm is experienced in terms of bodily movement, the body may not actually move. It helps, though, if it does. Movements are most satisfactory when chosen by listeners to accurately reflect perceived musical features. Rhythm can be experienced by hearing music or by visually examining a score.[54]

Mursell said less about rhythm in later writings. In 1948 he wrote that rhythmic response is a response to expressive patterns of stress, release, duration, and pause. It is not an arithmetical entity. Nor is it merely physical movement. Rather, it is "the expression of physical movement."[55] In 1956 he summarized the whole rhythmic issue. Rhythm is critical; its incorrect feel is usually the problem in an ineffective performance, and its correct feel is usually a major factor in an effective one. Since rhythm carries the rest of musical experience, understanding it increases pleasure. Mursell came full circle here in saying that listeners may need to feel rhythm in their muscles first to get the whole of a musical experience.[56] The beauty of music's tone and phrase structures must be felt; these factors should be neither overemphasized nor ignored.

6. *Musical experience may be affected by the study of music theory.*

Mursell's views on the role of music theory in helping to build musicianship are clear and consistent. Studies of key relationships, harmony, melody, timbre, and even imagery can help people perceive sounds if the intent is to clarify music. Theoretical study should include attention to dissonance and consonance, tension and release, but should not focus on rules that do not correspond to actual musical experience. At best, theory and counterpoint can help listeners understand how a beautiful piece of music was crafted; analysis can help them understand how it should sound: "A person who cannot hear tonality cannot hear music. His sense for intervals and for melody, and his apprehension of harmony and harmonic relations, is bound to be uncertain."[57] A music student should study — even by drill — scales, transpositions, harmony, and harmonic progressions, both by looking at scores and by listening to the sounds they represent. Score study normally should be preceded by aural familiarity with the music involved.

Ear training can enhance musical experience by helping a listener discriminate musical sounds. Authentic musical excerpts should be used in this study so that transfer to actual use can occur. The student should listen for tone quality, melodic flow, phrases, tonal relationships (expectations), harmony, and harmonic colors. The ability to image sounds should also be developed.[58]

7. *Musical experience can be affected by the study of technique.*

Technical study is another means to musical experience. Properly developed, technique increases a performer's ability to use an instrument or voice to achieve musically intelligible, beautiful results. If this goal is to be met, though, technical study must be musical. Technical study should never be based upon skill for its own sake. Facility must be learned for musical purposes:[59]

> Musicianship is an excellence of the mind, not of the muscles. The various instruments are no more than the mechanical means by which musical thought and musical feeling are transmuted into sound waves. The technique required to play or to sing is no more than the exquisite motor skill and control by means of which the musician comes to express his inner and mental apprehension of the meaning of the music itself. Indeed, as we shall see, the very development of executant technique is hardly possible apart from that mental grasp and insight which constitutes musicianship.[60]

If technical accuracy becomes the end, performers may become afraid to perform. Musical errors do detract from the musical effect. "But the great purpose . . . is precisely the creation of beauty, and not the avoidance of wrong notes."[61]

As in the case of theoretical knowledge, drill in technique can be valuable and even necessary, but it must be purposive. "Any and every technical and specific skill is learned best in a setting which calls for its expressive use; and when so learned it is retained longest, and is made most surely available for application in new situations."[62] If drill is strictly mechanical, it has "about the same cultural and educational value as cracking stones on a rock pile."[63]

The focus of musical experience is activity. Musical activity has musicianship as its end, and the end must not be confused with the means toward it:

> Of course, it is possible to listen in a crude and stupid way, and at a low musical level; but this simply means deficient musical-mindedness. And it is possible to play with some facility without any apparent musical meaning; but this simply means that the pupil has been drilled in empty technical tricks rather than disciplined in musicianship. And it is possible to write music "correctly" — that is, in accord with formal rules — but without any shade of artistic value. Each of these three outcomes involves a slightly different distribution and employment of the basic mental skills which constitute musicianship. But in so far as they are real musical outcomes at all, they are not possible without definite musical-mental training.[64]

All three musical involvements — listening, performing, and composing — can be distorted by an overemphasis on knowledge and/or technique. But when the means are kept in perspective they greatly enhance active, meaningful musical experience.

8. *Optimal musical experience is dependent upon appropriate literature.*

Only music literature of high artistic worth should be used in education. A wide range of such pieces is available for both listening and performing. Drill should not be used at all; it is musically meaningless because it was not intended to express feelings.[65] Whether or not people like the music chosen is not a significant issue, because liking and quality are unrelated. Music of the highest quality "enshrines the very spirit of an age."[66] It does more things and deeper things with feelings than lesser music. With emotional profundity goes subtlety of effect, and music that has these qualities survives social selection to remain in the repertoire.[67]

It is advisable, though, to use some music in popular styles. Modern popular music should be included in student musicians' repertoires because it attempts to embody modern feelings.[68] Music teachers should not deplore student tastes for popular music. Rather, teachers should use students' tastes to excite interest in musical art in general.[69]

Mursell's thinking in regard to appropriate levels of difficulty in music literature changed over time. In 1934 he wrote that the artistry of particular pieces of music is the only important issue, and excessive difficulty is not a serious problem.[70] In 1943 he wrote that music should not be too difficult for students to perform, or their renderings would inadequately represent the intended feelings. There is good music in the difficulty ranges appropriate for young musicians, he said.[71] In 1948 he clarified and synthesized previous ideas. On the one hand, music must be chosen in reference to pupils' capacity for enjoyment. If the literature studied is abstract or only remotely emotional, it may be impossible for the students to process and experience. On the other hand, teachers should not assume that student standards are low. It is better to stretch young musicians than not. Furthermore, students do not need to perceive everything in a piece or like it on first hearing to profit from the experience.[72]

With appropriate literature, people of any age can enjoy musical experience through the discovery of music's expressiveness, and they will gradually develop better musical tastes. Educated musical tastes are personal but not subjective or arbitrary. If people are exposed to expressive music, led to perceive the expressive point, and guided with analysis that serves aesthetic goals, each experience of music becomes a means to greater capacity for musical experience.[73]

9. *Musical experience is creative.*

"Music is essentially diversified, not uniform, and the better and more genuine musical experiences and activities become, the more they resist uniformity."[74] Musical experience requires personal initiative and identification with the sounds. Listeners feel the sounds as expressing their own feelings and attitudes, and they actively discover feelings in the sounds they hear.[75] In listening, a person "finds himself" in the music. In performance, personal choices and insights are clearly involved in producing musical sounds. In performing, musicians create the realization of a score through active, discerning responses. Composition is an exhibition of personal choices that is possible at any age and talent level. Creative ability in composition cannot be taught, but it can be encouraged, and use of the tools to compose can be directly taught. Since creativity is a reassembly of elements, an understanding of facts, various stimulations, and moods can help the musician who chooses to compose.[76]

To summarize Mursell's position on musical experience, it always occurs through activity: listening, performing, and composing. If it is to be significant, it must involve emotion that results from mental perception of auditory and physical stimuli. The experience can be enhanced by knowledge about music and by technical facility, but these aspects are never the main factors in the experience. Optimal musical experience depends on appropriate literature. Finally, musical experience is creative. Both feeling and intelligence combine in musical experience — a result with tremendous human value.

> So once again we need not hesitate; we need not apologize for music as an enriching influence in human life; we need not try to excuse it by reducing it to routines. The more courageously we emphasize its aesthetic values, its cultural values, its social values, its human values, the better for the cause we have at heart.[77]

Steve F. Werpy

NOTES

1. James Mursell, *Principles of Musical Education* (New York: Macmillan, 1927), p. 85.
2. James Mursell, *The Psychology of Music* (New York: Norton, 1937), pp. 36–42.
3. James Mursell, *Education for Musical Growth* (Boston: Ginn, 1948), pp. 26–148.
4. Ibid., pp. 35–38.
5. James Mursell, *Human Values in Music Education* (New York: Silver Burdett, 1934), pp. 162–163.
6. Ibid., p. 35.
7. Ibid., p. 51.
8. Mursell, *Principles of Musical Education,* pp. 236-237.
9. Ibid., pp. 91–92.
10. Ibid., p. 133.
11. Ibid., p. 60.
12. Mursell, *The Psychology of Music,* p. 221.
13. Ibid., pp. 221–222.
14. Ibid., pp. 18–20.

15. Ibid., p. 50.

16. Mursell, *Principles of Music Education*, p. 17.

17. James Mursell, *Music in American Schools* (New York: Silver Burdett, 1943), p. 147.

18. Mursell, *Human Values in Music Education*, pp. 46–47.

19. Mursell, *Music in American Schools*, pp. 11-29.

20. Mursell, *Human Values in Music Education*, pp. 89-91.

21. James Mursell, "Music and the Redefinition of Education in Postwar America," *Music Educators Journal* 29 (May/June 1943), p. 11.

22. Mursell, *Education for Musical Growth*, p. 74.

23. Mursell, *The Psychology of Music*, p. 277.

24. Mursell attributes these remarks to Schumann but fails to cite the source.

25. Mursell, *The Psychology of Music*, pp. 281–283.

26. Ibid., pp. 276–281.

27. Mursell, *Music in American Schools*, p. 170.

28. Ibid., pp. 144–170.

29. Mursell, *Principles of Musical Education*, pp. 134–136.

30. Ibid., p. 141.

31. Mursell, *The Psychology of Music*, p. 239.

32. Mursell, *Principles of Musical Education*, p. 141.

33. Mursell, *The Psychology of Music*, p. 238.

34. Mursell, *Music in American Schools*, pp. 168–170.

35. Mursell, *The Psychology of Music*, pp. 49–90.

36. Ibid., p. 106.

37. Ibid., p. 138.

38. Ibid., p. 139.

39. Ibid., p. 141.

40. Ibid., p. 146.

41. Ibid., p. 148.

42. Mursell, *Principles of Musical Education*, pp. 90–96.

43. Mursell, *The Psychology of Music*, pp. 18–21.

44. Ibid., p. 41.

45. Mursell, *Principles of Musical Education*, p. 39.

46. Ibid., p. 41.

47. Ibid., p. 47.

48. Ibid., p. 49.

49. Ibid., pp. 46–47.

50. Ibid., pp. 46–55.

51. Mursell, *The Psychology of Music*, p. 162.

52. Ibid.

53. Mursell, *Music in American Schools*, p. 205.

54. Ibid., pp. 205–218.

55. Mursell, *Education for Musical Growth*, pp. 43–46.

56. James Mursell, *Music Education: Principles and Programs* (Morristown, NJ: Silver Burdett, 1956), pp. 254–272.

57. Mursell, *Principles of Musical Education*, p. 178.

58. Mursell, *Music in American Schools*, pp. 160–167.

59. Mursell, *Principles of Musical Education*, p. 141.

60. Ibid., p. 7.

61. Mursell, *Human Values in Music Education*, p. 128.

62. Mursell, *Music in American Schools*, p. 47.

63. Mursell, "Music and Redefinition," p. 8.

64. Mursell, *Principles of Musical Education*, p. 9.

65. Ibid.

66. Mursell, *Human Values in Music Education*, p. 165.

67. Ibid.

68. Ibid., p. 60.

69. Mursell, *Music in American Schools*, pp. 113–114.

70. Mursell, *Human Values in Musical Education*, pp. 60–61.

71. Mursell, *Music in American Schools*, pp. 103–107.

72. Mursell, *Education for Musical Growth*, pp. 185–188.

73. Mursell, *Music in American Schools*, pp. 44–49.

74. Mursell, "Music and Redefinition," p. 9.

75. Mursell, *Music Education: Principles and Programs*, pp. 328–342.

76. Mursell, *Music in American Schools*, pp. 275–293.

77. Mursell, "Music and Redefinition," p. 15.

LOUIS ARNAUD REID
(1895-1986)

SOURCES

Louis Arnaud Reid followed a consistent impulse throughout his career — finding ways to synthesize modes of human thought and human feeling. In addition to his philosophical writings on such issues as knowledge, truth, and values, he also had a special interest in aesthetics and criticism. His major publications illustrate this: *A Study in Aesthetics* (1931), *Creative Morality* (1937), *Preface to Faith* (1939), *The Rediscovery of Belief* (1946), *Ways of Knowledge and Experience* (1961), *Philosophy and Education* (1962), *Meaning in the Arts* (1969), and *Ways of Understanding and Education* (1986). The majority of ideas in this essay were gleaned from *A Study in Aesthetics* and *Meaning in the Arts*. The latter clarified and, in some cases, altered the positions taken in the former. It is Reid's position that a clear description of an aesthetic experience should come before any discussion of individual art forms. Thus, Reid's discussion of the musical experience reflects a logical extension of his aesthetic theory and illustrates the uniqueness and integrity of the art of music.

GENERAL ORIENTATION TO AESTHETIC EXPERIENCE

"I have been told aesthetics is an impossible subject. I almost agree. Aesthetics, if not wholly impossible, is, I verily believe, as difficult as anything could be. It is difficult because it courts vagueness and evades precision."[1] Although Reid began his study of aesthetics with this statement, he quickly emphasized the sensitivity it takes to approach the arts, the competence it takes to witness the artistic with any degree of objectivity, and the skills it takes to approach the task of analysis clearly and philosophically. At the outset, Reid dismissed the obiter dicta of artist connoisseurs and the a priori pronouncements of system-making philosophers. His aesthetic posture lay between those two poles. He sought unnebulous generality that would reveal the essential in art. He pursued a utilitarian theory of the aesthetic.

The test of aesthetic definition, according to Reid, is in the working out of a viable description of an art experience and applying that to concrete instances. In his view, to approach a description of the musical experience before the proper aesthetic stance is achieved is premature, if not foolhardy.[2] Reid began his own task of analysis by finding ways to approach the ineffable in art. For him, approaching it with generality was justified if the attempt was based on immediately experienced aesthetic intuition. Without this, all is but "words and breath." The source for the development of aesthetic intuition rests securely in firsthand acquaintance with beautiful things. It is this relationship to beautiful things that Reid sought to define. For him, the function of definition was to allow for fruitful discussion, the results of which could then be applied to heightening our awareness of human feeling and how that awareness might be applied to practice.[3]

FEATURES OF AESTHETIC EXPERIENCE

1. *In aesthetic experience, feeling is a form of cognition.*
Throughout his career, Reid was concerned with defining *feeling* in the arts. In the beginning, Reid's forays into this arena were tightly allied with his interest in education and criticism. Because he believed that aesthetic appreciation could be trained, he took the position that aesthetic experience was more than mere feeling; it was knowledge.[4] Decades later, he enlarged his vision by concluding that cognitive feeling *must* be involved in aesthetic experience or, "instead of disciplined feeling and emotion instrumental to finer aesthetic perception, we get an indulgent wallowing in feeling, an emotionalism."[5] Reid became convinced that feeling was actively auxiliary in what we do and think. He described feeling as cognitive, a living process becoming

aware of itself — a mental happening, not an activity. For Reid, feeling was like awareness though more general, more open, and more exclusively subjective.

According to Reid's view, cognition and conation (the conscious drive to perform volitional acts) involve focusing, grasping, acting, and reacting functions with respect to the world. Feeling includes all of the above.[6] He arrived at this position, in part, because he thought Susanne Langer's view (that art expresses "the form of human feeling"[7]) too general. In art, attention should be directed to the object rather than the feeling. One should contemplate the works themselves to get a feeling of them. Meaning is what is apprehended; it is not a form of feeling.[8] In other words, feelings should be relevant to the perceived object. The form of the feeling in a work of art can only be the form of the feeling *of* that work of art. This distinction brought Reid to a central question in his aesthetic theory: what is the feeling of an art work and what is its source?

Reid postulated that there are two aspects to feeling — the intra-psycho-physical content of human beings and a cognitive relation to the independent world. Human beings feel their participation in life and feel, cognitively, something of the character of the world. There is an interaction at work here that involves the dynamics of the psycho-physical organism directed outward toward life situations.[9] The dynamic elements of this interaction between life situations and individual organisms lie at the heart of Reid's aesthetic theory. He cited a number of these elements to give an indication of the process:

> attack
> active elation
> rhythms of effort
> weariness
> depression
> sense of defeat
> dissonance and strain
> consonance and peace
> loudness
> softness
> rising
> falling[10]

The aesthetic in art cannot express exactly the feelings of life. The dynamics of experience, internally and externally, are like and unlike each other. Because the content of the feelings from life situations cannot be exactly reproduced in art, Reid found the discussion of the feelingful nature of art and life to be confusing.

Although Reid addressed feelings in this general way, he clarified by contrasting feeling with *emotion*. Feeling is a basic mental concept. Emotion is a derived one. Emotion is dependent for its character on distinguishable factors, excitations bound up in our relation to the world.[11] An emotion is an external reference to an objectification; feeling is the internal base from which emotion springs.

Reid recognized the temptation to describe the feeling of a work of art in emotional terms. Not only is that not possible, but also it is often shallow, if not misleading. In his view, there is no reason to assume that feelings need to be stirred up by an art work to such a pitch that they can be labeled *emotional*. Even when that occurs, it is specific to that art work and is not generalizable.[12] Again, Reid pointed out that aesthetic experience is related to an art work where psycho-physical experience is not.

Reid likened cognitive feeling to Michael Polanyi's concept of *tacit knowing*. As one who has internalized (automatized) technical understandings can "think with" a work of art, so also can one attend to a work of art by "feeling (cognitively) with" it.[13] Tacit knowing and tacit feeling are part of the same process. For example, suppose one is cooking a steak for a picnic. With a barbecue fork, one turns the steak so as to achieve "medium-rare." Assuming the cook is not a novice, what is attended to is sticking the tip of the fork into the meat. There is no conscious feeling of the handle of the fork in the palm of the hand, although the tactile feeling is there. The fork is simply not in attention. The handle is felt tacitly, while attending to the larger context.

Reid believed we focus on external things, but the total content is our "functioning-bodies-and-minds-in-relation-to-these-things."[14] More specifically, in aesthetic experience there is always both a focus *and* a margin, or those images that occupy the fringe of consciousness.[15] In that way, an aesthetic object can be said to express functionally our inner states of mind and body, the untranslatable parts of human experience.

Our knowledge of the arts shows sensitive feeling to be an added asset in knowing and coming to terms with the world. To "feel" structures of things (and their values) is a way to come to know them more positively. In this context, that of cognitive feeling, the aesthetic experience becomes something finer, more subtle, more accurate, less literal, and more imaginative than might otherwise be perceived.[16]

2. *Aesthetic experience is the imaginative contemplation of a work of art — perceptual, imaginal, or both.*

According to Reid, with "imaginary perceptual experience" we image as if we were perceiving.[17] Aesthetic experience is different from ordinary perception. What is the nature of that difference? Reid provides two answers to that question. First, with aesthetic experience there is no interest in a relationship to existence or reality. We are interested in what appears, isolated from the real world. Second, with aesthetic experience we are primarily spectators, untainted by practical need and interests.[18] For example, when we see an "ordinary tree," we do not walk into it; it is a thing of the world. When we see an "aesthetic tree," it is complete in its own way, irrespective of its position in the world. We bask in the contemplation of it.[19] The aesthetic experience, then, stops us. A new attitude to the world is presented for our contemplation.

Aesthetic contemplation forms the basis for aesthetic imagination. The aesthetic object, contemplated imaginatively, has intrinsic value for its own sake, not for its practical cognitive, existential implications.[20] The nonaesthetic object instills no such imaginative activity: "The basic fact about the aesthetically equipped person, which differentiates him from all other highly developed human beings, is a great sensitivity to the suggestiveness of the material which he perceives."[21]

Reid also made a distinction between artist and perceiver. The artist's imaginative contemplation is his own. If it becomes public, the connection is not from person to person but from contemplation to contemplation.[22] There are conditions for imaginative aesthetic apprehension: (1) the apprehension of perceptual data; (2) interest in appearance for the sake of meaning, a value that transcends the data itself; (3) the avoidance of referential associations that may nullify the aesthetic nature of the experience; and (4) feelings that are relevant to the perceived object.[23] Aesthetic seeing is imaginative seeing for the sheer interest of what we apprehend. Further, aesthetic experience is not about content but about the valuable meanings that are embodied in the content.[24]

Aside from the issues already addressed in the matter of contemplation, the aesthetic object itself (expressive form) must be discussed. Reid rejected his earlier use of the term *expression* because he believed it too vague and misleading. As Langer proved an able catalyst in the clarification of his thinking about feeling, Clive Bell provided such in the matter of form. As with the former, the ideas of the latter were altered somewhat in Reid's hands.

Aesthetic form is expressive form; form is the structure of expression. Reid recognized the slippery nature of this statement and set about to refine it.[25] He felt that expression, not form, was the primary notion, and form the manifestation of expression. The final form of a work of art reflects the unity of the whole. It is not just an imposition. Reid allied himself, at least in part, with Clive Bell's "significant form," which unites in conception the aspects of meaning and of perceived forms. Aesthetic imagination unites these two aspects in apprehension. Whereas Bell conceived the idea as common to the visual arts, Reid insisted that it was common to all works of art.[26] Form is the house in which art lives.

But what is expressed in form? In the aesthetic experience, form is the vehicle for the commingling of sensual data (colors, shapes, sounds, etc.) and mental activity (ideas, images, feelings and emotions, apprehension). Thus, an overemphasis on either the sensual properties of art or the formal is to be avoided.[27] In addition, association can also be unconscious and still have an effect on present apprehensions. Previous experiences and values are thought and felt with. That the object becomes transformed in imagination must be assumed, regardless of the degree of association present.[28]

3. *Aesthetic experience must "embody" some valuable meaning that moves, interests, and excites.*

How do perceived objects convey meanings they do not literally possess? Reid's answer was *embodied meaning*. In aesthetic experience, we apprehend patterns of paint or sound not as meaning something or expressing something, but as meaningful.[29] Neither body nor meaning are of concern here; rather, embodied meaning is important. Within the aesthetic object rests value. The perceived object appears (to the imaginative mind) to express values that seem to emanate from the

perceived object. For the artist, "it is the values *as embodied* in perceived stuff which matter."[30] Reid suggested that something new is
brought forth in a work of art. Thus, *embodiment* is a better term than
expression. In aesthetic embodiment, imaginative attention to the perception of sounds and shapes is instrumental and intrinsic to the
understanding of aesthetic meaning.[31]

At this point, the stage is set for the synthesis of thought and
feeling only hinted at earlier. In Reid's vision, psycho-physical embodiment is a good analogue of aesthetic embodiment. For example,
to feel angry is not mental only, not physical only, but psycho-physical. In creating, the artist discovers a new dimension of being, one
made possible by the manipulation of medium and materials that are
charged with meaning for his imaginative mind.[32] This is the aesthetic
embodiment of that meaning. For the perceiver, aesthetic embodiment is the actual presence of what we are sensibly aware of and
attending to, as well as the whole range of what we can imagine.[33]
Thus, the perceiver is no blind partner in the process.

While this process of aesthetic embodiment is present in all the
arts, Reid pointed out that each art has to exploit its own special media
of embodiment in its own way. Because of the specificity with which
this can be accomplished, "no single word could ever adequately
symbolize the manysidedness of art."[34] Embodiment occurs whenever
the creative manipulation of a medium is complete and successful.
Embodiment is appreciated, not made.[35] Although the artist sees his or
her work in the context of the experience of making it, and the
perceiver sees it in completed form, in both cases the appreciation of
embodiment provides the meaning. Aesthetic experience *is* embodiment and *means* embodiment; the two are identical.

It was Reid's conviction that all reductions of artistic meaning to
ordinary language are doomed to failure.[36] It is indescribable in words.
He used a well-known idea from Felix Mendelssohn to make this
point: "Music," in Mendelssohn's words, "is not too 'indefinite' but
too 'definite' to express life-feelings exactly."[37] Because a work of art
involves a personal embodied experience of meaning, one the perceiver may or may not fathom directly, feeling becomes an active
participant in the cognitive process. Reid cited three levels of participation — part intra-cognitive, part *in* the work itself, and part in the

feeling *of* the work. "To understand the nature of this embodiment in its untranslatableness is to understand the essence of the aesthetic."[38]

Reid mentioned value and meaning as he discussed aesthetic embodiment. Having defined how meaning is embodied in art, he turned to the issue of value. By clarifying further, he showed how meaning gets out of the artifact and becomes valuable. He began by stating that, in aesthetic experience, there is some release of inner tension (internal, physical, or both) by way of external behavior. This release is carried out for the satisfaction of some conscious desire (note the volition of conation cited earlier). Value comes from the fulfillment or the frustration of that tendency.[39] Reid's term for this was *tendency-fulfillment*.[40] Reid cited views from W. Olaf Stapledon's *A Modern Theory of Ethics*[41] to support a position that "the typical case of value within our experience, then, occurs when some hormic tendency of the organism is fulfilled or thwarted."[42]

According to Reid, we experience tendency-fulfillments relevant to the aesthetic object when a whole complex situation, including our own, is cognized by us.[43] Tendency-fulfillment is really "value," awakening imaginative contemplation. For the artist, his or her material is replete with tendencies to be fulfilled. Tendencies are stirred, fulfilled, and stirred again, and it is that dynamic in the arts that directly and/or indirectly affects organic and mental response.

4. *Aesthetic experience must be approached with some degree of psychical distance.*

Put simply, placing something at a psychical distance from ourselves ensures the experience will be outside the context of personal needs and ends.[44] The amount of distance varies. For example, greater distance is more appropriate for a classical attitude than for a romantic attitude. The amount of distance is relative, not absolute. Aesthetic experience ceases when the psychical distance is too great or too small.[45]

5. *Aesthetic experience is rooted in the principle of unity and synthesis.*

In a work of art, literal translation of meaning is impossible. An art work is an imaginative construction and, with its completion, more existed than before construction began. The embodiment of meaning contained within the finished work transcends the work — a greater "whole," of which everything else is a part. With aesthetic experience, there is a synthesis of what is perceived and what is embodied. Therefore, a new entity results. The contemplation of this aesthetic unity satisfies that fundamental urge that craves completion and perfection. The unity is a value, a means and end, an aid to the fulfillment of tendency.[46]

The elements of aesthetic experience are but parts of the whole — "which themselves are inadequate, imperfect, and not very significant, little wholes."[47] Although appreciating this fact is not always an easy task, Reid believed that, to the mature imagination, the complex of valuable meanings appears without effort. However, this too is a variable in aesthetic experience. The demand for imaginative synthesis is not constant. For example, what is demanded of the perceiver attending to an artist's rendition of a single wild rose is very much different from what is demanded when attending to Johann Sebastian Bach's complete Goldberg Variations. According to Reid, however, the difference is one of degree, not kind.[48]

Reid espoused a specific role for "fusion" in the aesthetic experience. Aesthetic fusion (synthesis) does not occur after the fact. In aesthetic experience, we start with the experientially indivisible. Upon reflection, however, we find it complex. What is apprehended are conceptually distinguishable aspects of an indivisible unity.[49] Further, Reid cited William Wordsworth, who embraced the idea of "similitudes in dissimilitude."[50] He accepted the notion of the art work as a single unity of indivisible meaning — a single symbol. It is with this sort of complexity that Reid believed we must continually grapple.

Reid applied all of this to the condition of "compound arts," such as opera. For him, assimilation and transformation did not mean elimination or annulment. That would have been contrary to his commitment to a synthesis among elements. In his view, the elements in compound art must be judged in relation to the compound as a whole. Reid felt that the confusion and difficulty with this idea came from a misunderstanding of such complex works. For example, he believed it takes many talents to appreciate opera and even more to create it. He insisted, however, that each element is transformed by its relation to the whole. While he admitted that compound arts like opera and dance are difficult to unify (sometimes extremely so), he stood by his previous statement. In a *mature* imagination, each aspect is apprehended by the perceiver so well and to such a degree (synthesis) that it is not compound, but single.[51] When this mature imagination contemplates with proper analysis, abstraction, and dissection, the experience "unifies a complex so that it seems that there is one rich, single, indivisible quality."[52]

MUSICAL EXPERIENCE

1. *In musical experience, feeling cognitively is of principal importance.*
Reid regarded music as the most impressive example of a highly complex and dynamic art form, one that is to be attended to cognitively and felt organically. Because we must feel our way through music with our whole being, musical experience is cognitive in the most important sense and unknowable except by way of feeling.[53] Because of the temporal nature of the art, "you are the music while the music lasts."[54] Music, then, has no existence except as lived through or with.

2. *In musical experience, imaginative instability heightens the expectation that tendencies will ultimately be fulfilled.*
During the musical experience, the perceiver is satisfied by what is given, yet demands more. This is because of the imaginativeness of instability that causes the contemplation of fulfillment possibilities. Reid likened the instability to the experience of life itself.[55] Put another way, instability demands stability not found until the end. Reaching the end is not the goal because it is in the process of reaching and apprehending the end that fulfillment comes. This becomes a lived aesthetic whole that is satisfying. The temporal nature of music makes this a unique attribute of the art.

3. *In musical experience, associations are possible that include a dimension not shared precisely the same way by the other arts.*
Reid considered two types of imitation, the incidental and the transformationally fused. When imitation is incidental, it is likely to be diversionary, distracting, and harmful to the musical experience. When that which is imitated is transformed by a fusion with the rest of the parts of the whole, nothing is encumbered.[56]

In addition to the purely musical imitation that can enhance (or hinder) the musical experience, other associations are possible. For example, knowing the particulars about Bach's employment might

lead a listener to focus on the protestant or catholic theological implications of his sacred music. That would surely distract from the whole.
On the other hand, one's ability to think with and feel with "religios-
ity" might well enhance musical apprehension. Reid continually reminded us that it is always a matter of context and degree.[57]

4. *In musical experience, meaning is embodied in sound.*

With music, sound is the source of values that are contemplated
by imagination. Meaning is embodied in those sounds. While the
material and the construction of the material are of immediate focus,
we get a feeling of the music, which is untranslatable except in the
crudest language.[58] Music has no "subject matter" in real life: it
represents nothing, in the sense that drama represents. However,
music is the embodiment of the values of life that exist outside
music.[59]

5. *In the musical experience, musical meaning (the content of the cognitive
feelings of music) is both concretely different from all life feelings and meanings
and is related to life feelings and meanings, sometimes suggesting and echoing
them, though never reproducing them.*[60]

Musical meaning cannot be translated into life meanings. That
is basic to the hypothesis. Life meanings go into human creation
(indirectly), a transformation takes place, and life meanings become
embodied meanings. The perceiver experiences psycho-physical
manifestations while listening to music. At the same time, the perceiver is cognitively feeling the music itself, aware of subjective aspects
only by effect and retrospectively. This is because one cannot attend to
the music and attend to the specifics of one's own dynamics at the
same time. Such a divided attention would not only slow the process,
but would also rob the perceiver of the impact of the whole. Aesthetic
fusion does not occur after the fact. What is essential is that the
perceiver be able to bring his psycho-physical being to the experience
tacitly. It is intrinsic to the experience.[61]

While perceiving the unique aesthetic object (which is music),
feelings and emotions arise from the life feelings of the musical experience, not from life feelings themselves. Reid believed it would be
too simple to say that music could express them. With regard to
program and pure music, Reid added that the "stuff" of pure music is
the "stuff" of music with text. Program music transforms explicit life
meanings; pure music transforms implicit life meanings.[62] There is no

working backwards from music to life. At best, all one can say is that there is a relationship between the feelings of the statics and dynamics of some music and the feelings that are present in the statics and dynamics of some life situations. Reid cautioned, however, that one leaves solid ground when one begins to think that "life generates art."[63] Still, there is some importance to that relationship. It is to that relationship that Reid next turned.

Reid believed that the human psycho-physical organism is the "common centre" from which we deal with the world and with music. We live inside that centre. We cognitively feel it. And the experience is self-transcending. It is inevitable, according to Reid, that the musician gets caught up in the shared dynamics of life and music. "A musician cannot escape from his human skin."[64] There are traces, flavors, and echoes of life meanings intrinsic to the musical experience. The dynamics of human response form a very large part of the material out of which music is built; it is the raw material that is transformed into new embodied meaning.

In summary, Reid stated:

> Art is not everything but to miss out on it is to be deprived of a whole world of values brought to the senses.
>
> Aesthetic experience is not the stopping or ending of a process, but a life of appetite and satisfaction more intense than ordinary earth life and rounded to unearthly perfection.[65]

John T. Langfeld

NOTES

1. Louis Arnaud Reid, *A Study in Aesthetics* (Westport, CT: Greenwood Press, 1931), p. 3.
2. Ibid., p. 5.
3. Ibid., p. 27.
4. Ibid.
5. Louis Arnaud Reid, *Meaning in the Arts* (New York: Humanities Press, 1969), p. 157.
6. Ibid., p. 144.

7. Susanne K. Langer, *Problems of Art* (New York: Charles Scribner's Sons, 1957), p. 15.
8. Reid, *Meaning in the Arts,* p. 64.
9. Ibid., p. 163.
10. Ibid., p. 164.
11. Ibid., p. 150.
12. Ibid., p. 156.
13. Ibid., p. 146.
14. Reid, *A Study in Aesthetics,* p. 80.
15. Ibid., p. 107.
16. Ibid., p. 50.
17. Ibid., p. 33.
18. Ibid., p. 37.
19. Ibid., p. 38
20. Ibid., p. 43.
21. Ibid., p. 160.
22. Ibid., p. 184.
23. Ibid., p. 41.
24. Ibid., p. 42.
25. Ibid., p. 197.
26. Ibid., p. 43.
27. Reid, *Meaning in the Arts,* p. 50.
28. Reid, *A Study in Aesthetics,* p. 105.
29. Reid, *Meaning in the Arts,* p. 70.
30. Reid, *A Study of Aesthetics,* p. 160.
31. Reid, *Meaning in the Arts,* p. 78.
32. Ibid., p. 77.
33. Ibid., p. 78.
34. Ibid., p. 80.
35. Ibid., p. 81.
36. Ibid., p. 134.
37. Ibid., p. 156.
38. Reid, *A Study in Aesthetics,* p. 42.
39. Ibid., p. 139.
40. Ibid., p. 131

41. W. Olaf Stapledon, *A Modern Theory of Ethics, a Study of the Relations of Ethics and Psychology* (London: Methuen and Co., 1929).

42. Reid, *A Study in Aesthetics*, p. 124.

43. Ibid., p. 142.

44. Ibid., p. 55.

45. Ibid., p. 56.

46. Ibid., p. 189.

47. Ibid., p. 68.

48. Reid, *Meaning in the Arts*, p. 217.

49. Ibid., p. 51.

50. Ibid., p. 78.

51. Ibid., p. 184.

52. Ibid.

53. Ibid., p. 150.

54. Reid, *A Study in Aesthetics*, p. 18.

55. Ibid., p. 161.

56. Ibid., p. 180.

57. Ibid.

58. Ibid., p. 279.

59. Ibid., p. 280.

60. Reid, *Meaning in the Arts*, p. 162.

61. Ibid., p. 149.

62. Ibid., p. 160.

63. Ibid., p. 161.

64. Ibid., p. 165.

65. Reid, *A Study in Aesthetics*, p. 91.

BENNETT REIMER
(1932–   )

SOURCES

The major book dealing with Bennett Reimer's views on the arts in general, music in particular, and educational implications is *A Philosophy of Music Education* (1970, 1989). Many of the journal articles he published between 1959 and the present (see bibliography) stem from or contain allusions to various concepts he has unified in that book. Numerous applications of these concepts to music education have been made in the final report of his research project sponsored by the United States Office of Education (1967), *Learning to Listen to Music* (1970), Silver Burdett *MUSIC* series (1974, 1978, 1981, 1985), *The Experience of Music* (1973), and *Developing the Experience of Music* (1984). Distinctions between conceptualization and perceptual structuring are explained in "The Nonconceptual Nature of Aesthetic Cognition" (1986) and comparisons between music education in the United States and China are offered in "Music Education and Music in China: An Overview and Some Issues" (1989). Reimer refines his explanation of extra-aesthetic content and social context as factors in musical experience in "What Knowledge Is of Most Worth in the Arts?" (1992), and in "Selfness and Otherness in Experiencing Music of Foreign Cultures" (1991).

GENERAL ORIENTATION TO MUSICAL EXPERIENCE

Reimer approaches his study of the arts and music through two central questions that map out the terrain in which he is interested: (1) where does one go in music to find what is uniquely valuable about it? and (2) what does one get from music when one goes there?

These questions cut through the many sociological, anthropological, psychological, and cultural-historical issues surrounding music and get directly to the intrinsic nature. While Reimer recognizes that music plays many important personal and cultural roles, he insists that all these are transformed by music into meanings peculiar to music — meanings made musical through sounds purposively deployed.[1] Until the essential nature of music is recognized (underlying and supporting its additional qualities and utilities), one has not built a foundation for understanding it deeply, experiencing it appropriately, and teaching it effectively.[2]

Three aestheticians have been of particular influence on Reimer's thought. From John Dewey he appropriates basic concepts dealing with the embodied, phenomenon-specific nature of musical meaning, the act of creation as transformative rather than self-expressive, the role of feeling in unifying the creative act, the intelligent nature of artistic work, the creativity of aesthetic experience, and the social function of art as providing a basis for shared subjective responsiveness to our common world.[3]

From Susanne Langer, Reimer takes the central idea that art transforms experience through its power to capture the vital nature of feeling in objectified, dynamic, artistic forms. The significance of art — the reason we care so much about it and are compelled to share it with each new generation of children — lies in its relation to our inner, subjective lives.[4] Art gives outer form to inner affect and allows us, through creative and disciplined shaping of artistic materials, to refine, clarify, deepen, and extend the quality of our inner subjectivities.[5] Following Langer, Reimer is careful to explain that feeling is a far broader concept than emotion, encompassing emotion but extending to all conscious awareness of ourselves as live, experiencing creatures.[6]

Reimer borrows from Leonard Meyer the technical terms dealing with the questions of where one goes in music and what one gets from music.[7] *Referentialism* argues that one goes outside the work itself and attains values that are nonaesthetic in nature. *Formalism* discounts any nonaesthetic content in music and claims an intellectual value from musical experience. *Absolute Expressionism* argues that music transforms any referential content and all social-contextual aspects into musical content but is influenced by what references and social uses add to the work. Musical meaning assimilates nonartistic and socially determined meanings, embodying them in dynamic forms themselves meaningful and valuable. This value (essentially a mode of cognition) relates to the clarification, refinement, extension, and internalization of affect — a "knowing of" feeling.[8]

Also influenced by Meyer is Reimer's view that musical affect is aroused by tension/inhibition patterns of sound,[9] including sound-forms not limited to common practice, goal-oriented musical tendencies. The affect-arousing components of sound are culturally embedded, identifiable, and teachable: this is what aesthetically valid music teaching must concentrate on at all levels of instruction and in all activities.

Reimer asserts that musicality is not a capacity limited to the talented but is the natural propensity all people have to respond to musical sounds as affective. The ability to enjoy music aesthetically — that is, for its intrinsic power to cause feelingful responses — is ubiquitous. Human capacities for aesthetic experience in general and musical experience in particular are conceived as robust, natural, primal to the human condition, and not limited to "art and music of the elite."[10] All people in all cultures at all levels of sophistication or education can and do experience their world aesthetically and have rich artistic/musical cultures including folk and popular forms in addition to more learned forms. A rich artistic/musical life is one that can share broadly and deeply from what one's own culture offers and, to the extent possible, what one can glean from other cultures.[11] This populist notion has broadranging effects on Reimer's approach to music education, leading him to include in his text materials for children a wide spectrum of musical literature and a focus on behaviors all children can develop. Perceptual activities that promote more discriminating listening are especially important in Reimer's music curricula.[12]

FEATURES OF MUSICAL EXPERIENCE

1. *Musical experience requires the perception of sounds as being artistically (aesthetically) organized.*

Musical perception entails noticing how the sounds in a piece of music are interrelated as determined by the particular historical-cultural context in which they exist. This kind of noticing is active, discriminating, discerning, appraising; it is, in short, intelligent. But it is a nonconceptual form of intelligent cognition because it functions without concepts as that term is commonly employed. Verbal, symbolic concepts require an interrelation among three components: (1) a phenomenon that exists in more than one instance; (2) a name or symbol for the phenomenon; and (3) the regular use of the name or symbol applied to the phenomenon. Musical perception is a noticing without naming in that no symbolic intermediary intrudes on the immediacy of discerned sound-relationships.[13]

The term *perceptual structuring* indicates the mental activity in which sensory/formal percepts are processed as meaningfully organized. (This is preferred over the generally recognized term *intuition* because it emphasizes the active, educable nature of musical perception.) A particular sound-relationship noticed as a phenomenon is termed a *perceptual construct* (for example, a theme, a tone color, a rhythm pattern, a textural organization, a harmonic relationship, or a variation).[14] Musical perceptual constructs, analogously to concepts, exist at levels from the very simple (a tone repeated) to the very complex (all possible musical events unified by the term *Western cultural tradition*). The ability to perceptually structure musical sounds, like the ability to conceptualize, is capable of extensive development and is limited only by (1) the level of each person's inherent perceptual intelligence, and (2) the opportunities afforded by that person's society to actualize his or her potential. Musical perceptual intelligence is subject, therefore, to the same forces of nature and nurture as all other forms of human intelligence. Music education is a society's organized attempt to nurture all peoples' inherent capacity for musical perceptual intelligence. It also nurtures peoples' musical talent for performance and composition.[15]

2. *Musical experience requires affective responsiveness to the expressive nature of sounds perceived as artistically (aesthetically) organized.*

It is possible to perceive the structured nature of sounds with no affective involvement whatsoever, as in taking musical dictation. This does not constitute musical experience (except in a technical, limited sense) because it does not include the perception of those sounds as *artistically/aesthetically* organized. The words *artistically* and *aesthetically* refer to the organization of sounds according to decisions as to their affective arousal possibilities, including any societal-functional aspects. Sounds artistically organized are specifically and consciously intended to be experienced affectively as an inseparable quality of their structure.[16]

Sounds can arouse affect by referring to a nonsound idea, event, or object (a police car siren, a fire alarm). No such sounds are musical (although any such sounds can be used for musical purposes). Sounds are musical when they embody possibilities for expectation of further, related sounds and develop those further relations in some perceptible configuration of tendencies and energies. References to nonsound affects (program music, vocal music, explicit social values incorporated within the music) can pervade the intrinsic tendency-relations of sounds, thereby influencing the affective experience of them.[17]

The ability to experience sounds as intrinsically affective is inborn to the same degree as the ability to perceptually structure such sounds. So music education must nurture each person's capacity to respond feelingfully to music through systematic improvement of the capacity to perceptually structure music. Music education is a society's organized attempt to nurture people's inherent capacity for musical affective responsiveness, through more discerning perceptions of the culturally affirmed sound structures in which affect is embodied, and through more expert abilities to create such sound structures as through performing, composing, and improvising.[18]

3. *Musical experience includes a sensuous dimension.*

The processing of artistically organized sounds entails, as a necessary component, the experience of sound as sensorily affecting. While sound must be processed by the brain, the *experience* at the sensuous level is of sound as if processed by the body. Loudness as such is a sensory experience, as are different tone colors, strong beats, dynamic changes, sweeping melodic contours, lush chromatic harmonies, sudden accents, accelerandos, ongoing rhythmic ostinati, and so on.

These are only obvious examples: it is likely that all experiences with musical sound are pervaded with sensuous responsiveness.

Sensuous responses are a necessary aspect of the intelligent processing of music. They are intimately related to the experience of music as "indwelling" within the self of the body. They can be enhanced through music education, which sensitizes people to the breadth, subtleties, and depths of musical sensory possibilities.[19]

4. *Musical experience includes a creative dimension.*

All musical experience, including listening to a piece composed and performed by others, requires an individual to exercise control over what is heard, the levels of subtlety of what is heard, and the levels of affective involvement in what is heard. Each experience of music is, in this sense, created by the person experiencing.

Composers create by giving direction to, and following, musical impulses as they are imagined. Performers create by shaping a composer's imagined sound events into expressive sonorities. (The two functions can coexist as when composers perform their own works or when a performer composes in improvisation.) Listeners create by selective attention and self-generated affect as they share the expressive possibilities made tangible by the composer and performer. In this creativity of "constructing one's own experience," the listener not only notices musical events as they occur, but "listens forward," anticipating what might occur, and "listens backward," checking what is now occurring against what has already occurred. Creativity at this level entails selective attention at various levels of inclusiveness, anticipatory projection, reflective reappraisal, and affective self-investment.[20] Whatever a person's involvement with music, whether creating it or experiencing what others have created, that involvement has consequences for the quality of felt experience. "The higher quality of affective experience is a direct result of a process that enables feelings to be precise, accurate, detailed, meticulous, subtle, lucid, complex, discriminating, powerful, meaningful. In this profound sense, creating art and experiencing art educate feeling."[21]

5. *Musical experience includes a contextual/social dimension.*

Musical experience, like all other human experience, is a product of each individual's inherent capabilities, but also of each individual's membership in a culture that shapes those capabilities in ways indigenous to that culture. So, while musical experience is in one sense unique to each individual having it, in another sense it is profoundly affected by its cultural setting. Reimer "insists that [musical] meaning and value are internal; they are functions of the artistic qualities themselves and how they are organized. But the artistic/cultural influences surrounding a work of art may indeed be strongly involved in the experience the work gives, because they become part of the internal experience for those aware of these influences."[22] Music, as all the other arts, resides in belief systems and community mores directly impinging on and determining the sensibilities of those who make art and those who experience it:

> Every work of art is influenced by a variety of circumstances impinging on the choices the artist made in creating it. Some of these stem from the artist — his or her personal and professional history, present life situation, characteristic interests, internalized influences from other artists, and so on. Other circumstances stem from the culture within which the artist works — the general belief system about the arts, important past and present political events, the existing social structure within which the artist plays a part, and so on.[23]

But while music shares with all other human activities a cultural basis, music is not identical with all other cultural activities — it has an identity making it musical. Music transcends the general culture, by adding a quality that only art exists to provide:

> That quality, I am convinced, is indeed its capacity to create intrinsically meaningful structures and to transform anything else it chooses to incorporate, such as conventional symbols, political statements, moral exhortations, stories and icons and whatever else, by setting such material as one dimension of — often an important dimension of — its intrinsic structure. The transformation of meaning through formed interrelationships occurs particularly and necessarily with emotions, I would argue. Emotional states or moods, like any other incorporated materials, can influence aesthetic expressiveness, but such expressiveness always transmutes, through the structures into which it is cast, any representation of an emotion as it might exist in experiences outside art. [24]

While all music is embedded in culture, it is possible for people outside a particular culture to experience its music with some degree of sympathetic understanding, through a process of confrontation with the otherness of that music in the context of qualities all music shares. So, while music education is responsible for making more available to all people the richness of music in their own culture, it is also responsible for introducing them to music from a variety of foreign cultures, to expand their understanding of both music and themselves:

> Music manifests powerfully this fundamental reality of human consciousness — that we exist in a world of meanings we experience alone in our own skins, while also being capable of recognizing and being influenced by the coexperience of those with whom we share the world. The expansion within us of that coexisting world is thus an expansion of our selves. Every act of musical experience expands our inner world. The experience of foreign musics does so dramatically in forcing us to push beyond the circle of assumptions more easily accommodated within a familiar system to a circle incommensurable with the familiar yet understandable through sympathetic effort. In studying the musics of others — especially foreign others — we come to a deeper understanding both of our selves as individuals and our selves as relative to other systems of being we can experience meaningfully.[25]

Bennett Reimer

NOTES

1. Bennett Reimer, "Selfness and Otherness in Experiencing Music of Foreign Cultures," *The Quarterly Journal of Teaching and Learning* (Fall 1991), p. 7.
2. Bennett Reimer, *A Philosophy of Music Education,* 2nd ed. (Englewood Cliffs, NJ: Prentice Hall, 1989), p. 93.
3. John Dewey, *Art as Experience* (New York: Capricorn Books, 1958), pp. 35–106.
4. Susanne K. Langer, *Feeling and Form* (New York: Charles Scribner's Sons, 1953), pp. 24–41.
5. Reimer, *A Philosophy*, pp. 32–34.
6. Ibid., pp. 45–49.

7. Leonard B. Meyer, *Emotion and Meaning in Music* (Chicago: University of Chicago Press, 1956), pp. 1–3.

8. Reimer, *A Philosophy,* p. 53.

9. Meyer, *Emotion and Meaning,* pp. 13–14.

10. Reimer, *A Philosophy,* p. 144–146.

11. Reimer, "Selfness and Otherness," p. 12.

12. For examples of the breadth of musical styles and listening tasks in Reimer's teaching materials, see the Indexes in *Silver Burdett MUSIC* (Morristown, NJ: Silver Burdett, 1974, 1978, 1981, 1985), Books 1–8, and *Developing the Experience of Music* (Englewood Cliffs, NJ: Prentice-Hall, 1984).

13. Reimer, *A Philosophy,* pp. 81–84.

14. Ibid., p. 83.

15. Ibid., pp. 97, 180–188, 207–213.

16. Ibid., pp. 49–53.

17. Bennett Reimer, "What Knowledge Is of Most Worth in the Arts?" in *The Arts, Education, and Aesthetic Knowing,* ed. Bennett Reimer and Ralph A. Smith (Chicago: University of Chicago Press, 1992), pp. 32–35.

18. Reimer, *A Philosophy,* pp. 53–54.

19. Ibid., pp. 126–128.

20. Ibid., pp. 70–71, 129–30, 168.

21. Ibid., p. 37.

22. Ibid., p. 27.

23. Ibid., p. 17.

24. Bennett Reimer, "Essential and Nonessential Characteristics of Aesthetic Education," *The Journal of Aesthetic Education* 25 (Fall 1991), p. 202. Also see the discussion of the power of art to transform social contents, functions, and emotions into aesthetic cognitions, in Reimer, "What Knowledge Is of Most Worth?", pp. 32–39.

25. Reimer, "Selfness and Otherness," p. 12.

ARNOLD SCHOENBERG
(1874–1951)

SOURCES

Arnold Schoenberg has had a profound influence on the music of the twentieth century. This influence has resulted from his work as composer, teacher, philosopher, and interpreter of the age. His literary contribution includes books, letters, lectures, and hundreds of essays. *Style and Idea,* selected writings of Arnold Schoenberg, was first published in 1975. It is an expansion of a 1950 collection of essays by the same title. The new edition of *Style and Idea* (1984) is the definitive source through which to examine the composer's orientation to musical experience.

GENERAL ORIENTATION TO MUSICAL EXPERIENCE

Style and Idea, containing articles that date from 1909 to 1950, provides a focus to the many facets of Schoenberg's thoughts and succinctly collates the massive literary output of this intensely curious and passionately involved musician. While there is no specific reference to the musical experience in *Style and Idea,* it contains statements pertinent to the subject. As is the case with many composers, Schoenberg's general orientation to the musical experience is that the listener must understand the composer's intent and that composers, historians, critics, and teachers should concern themselves with the communication of ideas. Schoenberg suggests that the most important aspect of musical participation is the involvement of the mind in comprehending ideas.[1]

He also feels that music pleases even though it is not necessarily created for this purpose. Most of his writings attempt to define the compositional process and direct the listener to matters in the score. "Nowadays I make a point of keeping my ideas at a decent distance from the feelings accompanying them," writes Schoenberg.[2]

His primary thesis is that composers create, express, and write ideas that must be heard and understood. Participation in music through the communication of and interaction with these ideas is the essence of the musical experience. Style manifests the character of the ideas being conceived. Schoenberg uses the term *idea* as a synonym for theme, melody, phrase, or motive. However, he also considers "the totality of a piece as the idea: the idea which its creator wanted to present."[3] The idea of the composition manifests itself when the craftsman brings into balance the inherent tension created by the development of a musical line from a series of notes in rhythmic, harmonic, and structural interaction. Regarding the present state of compositional efforts, Schoenberg writes, "It is very regrettable that so many contemporary composers care so much about style and so little about idea."[4]

FEATURES OF MUSICAL EXPERIENCE

1. *The musical experience is enhanced by memory.*
The role of memory in musical experience is more important than most people realize. Schoenberg feels that one starts to understand a piece only when one can remember it — at least partially. As one who grew up in close proximity to Johannes Brahms, Schoenberg learned early that it was customary for a musician to understand the construction of a composition on first hearing. The layman was expected to take a melody home in his memory.[5]

2. *The musical experience is enhanced by an awareness of musical structure — a requirement for proper cognition.*
Comprehending the structure of a composition requires following the elaboration and derivation of its themes and its modulations, as well as recognizing the number of voices in canons and the presence of the theme in a variation.[6] In defense of the twelve-tone system,

Schoenberg states that this method of composition provides the structure once furnished by harmony. However, he realizes that it cannot replace all that harmony has accomplished from the time of Bach to the contemporary period.[7]

3. *The musical experience is enhanced when unity is present and perceived, making the composition comprehensible.*

Can unification be achieved without the missing power of harmony? Can twelve-tone technique create its own center of gravitation which has the power to permit lines to go astray but the inherent capacity to recall them and envelop them in a unified work?[8] The effort of the composer is solely for the purpose of making the idea comprehensible to the listener. For the latter's sake the artist must divide the whole into surveyable parts, and then add them together again into a whole that is conceivable in spite of hampering details. Experience teaches that the understanding of the listener is an unstable quantity — that is, it is not permanently fixed. For this reason it does not always accommodate the development of the art form.[9]

4. *The musical experience requires that an interaction of the product, producer, and receiver take place.*

An artistic impression is the result of two components: that which the work of art gives to the onlooker and that which the onlooker is able to give to the work of art. The musical product is merely the external stimulus that awakens those forces sensed by us as an artistic impression. The intensity of an artistic impression depends on the onlooker's ability to receive even while giving to the work of art.[10] Music is only understood when one goes away singing it and only loved when one falls asleep with it in one's head, and finds it still there on waking up the next morning.[11]

5. *The musical experience requires that a prophetic message be present.*

Music conveys a prophetic message revealing a higher form of life toward which humankind evolves. It is because of this message that music appeals to people of all races and cultures.[12]

6. *The musical experience can happen only when the sensual is communicated from the composer to the listener.*

The intellectual is skeptical and untrusting of the sensual. If one is overwhelmed, the intellect maintains that there are many means that might bring forth such an overwhelming emotion. A work of art can produce no greater effect than when it transmits to and reproduces within the listener the emotions that raged in the creator.[13] Schoenberg admits that he was completely overwhelmed when he first heard Gustav Mahler's Second Symphony, seized with an excitement that expressed itself physically (in the violent throbbing of his heart) as well as intellectually.[14]

7. *The musical experience requires understanding, which is the result of proper education.*

Art teachers typically pass on only artistic methods and aesthetics, mixing the two in a proportion according to their degrees of insight. When they can get no further with the one, the other comes to the rescue.[15] As long as teachers provide artistic methods, this process may function effectively. However, when teachers turn to the function of feeling and sensitivity, they becomes nebulous, unclear, and lose control.[16] Schoenberg criticizes those who teach nothing but the peculiarities of a certain style. He contends that it is important to provide student composers with the tools of their art, and with the technical, aesthetic, and moral basis of true artistry.[17]

8. *The musical experience requires that beauty be perceived; this can only happen when the form is understood.*

It is a great mistake to believe that form exists to create beauty. On the contrary, the principal function of form is to advance our understanding. Music should be enjoyed, and understanding offers the most enjoyable of pleasures: "Though the object of form is not beauty, by providing comprehensibility, form produces beauty."[18]

9. *The musical experience (closely tied to musical cognition) is enhanced when the principle of repetition is judiciously employed.*

Forms are primarily organizations that express ideas in a comprehensible manner. A student knows by experience that the repetition of a section may be good, useful, or inevitable and recognizes the meaning of repetition in the works of others. Anyone trained to vary the basic motive of a composition will probably be able to follow a complicated melody without involuntarily dreaming of irrelevant images.[19]

Paul A. Aliapoulios

NOTES

1. Arnold Schoenberg, *Style and Idea,* trans. Leo Black, ed. Leonard Stein (Berkeley: University of California Press, 1984), pp. 53–54.

2. Ibid., p. 138.

3. Ibid., p. 122.

4. Ibid., p. 123.

5. Ibid., p. 121.

6. Ibid.

7. Ibid., p. 245.

8. Ibid.

9. Ibid., pp. 103–104.

10. Ibid., p. 189

11. Ibid., p. 180.

12. Ibid., p. 136.

13. Ibid., p. 450.

14. Ibid.

15. Ibid., p. 365.

16. Ibid.

17. Ibid., p. 390.

18. Ibid., p. 380.

19. Ibid., pp. 380–381.

ROGER SESSIONS
(1896–1985)

SOURCES

Roger Huntington Sessions is often regarded as the leading teacher of composition of his era: 1935 to 1980. In addition to his work as composer and teacher, Sessions also established himself as a writer about music and the musical experience. He was editor of the *Harvard Musical Review* from 1915 until 1917, and he contributed regularly to *Modern Music* from 1927 until the early 1940s. His books include *The Musical Experience of Composer, Performer, Listener* (1950), which was based on lectures given at the Julliard School of Music; an exposition of his aesthetics entitled *Questions About Music* (1970); *Harmonic Practice* (1970), a work based on his teaching experience at Berkeley in the 1940s; and *Roger Sessions on Music* (1979), a collection of essays covering a variety of topics. While this discussion follows the basic progression of ideas as outlined in *The Musical Experience,* it also incorporates thoughts from other sources mentioned above.

GENERAL ORIENTATION TO MUSICAL EXPERIENCE

Sessions is careful to stress the fact that he writes not as a scholar or critic, but as a practicing artist — a composer. While his choice of

---

The quotations in this chapter from Roger Sessions's *The Musical Experience of Composer, Performer, Listener* are reprinted with permission of Princeton University Press.

words could sometimes be criticized by the philosopher or aesthetician, his insight into the musical process remains valuable. Speaking as
one who has "dirtied his hands" with the reality of musical problems,
Sessions's words find credibility in their practicality. He addresses
issues that every mature musician should face and ponder. With no
desire to shroud his thoughts in mystery or ambiguity, Sessions speaks
simply and directly. He strikes a sympathetic chord with all who have
wondered about that which lies beneath the musical experience.

Sessions notes that at one point in the history of musical development, all facets of the musical process as practiced in Western music
were executed by a single individual. The composer, performer, and
listener were all the same person. It was a relatively recent development in the history of Western music that these tasks were divided,
thereby allowing the advent of the musical specialist.[1] While he does
not argue for a return to the former practices of music, Sessions does
seem to realize the importance of maintaining unity and continuity
among these phases of the musical experience. It is necessary that
composers view their work as the first step of a larger process that
eventually will involve both the performer and the listener. It is the
composers' responsibility to master their craft to such a degree that
their products may be realistically re-created by the performer and
meaningfully apprehended by the listener. Only when the cycle of
composition, performance, and perception is complete can there be a
satisfying musical experience.

FEATURES OF MUSICAL EXPERIENCE

1. *The musical experience as manifested in composition involves the
crafting of a complex structure from a musical idea.*
Sessions begins his exploration of the compositional process by
addressing the issue of *inspiration,* even though he feels that the word
inspiration is often laden with connotations that are unrealistic and
fanciful. For some, this word denotes a sudden flash of musical activity
thrust upon the composer from an external source. Sessions, however,
holds that inspiration comes in the form of an idea that can create
momentum for the musical thoughts of the composer. It is inspiration
that sets the creative process in motion and supplies the energy needed

to keep it in motion. Inspiration is internally motivated rather than externally derived by the composer. This impulse toward a musical goal may come easily and quickly or it may require a time of growth and development. Sketches made by composers often reveal the birth process of a musical idea, confirming the fact that these ideas sometimes require a great deal of revision. Regardless of the generative process, when an inspired idea finally arrives, it is immediately recognized by the composer. The problem now becomes one of structuring an entire work from this kernel. Each phrase of the completed work must recapture the energy and spirit of the original idea while fitting into the composer's vision of the whole creation.[2]

According to Sessions, a composer is someone who constantly has "tones in his head."[3] Obviously, anyone who remembers a melody is exercising the same capacity, but the difference for the composer is the pervasive nature of this musical activity. Musical patterns are somewhere in the minds of composers at all times and may be brought into consciousness without difficulty. When consciously focusing upon these musical ideas, composers are, in a way, improvising on them. They are shaping and amending, elaborating and changing until a fragment reaches the point at which it no longer permits these formative processes to continue. Rather, the fragment demands to be left in its present state. At this point the process changes from one of shaping to one of following the fragment. It now becomes an entity — an independent musical idea.[4]

A musical idea is a segment of music that serves as a point of departure for the composer. It is the starting point from which one may develop some aspect of a composition or even an entire composition. This seminal idea may take any of several forms. It may be a particular sonority, a rhythmic movement, a texture, or even a single note in a particular context. Whatever the manifestation of the musical idea, it is the unit that serves as the "glue" or unifying agent of the composition. In some works of great maturity this may even take the shape of recurring relationships between harmonies or keys, or some other predominant feature of the musical work. It should be noted, however, that a musical idea is not necessarily the same as a musical motif. In some cases, the two may be a single unit, but Sessions feels that the motif (or theme) is often separate from or perhaps even a manifestation of the central musical idea.[5]

The musical idea, once it is set in place, will prescribe the thoughts of the composer and the development of the musical composition. All succeeding ideas will bear some close relationship to the initial idea and should, in some way, develop or extend that point of departure. Sessions discusses this concept in several places in his writings (sometimes at great length) because he feels it is important to dispel the myths that surround the process of artistic creation. He insists that composition involves thought and action. Though the pattern or method of this deliberative process may vary among composers, there is overwhelming evidence that the basic process is common across cultures and generations. Sessions believes that there is a strong correlation between the character and quality of the composer's product and the intensity of his or her activity.[6]

If the compositional process is set in motion by the formation of a musical idea, then the problem the composer faces is that of extending and developing the idea, bringing its energy to bear not only on each detail of the work, but also on its overall structure. Sessions refers to this vision of the whole of the work as the *conception* of the composition. This aspect of the compositional process differs from inspiration in that it cannot be realized in a short amount of time. It is a result of the inspiration and an extension of it. Just as inspiration manifests itself in the style of the music, the conception determines the form of the music. It is important to note, however, that neither style nor form is established on the basis of convention. Sessions feels that, even though certain periods of music established clearly defined patterns from which the composer could freely improvise, ultimately the essence of the music itself determines the overall shape of the composition. These standards, however, are vital only as long as they are in process of development. Once they have diminished, it is most difficult to revive them because they were the result of a unique and irretrievable impulse. They were specifically suited for the situation in which they developed.[7]

It is essential that composers reach a point at which they can see the entire work as a whole and become aware of how its components fit together. With this in place, it is possible for composers to move toward the structural goals they have established. These goals determine a yet larger pattern (or layers of patterns) that come to constitute a large-scale entity.[8]

After inspiration and conception, the next step in the compositional process is *execution*. It is in this stage that the music expands and develops, following wherever it may be led by inspiration and conception. It is at this point that the momentum of the musical idea is given the opportunity to flourish and expand, propelling itself into new phrases, motifs, and harmonies. Inspiration has been linked with style, and conception with form. Execution determines the structure of the musical product.[9]

It may be helpful at this point to articulate some of the principles of musical structure that serve to establish the general characteristics of the music.

Association. The term as it is used here refers strictly to the music itself and not to extra-musical associations or references. Sessions states that certain features of the music must be repeated and, by virtue of this recurrence, will gain significance and provide coherence for the piece at large. Therefore, these associative elements must span more than a single phrase. As the listener detects the associations within the music, a sense of unity within the musical product will result.[10]

Progression. Because music is an art form that is based on the passage of time, the principle of progression is of vital importance in music. Generally speaking, each moment of the music must be of greater intensity and significance than the one that came before it. This is executed through the movement of the music toward a clearly defined musical goal. This means that music of large dimensions must be organized in such a way that the music moves logically and expressively through a progression of goals.[11]

Contrast. This element is essential to the development of the composition in that it serves hand-in-hand with the concept of progression. Once the music has accomplished a goal by means of a progression, the need for contrast arises. Contrast could manifest itself in the form of a variation on the previous material or a departure from that which happened before. The decision regarding the form of the contrast depends entirely upon the composer's conception of the work. The alternation of contrasting musical ideas is the process through which the outline of the musical product becomes apparent. Contrast gives the work its largest rhythm.[12]

Continuity. The concept of continuity is used here to refer to everything that relates to the logical flow of events in the composition.

It includes the relationships of tones, sonorities, patterns, colors, or nuance to that which comes before and after it. It also encompasses proportion, balance, tension, relaxation, and contrast. Perhaps more than any other element, continuity determines the ultimate character of the music.[13]

Articulation. This principle involves giving the clearest possible definition (in terms of function) to each of the compositional elements. With the term *compositional element,* Sessions is referring to the units or gestures that combine to create the structure of the music. These gestures exist on various levels so that small gestures combine to create larger ones, and so on until the overall design is created. While this is a simplistic representation of the complex matter of bringing proportion and equilibrium to music, Sessions feels it is of the utmost urgency to clearly articulate the components of the music. While we can become thoroughly acquainted with music as it was defined in previous periods of history, today's composers are obligated to discover their own vocabulary for the articulation of their music.[14]

After a rather lengthy discussion of the elements and principles of musical composition, Sessions is careful to point out that composers do not actually think in terms of these or any other words when they are practicing their craft. Rather, the composer thinks abstractly in terms of sounds and shapes. These elements interact with each other and are all facets of the organic process of creating music. While they may be isolated and identified as distinguishable factors, composers are seldom conscious of them as such. They turn their ears in a particular direction that ultimately will lead to a musical result. The composer pursues a creative goal, one that cannot be achieved through rational thought.[15]

2. *The musical experience as manifested in performance is expressive through movement.*

For Sessions it is important to establish those criteria that separate music from other forms of artistic creation. Only when this is done can one determine what music does for people that no other art form can do. It is then that we can understand the human need for music.

The essential aspect of music that makes it unique among the arts is, according to Sessions, its ability to make time come alive through its expressive essence — movement. Because music is apprehended through the ear, it is different from visual or literary creations that may be contemplated and scrutinized as long as one likes. The musical experience is fleeting and elusive.[16]

Because music exists only in time, it is a temporal art in which the ear coordinates and labels its elements so that they can be retained and identified. In this way, as listeners become aware of patterns of structure such as continuity and contrast, tension and release, they become aware of a progressive movement through time:[17]

> Once more I should like to emphasize that it is through our perception of these elements, our awareness of them, that they have meaning for us, and that we gain this perception through the experience of our psycho-physical organism. Here it is not a question of the alternation of tension and relaxation but of our experience of time itself. We gain our experience, our sensation of time through movement, and it is movement, primarily, which gives it contrast for us.[18]

Sessions gives considerable attention to what he regards as the primary sources or raw materials of music — sound and rhythm. It is not sound and rhythm as such that are his concern, but their nature as human factors. For instance, he refers to the fact that people are immersed in rhythm from conception. They are surrounded by a universe characterized by multiple layers of rhythmic activity, from the limited scope of their walking and breathing to the overwhelming thought of interplanetary motion. It is the alternation of rhythm in the form of tension and release that so deeply affects people as movement is experienced. The multiple layers of rhythmic activity that fit together on various levels to create a large-scale musical structure are a direct reflection of the multi-layered rhythmic activity of the human environment.[19]

The impulse to create musical sounds is also one of our earliest, most pervasive, and most intimate experiences. The production of vocal sound is rooted in our initial moments of existence and gradually undergoes a process of growth and refinement as the mind and body mature. This human function stems directly from rhythmic activity (breathing) and relates, in and of itself, a rhythmic quality — the rise and fall of the voice, the tension and release of a phrase. It is the essence of the vocal gesture that is the paradigm of the melodic motif or phrase. Once again, the basic material of music finds its beginning in the essence of humanity.[20]

While Sessions admits that this discussion greatly simplifies a complex matter, he justifies himself with these words:

> These are not the only elements in musical expression, but I am deliberately restricting the discussion here to primitive, direct, and simple responses to music. Even at this level, may we not say that the basic ingredient of music is not so much sound as movement, conceived in terms I have indicated? I would even go a step further and say that music is significant for us as human beings principally because it embodies movement of a specifically human type that goes to the roots of our being and takes shape in the inner gestures which embody our deepest and most intimate responses. This is of itself not yet art; it is not yet even language. But it is the material of which musical art is made, and to which musical art gives significance.[21]

Having established that there is human responsiveness to the primitive elements of musical movement, Sessions embarks upon a discussion of how this movement serves as an avenue of expression in music. This matter is difficult to describe in discursive terms since, as was noted earlier, composers think with sounds that will capture the essence of what they have to say. To recode these ideas into a format that they were never meant to occupy results in an approximation at best. Sessions feels, however, that it is the quality and character of movement that brings meaning to music. If music is a design of controlled movement and time, then we must ask "why this specific movement?" and "why this particular sound?"[22] While precise answers to these questions are impossible, it is possible to state that what music expresses is, to a great extent, determined by the individual listener. However, Sessions is adamant in the belief that music does not express emotion. Though humans react to the immense power of movement and sound (musical or nonmusical), this power is "beneath the realm of emotion, in the sphere of movement itself, and the vital significance of movement for us."[23] Music conveys to us (through the nature of the medium and not through the intent of the composer) the essence of our existence as embodied in the movement that makes up our existence and lies beneath emotion, impulse, and action.[24]

Sessions summarizes his views on musical expression as follows:

> "Emotion" is specific, individual, conscious; music goes deeper than this, to the energies which animate our psychic life, and out of these creates a pattern which has an existence, laws and human significance of its own. It reproduces for us the most intimate essence, the tempo and the energy, of our own spiritual being; our tranquility and our restlessness, our animation and our discourage-ment, our vitality and our weakness — all, in fact, of the fine shades of dynamic variation of our inner life. It reproduces these far more directly and more specifically than is possible through any other medium of human communication.[25]

3. *The musical experience, as manifested in perception, makes use of the musical ear.*

Sessions gives considerable attention to the concept of the musical ear, that is, a method of hearing music that need not be restricted to the musician. While it may be true that musicians sometimes develop a more discriminating musical ear than nonmusicians (though certainly not in every case), auditory functions are possessed by the human race as a whole. The musical ear, first of all, discriminates between sounds and does so on a number of levels (pitch, tone quality, intensity, timbre, duration). Second, once pitches have been distinguished, the musical ear relates and associates the musical impressions. Again, these associations are possible on the basis of a great many criteria. Finally, the ear is responsible for ordering these associations into hierarchical levels that combine to create an overall image of the work.[26]

Before this final step (ordering of musical events) can take place, however, we must define the features of the musical product that allow it to be grasped and arranged by the listener. The principle means by which this happens, according to Sessions, is through the perception of harmony. While music embodies movement, harmony provides a static element that allows the music to be organized. Harmony, more than any other element of music, affords the possibil-ity of extension and growth by virtue of the almost inexhaustible variety of tonal relationships. The development of tonality and modulations suddenly made it possible to develop large-scale sections of contrast. As tonality is perceived by the musical ear, it becomes possible to compare areas of tonal contrast and put them in the perspective of the overall design. When the composer has exercised clear articulation, it is possible for the listener both to perceive aurally and feel empathetically the impact of the composer's work.[27]

With this overview of the musical experience, one must not lose sight of Sessions's concern for the essential unity of its component parts:

> The unity of the musical experience can be regarded from several angles. First of all, the composer, the performer, and the listener are in a certain sense collaborators in a total musical experience, to which each makes his individual contribution. Secondly, not only are the performer and the listener, in a real sense, re-experiencing and re-creating the musical thought of the composer, but they are, also in a real sense, adding to it. We might even say that, according to the various gifts involved, the three functions sometimes overlap, with the performer supplying whatever for him is missing in the work of the composer, the listener hearing the composition sometimes beyond the performer, and the composer, to a very important degree, visualizing (with his ears and not with his eyes, be it understood!) his work in terms of both performance and sounds heard. Finally, a given musical environment produces all of these phases if it is, as we might say, musically alive; if, that is, the love for music is a strong and vital factor in people's lives. In such an environment all these — composer, performer, and listener — are subject to similar influences, and hence may always be presumed to show somewhat similar trends. A similar musical spirit or musical mentality will operate through them all — all of them, that is, whose musical activities embody values that are new, and hence characteristic of that environment.[28]

Jeffrey E. Wright

NOTES

1. Roger Sessions, *The Musical Experience of Composer, Performer, Listener* (Princeton, NJ: Princeton University Press, 1950), pp. 4–7.

2. Roger Sessions, *Roger Sessions on Music,* ed. Edward T. Cone (Princeton, NJ: Princeton University Press, 1979), p. 21.

3. Roger Sessions, *Questions About Music* (New York: W. W. Norton, 1970), p. 76.

4. Ibid., pp. 74–76.

5. Sessions, *The Musical Experience,* pp. 46–47.

6. Sessions, *Questions About Music,* pp. 82–84.

7. Sessions, *Roger Sessions on Music,* p. 22.

8. Sessions, *Questions About Music,* p. 89.

9. Sessions, *Roger Sessions on Music,* pp. 22–25.

10. Ibid., pp. 23–24.

11. Ibid., pp. 24–25.

12. Ibid., pp. 25–26.

13. Sessions, *Questions About Music,* pp. 103–105.

14. Ibid., pp. 105–108.

15. Ibid., pp. 108–110.

16. Sessions, *Roger Sessions on Music,* pp. 6–8.

17. Sessions, *Questions About Music,* pp. 39–40.

18. Sessions, *The Musical Experience,* p. 15.

19. Ibid., pp. 11–17.

20. Ibid., pp. 17–19.

21. Ibid., p. 19.

22. Sessions, *Questions About Music,* pp. 40–45.

23. Ibid., p. 44.

24. Ibid., pp. 40–45.

25. Sessions, *Roger Sessions on Music,* p. 19.

26. Sessions, *The Musical Experience,* pp. 31–33.

27. Ibid., pp. 33–42.

28. Ibid., pp. 107–108.

IGOR STRAVINSKY
(1882–1971)

SOURCES

Igor Stravinsky was a prolific and extremely influential composer, his compositions reflecting his evolutionary passage through most of the familiar twentieth-century compositional techniques. Though a copious composer, Stravinsky's writings are much more limited. They consist almost entirely of six books of interview transcripts compiled with Robert Craft, an autobiography, and his *Poetics of Music* (1947), which is based on transcripts of six "lessons on music" presented at Harvard University during the 1939–1940 school year as part of the Norton Lecture Series. The second lesson from the *Poetics* is entitled "The Phenomenon of Music" and contains Stravinsky's only comprehensive description of the musical experience. It is the primary source of the following discussion.

GENERAL ORIENTATION TO MUSICAL EXPERIENCE

Not surprisingly, Stravinsky approaches his descriptions of the musical experience from his perspective as a composer. He talks at length about aspects of musical effects on the listener, but retains a compositional outlook by modulating from these commentaries to their implication for musical creation. For Stravinsky, musical creation resides with the composer alone; elsewhere in the *Poetics*[1] and in interviews with Craft,[2] he expounds at length about the proper role of the interpreter, which he considers to be exclusively "re-creative" of the composer's original vision rather than creative in the sense of an independent artistic entity. Stravinsky's challenge to the interpreter is to be fully aware of the compositional intent, well versed in style and historical perspective, but subservient to the composer's vision. His argument here is mostly one of equity. The great care and thoughtful detail provided by the composer should not be capriciously disregarded, amended, or in any way altered by another. The composer's investment is complete and normally far exceeds that of the interpreter on any one piece. In short, due to their enormous investment, composers' visions deserve to be heard without alteration.[3]

FEATURES OF MUSICAL EXPERIENCE

1. *The musical experience is available only to those people (composers, listeners) who are armed with the full resources of their aural senses, psychological faculties, and intellect, and are capable of a kind of higher "speculation."*
   The phenomenon of music (musical experience) is, to Stravinsky, nothing other than speculation. This reflects the creative process in music that presupposes a preliminary "feeling out," an exploration in the abstract with the ultimate objective of giving shape to something concrete. The elements with which this speculation deals are *sound* and *time*. Music is not possible without them.[4]
   2. *The musical experience is made possible through two key elements of music — sound and time. Of the two, time is the more immediate.*
   Plastic arts exist in space. The perceiver is able to receive an overall and general impression of the work initially, and then is able to begin to discover details about the work, entirely at his or her own leisure and pace. In the plastic arts, time, when it is of any importance, is manipulated by the perceiver. Music, though, exists wholly in time and, as shall be seen, relates to it. Music is based on temporal successions of sonic events and requires retention by the perceiver. Before all else, music presupposes an organization in time — what Stravinsky terms a *chrononomy*.[5]
   The movement of sounds that can be music requires a constant and measurable value: *meter*. Through meter, rhythm is realized. Meter reflects the number of equal parts into which the musical unit we call a measure is divided; rhythm reflects part groupings within the measure.

Meter offers only symmetry, but is utilized by rhythm, whose "function it is to establish order in the movement of sounds."[6]

Stravinsky suggests an example of jazz music as producing relationships between rhythm and meter that can clarify the connection between the two. In jazz, melodic lines often persistently stress irregular accents or note groupings above the regular pulsation of the rhythm section. Here the isochronous beats (of meter) serve to throw the rhythmic invention of the melodic material into relief. Without the real or implied presence of the regular beats, the invention would lose its meaning. The function is one of a relationship between the two.[7]

3. *The musical experience is dependent upon the counterpoint between real time and musical time.*

"Musical creation is an innate complex of intuitions and possibilities based primarily upon an exclusively musical experiencing of time, . . . of which the musical work merely gives us the functional realization."[8] Stravinsky embraces the concept developed by Pierre Souvtchinsky, philosopher and friend, on the problem of musical time — that which Souvtchinsky calls the "chronos of music." Souvtchinsky reminds us that time is perceived to pass at rates that vary according to disposition and events. Expectation, boredom, anguish, pleasure, and pain each helps to determine a particular "tempo" in the perceived passing of time. This he terms *psychological time*. Variance in psychological time is apparent only when compared with real, ontological time.[9]

All music, whether it follows the normal flow of real time or disassociates itself from it, establishes a "counterpoint between the passing of real time and the material and technical means through which music is made manifest."[10] We can identify, though, two kinds of music — one that runs parallel to the passing of real time, "embracing and penetrating it and inducing in the mind of the listener a feeling of euphoria and, so to speak, of 'dynamic calm.' " The second sort runs counter to this process. It is not self-contained in each momentary tonal unit, but rather dislocates the centers of attraction and "gravity," establishing itself in the realm of the unstable. This characteristic makes this second sort of music particularly adaptable to the translation of the composer's emotive impulses; indeed, all music in which the will to expression is dominant belongs to this second type.[11]

4. *The musical experience is dependent upon the composer's use of unity and variety.*

Music that is based on real time is generally dominated by the principle of similarity. Music that is based upon psychological time, though, tends to proceed by contrast. From examination of the problem of time in music, therefore, emerges the fundamental creative concepts of variety and unity.[12] Stravinsky describes his working posture as one favoring unity. Through unity in music, he finds strength. What compositional choices he rejects from "the seductions of variety"[13] are more than compensated by gains in true solidity.

Contrast is an element of variety and produces an immediate effect. Contrast, though, divides the listener's attention. Similarity is born of the pursuit of unity and tends to satisfy "in the long run." Though both elements must coexist within a work, Stravinsky values variety only as a means of obtaining similarity: "When variety tempts me, I am uneasy about the facile solutions it offers me. Similarity, on the other hand, poses more difficult problems but also offers results that are more solid and hence more valuable to me."[14]

5. *The musical experience is reliant upon sets of musical impulses and points of musical repose.*

"Music is nothing more than a succession of impulses that converge toward a definite point of repose."[15] In the classical sense, consonance was partner to repose; dissonance served as an element of transition, a set of tones not complete in and of itself that had to be resolved into perfect consonance. During the last century, this function of dissonance has largely disappeared. Dissonance now need not prepare or anticipate anything. This is a new musical logic that would have been unthinkable to past masters but that has opened our eyes to sonic riches we had not suspected. The new logic requires an affirmation of an "axis in our music" and the existence of certain "poles of attraction." Diatonic tonality remains one means of orienting music to these poles but has long ago ceased to be the only proper means.[16]

Our chief concern is not so much what is known as tonality as it is the polar attraction of sound, of an interval, or even of a complex of tones. As all music is nothing but a succession of impulses and repose, it is easy to see that the drawing together and separation of poles of attraction determines the "respiration of music."[17] Stravinsky describes composing as putting into an order a certain group of sounds according to their interval relationships. This activity leads to a search for the center, the pole, upon which the series of sounds must ultimately converge.[18]

Donald E. Casey

NOTES

1. Igor Stravinsky, *Poetics of Music* (New York: Vintage Books, Random House, 1947), pp. 122–133.
2. Igor Stravinsky and Robert Craft, *Conversations with Igor Stravinsky* (London: Faber Music Ltd., 1959), pp. 117–121.
3. Ibid., p. 121.
4. Stravinsky, *Poetics of Music,* p. 27.
5. Ibid., p. 28.
6. Ibid.
7. Ibid., p. 29.
8. Ibid., p. 30.
9. Ibid.
10. Ibid., pp. 30–31.
11. Ibid., p. 31.
12. Ibid.
13. Ibid., p. 32.
14. Ibid., pp. 32–33.
15. Ibid., p. 35.
16. Ibid.
17. Ibid., p. 36.
18. Ibid., p. 37.

PART II

FEATURES OF MUSICAL EXPERIENCE HELD IN COMMON AND IMPLICATIONS FOR RESEARCH

INTRODUCTION

Part I of this study attempted to clarify the nature of musical experience by summarizing what a group of influential thinkers has said on this topic. Part II explores those features identified by many, if not most, of the thinkers. The last section of the introduction to Part I, "The Present Study," explains the process by which the "feature essays" in Part II were generated.

Each of the following essays is preceded by a short overview highlighting the major points in that essay. Following each essay is a list of research topics suggested by that essay. These topics range from large, broadly based research issues that would require many sub-studies over a period of years to more specific suggestions for studies such as would be appropriate for doctoral dissertations. No attempt has been made to exhaust the research implications of each essay, for each is essentially inexhaustible.

The suggestions given are for illustrative purposes only. It is hoped that these essays and the research implications listed will stimulate thought among music education researchers and other scholars and subsequently lead to ideas for a great number and variety of research studies related to the nature and cultivation of musical experience. The recommendations section, Part III of this volume, offers some suggestions for further research at a more general level than the essay-related implications given in Section II.

The essays of Part II condense and coordinate the material from all the separate author essays of Part I. Therefore, footnotes are not given in Part II because they would be redundant and because practically every sentence would have to be footnoted. Instead, at the bottom of the first page of each feature essay a listing is given, by author, of the Part I pages on which citations may be found.

INTRINSICALITY

Perhaps the most salient characteristic of the art of music and the experience of music is that sounds can be, and are, attended to for their intrinsic interrelationships. It is possible, of course, for sounds to have reference, but none of these writers on musical experience suggests that reference is either an essential or a defining component of musical experience. Intrinsically related sounds, on the other hand, are essential to music, and the noticing of them and response to them are essential to musical experience. Sounds, in music, create a dynamicism by virtue of their ability to imply other sounds and by the ways a particular piece plays out those implications. Musical experience requires attending to sounds as meaningful because they are part of a structured interplay of related implications.

★ ★ ★

According to many authors, the single most essential characteristic of musical experience is that it is caused by sounds perceived as being related to one another in meaningful ways. A piece of music is a particular episode of sounds organized to create dynamic interrelationships. The perception of these interrelationships and the internalized experience of their dynamicism (their expressiveness) constitutes musical experience.

Citations for the material in this section of Part II will be found on the following pages of Part I: Reimer, 153–156; Langer, 87–88; Beardsley, 4–5, 7, 9–11; Bernstein, 17–18; Copland, 63, 65; Hindemith, 82–84; Sessions, 171–174; Meyer, 113–114; Mursell, 122–125, 131–133; Reid, 142–145; Broudy, 37–39; Blacking, 27–28; Clifton, 54–58.

For Bennett Reimer, sounds and their interactions, as each culture determines them, embody dynamic qualities that capture a sense of the organicism (the "livingness") of our affective lives. When we experience music "musically," it is to these embodied interactions that we are paying attention, with both perceptual and affective involvement ("perceptual structuring"). Other things may influence the perceptual structuring process (such as references external to the sounds, associations with life events, and accompanying fantasies). The reason we regard music as significant rather than only pleasurable is that expressively organized sound (music) lets us experience the depths and breadths of our inner subjectivities.

Susanne Langer explains the significance of musical experience as being dependent on the intrinsic dynamicism of sounds. Music, she says, is "significant form" because it is a highly articulated sensuous object that, by virtue of its intrinsic dynamic structure, can express the forms of vital experience in ways language cannot. The import of music, experienced through its embodied sound-relations, is the sense it gives us of feeling, organized passage of events, life as intrinsically experienced. Music articulates, in its dynamic forms, the forms of growth, conflict, resolution, speed, and attenuation. In music, these vital forms are worked out in pure, measured sounds and silences. Thus, music is a "tonal analogue of emotive life." The forms of music (embodied sound-complexes) are virtual rather than actual, their motions are virtual, and compositions are semblances. A piece of music is a developed "metaphor" of feeling, articulating what is verbally ineffable. When we contemplate the embodied, virtual, dynamic forms that are pieces of music, our own experience is formulated analogously.

Monroe Beardsley adds several insights to the notion of intrinsicality. Music, he suggests, is not capable of pointing beyond itself to specific events, emotions, images, or psychological states, and therefore does not function as a natural or conventional sign. Music exists as process — not as *about* process, but as process itself. Intrinsic sound qualities (such as tempo or variations of intensity) have features that mental life also has. Further, when these qualities, or elements, combine to form complexes, these complexes take on new qualities that were not qualities of the constituent elements. These "regional qualities" allow us to perceive art works as unified, coherent, aesthetic phenomena. Some musical qualities seem to resemble qualities of human beings or of their states of mind, or actions or activities ("the music is schizoid, or it rushes headlong"); these human qualities are *metaphorical* (more specifically than in Langer's very general use of that term). But music need not refer to anything besides its own intrinsic qualities in order to play its role in helping us understand our inner world.

For Beardsley, a fundamental aspect of music is change. In a sense, music is nothing more than change (for Langer, dynamic form) in its myriad forms and ways, and in this respect it is a mirror of the most fundamental features of our personal lives and social histories. Music, in exemplifying change (process), entails continuation. Because music can make extremely precise distinctions among kinds of continuation, our experience of it can bring fresh perceptiveness and clearer cognitive grasp to this essential quality of our lives. Beardsley summarizes an experience with markedly aesthetic character (that is, musical experience) as having the following features (the first always included and the fifth preferably included): (1) object-directedness, which requires attention to the phenomenally objective properties (intrinsic qualities and relations) of a work of art; (2) felt freedom, which is freedom from concerns about matters extrinsic to the experience itself; (3) detached affect, which has no practical ends other than the intrinsic experience; (4) active discovery, which requires the exercise of one's own powers to search out the qualities and relations in the work; and (5) sense of wholeness, which integrates the self and the work in the experience of the work.

Like Beardsley and Langer, Leonard Bernstein repeatedly insists that musical experience be focused on the intrinsic qualities of music itself. He objects to two approaches to the cultivation of musical experiences — the "music appreciation racket" on the one hand, and the overly technical discussion on the other. The first invokes anything under the sun to describe extra-musical references, effectively taking the experiencer's mind off the music itself. But excessive technicality can be equally distracting because it focuses on meaningless detail to the exclusion of larger, expressive gestures. While Bernstein is not clear about how, precisely, to deal with music's expressive values directly, he is insistent that these are essentially intramusical.

Aaron Copland is somewhat more specific. He locates the intramusical experience in three interrelated planes. The sensuous plane offers the sheer pleasure of musical sound itself. The expressive plane includes the affective response to musical meaning — the structured events that form a composition and the experiences these events give. Finally, the sheerly musical plane includes a responsiveness to the details of the notes and their manipulation. So musical experience encompasses three planes of intrinsicality — the sounds, their overall expressiveness, and their detailed expressiveness. The total experience, when attached to a musical masterwork, arouses in us a spiritual response because of the depth and breadth of the piece and of our concomitant experience of it.

Another composer speaking of the intrinsic nature of musical experience is Paul Hindemith, who insists that the relationship of music to feeling is not one based on programmatic references or on onomatopoetic devices, nor is it symptomatic of what a composer's emotional state happens to be at the moment of composition. The reactions music causes in the experiencer are not feelings as such, but images or generalized memories of the dynamic qualities of feeling. The basic factor linking music with felt experience is motion (change, dynamicism, process, continuation). The actual motion caused by sounds in ongoing relationships equals the feeling of motion on the part of the person experiencing those sounds.

Still another composer who explains the relation of music to feeling as based on intrinsically experienced sound-in-motion is Roger Sessions. Movement itself, internalized by both composer and experiencer as expressive, is what sets music apart from other genres of art. The significance of music comes principally from its power to embody movement of a specifically human type. This movement goes to the roots of our being. It takes its shape in the inner gestures embodied in our deepest, most intimate responses to ourselves and our world. The sounds and rhythmic organizations of music manifest that movement in infinite variety.

How, precisely, do sounds produce a sense of movement in the experiencer of those sounds? While many if not most thinkers about musical experience claim the relationship between moving sounds and felt experience, few explain it in detail. Perhaps the most precise descriptions of the process involved is given by Leonard Meyer. According to Meyer, there are two different ways for meaning to be produced. In the first way, a stimulus points to something different from itself (as do, for example, words). Such meaning is designative. In the second way, a stimulus implies an event of the same kind as itself (as do musical sounds). Such meaning is embodied in the sounds themselves and in what the sounds cause the listener to expect other sounds to be. To "mean," in this musical context, is to "expect."

An expectation implies a tendency. Sounds have tendencies to do this or that within style systems, in which certain continuations are more or less probable. Whether overtly conscious of the probabilities or tacitly aware of them, the listener becomes engaged in their playing out. Unexpected events cause tensions, resolved by musical arrivals. The interplay of tendencies, delays, inhibitions, and resolutions within a particular piece, as constrained by style possibilities, allows the listener to experience those tendencies and delays as affect. Sound implications, processed affectively, constitute embodied, intrinsic, meaningful musical experience.

In less technical terms this explanation is the basis for many other claims about the intrinsic nature of musical meaning, musical significance, and musical experience. James Mursell, for example, suggests that significant musical experience involves emotion being felt from the perception of auditory stimuli. These stimuli can arouse associations and images external to the sound tendencies themselves, but those should not be understood as the significant part of the experience. Knowledge of musical techniques, music theory, and music history can also impinge on the experience, but these are also not to be mistaken for the intrinsic experience itself, however much they can influence that experience positively.

Louis Arnaud Reid makes a similar if not identical claim. In aesthetic experience, he explains, we apprehend patterns not as referring to things or "expressing" things, but as meaningful in and of themselves (embodied meaning). The object perceived appears to the imaginative mind (the mind attuned to the expressive potentials of intrinsic meanings) to embody values emanating from the object itself. The artist creating the object discovers, in the act of creation, a new dimension of being, made possible by the manipulation of his or her medium, which is charged with possibilities for affective interrelationships. The meaning embodied in a finished work transcends any particulars in the work, and the experience of the work's meaning causes a new entity — a new value — in the experience of the perceiver. To understand that this value is untranslatable is to comprehend the essence of art.

For Harry Broudy, two fundamental properties of art works enable them to present conditions that are at one and the same time intrinsic to their materials and characteristic of human life as experienced. The first are sensory properties (sounds, colors, shapes) presented directly to sense. These sensory properties can be subtle and complex, so that the experience of them can be enhanced by increasing discrimination of them. A particular aesthetic object, with its richness of sensory stimuli, must be perceived both in its details and as a whole. This has great significance to the aesthetic educator, whose responsibility includes sensitizing people to this sensory richness so they can experience it more fully. That is the first concern of aesthetic education.

The second property of art works, both intrinsic to their materials and characteristic of human experience, is their formal organization, which is the arrangement of elements in a manner peculiar to each work. The form of a work — its design or composition — is the result of conscious choices made by the artist. Certain formal arrangements are powerful and pleasing to the perceiver because comparable arrangements are inherent in nature and in our inner experiences, so that we respond sympathetically to them when they are encountered in an aesthetic object. The overall form of a work is its dramatic structure, giving the work its inherent unified quality, which requires no further justification for its existence than its own completeness. Sensitivity to this intrinsic dramatic structure distinguishes the aesthetically developed person from the undeveloped.

Every aesthetic object, says Broudy, consists of images or clusters of images constituted of its sensory and formal properties and the dramatic structure they create. These images need not be representational; they may be images of ideas or feelings, unrecognizable as actual objects. Each image carries a particular value import embodied in it, which is sharable by the person sensitive to its nature. The aesthetic image is not *like* something other than itself; it presents itself as actually *being* a particular quality of human experience. In this way, art is intrinsically meaningful rather than consisting of signs pointing to things outside itself.

John Blacking points out that music draws on man's own nature for many of its forms. Human feeling is structured. Pieces of music transform these structured feelings into structured patterns of sounds; and the experience of a piece of music transforms structured sounds into experienced, structured feelings. Implicated in these transformations are the innate structures of the body, the particular musical experiences of individual composers and listeners, and the musical conventions of particular societies. All converge to allow music to be experienced as a metaphor (not a sign) of feeling.

Finally, Thomas Clifton provides a phenomenological analysis of the intrinsic nature of musical experience. He defines music as an ordered arrangement of sounds and silences whose meaning is presentative rather than denotative. Music, he suggests, is the actualization of the possibility for any sound whatsoever to present to human beings a meaning they can experience with their minds, feelings, senses, and wills (these constitute the "body"). In a piece of music, feeling, like space and time, is a necessary constituent. The creation of a piece is determined by human acts that always include acts of feeling.

The formal traits of pieces of music are, in fact, the shapes of human experience itself, as are the basic materials of music. Pitch, for example, is not experienced as such; we experience the music *through* pitch, hearing the activity created by pitches. Tonality, likewise, is not simply a system of pitches creating a center around which other pitches arrange themselves. It is, instead, a habit, an aptitude acquired by the body, a sensuous experience, a feeling complex, all of which combine in the intuitive "givenness" of what we experience as tonality.

Clifton argues that music is not purely auditory; it must be understood as synaesthetic perception engaging the body (see above) with sound. Music creates a "lived space," fields of action in which a listener participates.

Musical line helps form musical space. It includes contour, width (thinness and thickness), distance, timbre, rhythmic level, and, potentially, text.

Also forming musical space — the lived, experienced domain of musical engagements — is surface, which is a type of texture. A surface is undifferentiated in texture when there is no movement, no dynamic contrasts, no timbral complexity. Changes in these conditions occur within every composition, forming surfaces from low relief (some movement, contrast, etc.) to high relief (pronounced changes in movement, etc.). All of this creates a dynamic space for musical experiencing.

Musical depth adds to the formal traits of pieces (traits that are the shapes of human experiences). Depth includes distance (sounds experienced as close or far away), penetration (silence can penetrate volume without interrupting the level of volume), sounds "in front of" or "behind" other sounds, yet still heard with the same magnitude. And faceting as a formal trait involves shifts in perspective where the movement suddenly appears to the listener from another point of view (caused by movement to an unexpected chord or from sound to silence).

All these traits of sounds as experience require what Clifton calls *possession*. To experience music requires a belief that there is an object (music) and that I am the one experiencing it. Musical experience cannot occur without belief that it can occur. When we experience music we are affirming our belief in its existence. This requires an act of commitment. In this sense we "possess" the moment that makes musical experience possible — we own the moment. At such moments it is possible for music to have intrinsic, meaningful structure because we believe it does, and we respond within this belief.

Intrinsicality (embodiment), it would seem, is a fundamental characteristic of musical experience. Regardless of how it is explained, intrinsicality is recognized as accounting for the power of organized sounds to be experienced as humanly significant.

IMPLICATIONS FOR RESEARCH

How early in a child's development can the ability to perceive intrinsically related sounds in music be detected? How would evidence of this ability be obtained?

What effects do the following factors (and others) have on the ability to perceptually structure intrinsic sound qualities in music: (a) directed listening instruction, (b) performance instruction, (c) composition instruction, and (d) improvisation instruction?

Are there correlations between mode of instruction and age?

How can various dimensions of intrinsic musical sound processing (such as sensuous, syntactical, creative, affective, object-directedness, sense of wholeness, dynamic motion, tendency-expectation) be (a) identified as existing in musical experience, (b) measured as to quantity, and (c) measured as to quality?

To what extent does the response of people to music consist of nonintrinsic factors (such as references, associations, fantasies, psychological states, technicalities, onomatopoetic devices, conceptual knowledge)? Is there a relation between degree of intrinsic versus extrinsic response according to (a) musical training, (b) cultural background, (c) age, and (d) musical preferences?

AFFECT

The experience of music does not consist of the perception of intrinsically related sound-relationships as a disengaged mental exercise (see the preceding feature essay). The second most salient feature of musical experience, directly dependent on the first, is that the perceived interrelations of sounds give rise to an internalized, or "possessed," experience of the dynamicisms created by the sound implications. A useful term for the inner experience of music's exemplification of process-as-such is *affect*. What we feel in musical experience, as a consequence of our engagement with sounds in process of being or becoming, is not this or that particular emotion, but the internal basis for our ability to feel. We experience, from music, the dynamics of consciousness as, at one and the same time, a feature of sounds themselves and a feature of our experience "selfhood." *Affect, expressiveness, feeling, musical responsiveness, artistic utterance* — all these and many more terms suggested by the writers call attention to the subjective dimension of musical experience as an essential component of such experience.

★　★　★

Citations for the material in this section of Part II will be found on the following pages of Part I: Mursell, 122; Meyer, 113–114; Reimer, 153–155; Sessions, 173–174; Reid, 139–142, 144–145, 147, 148–149; Blacking, 28–30; Clifton, 52–54, 57–58; Beardsley, 7, 11–12; Cage, 45; Langer, 86–91, 94, 95; Goodman, 75–77; Schoenberg, 163; Bernstein, 18–19; Hindemith, 81–82; Broudy, 38–39; Maslow, 107; Copland, 64.

The presence and impact of affect in musical experience is a popular topic of discussion among those who write about music. In music education, one of the first writers to articulate the difficulties of a precise definition of musical affect was James Mursell. He describes feeling as the central quality of musical experience. If feeling is not present, the experience cannot be considered musical. Mursell believes musical feeling to be non–mood-specific and ineffable; thus, it is difficult to define.

More recent writers about music have helped clarify the role of affect in musical experience. Leonard Meyer, for example, distinguishes affect from affective experience. For him, the difference is critical. Affective experience (resulting from an awareness of the pertinent stimulus) can be differentiated, whereas affect alone cannot. Meyer believes that we merely group instances of affect according to similarities among the stimuli that are responsible for affective arousal. More specifically, affect itself is neither pleasant nor unpleasant. Only affective experience can be described as such.

Bennett Reimer concurs that musical experience must always include an affective dimension. However, he goes on to explain how feeling and emotion are related to this dimension. Reimer states that the perception of embodied sound-relationships is the cause of feeling. He distinguishes feeling from emotion by stating that emotions are broad categories that can be named, while feelings cannot be named. Emotions are surface manifestations that can be verbally conceptualized. Feelings are dynamic mixtures of subjectivities that exist below (and often far beyond) the level of emotions. Musical feeling, Reimer claims, is an essential aspect of musical cognition. We cannot "know" as music allows us to if our engagements with music, whether as listeners, performers, or composers, are not feelingful.

Roger Sessions expresses a notion similar to that of Reimer. He claims that human beings respond to the power of music beneath the realm of emotion because of the significance that musical movement has for us. For him, emotion is specific, individual, and conscious. Music, however, carries us to a deeper level of energy that animates more subtle arenas of our psychic life.

Louis Arnaud Reid puts it another way. He claims that emotion is dependent for its character on distinguishable factors, excitations bound up in our relation to the world. Reid believes emotion to be an external reference to an objectification; feeling is the internal base from which emotion springs. Emotions are derived from feeling. In musical experience, feeling is the basis from which emotions arise.

Other writers have advocated the idea that feeling in music is a metaphor for life feelings. John Blacking, for example, thinks of music as a metaphor of feeling that draws on mankind's own nature. For him, the transformation of feelings into patterns of sound, and vice versa, resonates with the ways in which human feelings in general are structured. The innate structuring of feelings and sounds makes the connection possible.

Thomas Clifton's phenomenological description of musical experience also directly implicates feeling. For him, it is a necessary component of the experience, not a psychological by-product of a listener. Clifton views what usually are regarded as formal aspects of musical objects as being shapes of human experience. Music presents (but does not denote) meanings that are experienced mentally, feelingfully, sensually, and willfully.

Monroe Beardsley's idea of "modes of continuation" addresses this metaphorical treatment of feeling in music. In his view, music is change, a mirror or match for some of the fundamental features of our personal lives. One such feature is that of continuation, that is, the question of where life will take us next. Change (or lack thereof) is a mode of continuation. Beardsley feels that an awareness of subtle variances of continuation in music can sharpen our apprehension of such fluctuations in our personal lives, differences that we might miss in ordinary experience.

For John Cage, the purpose of music is to affirm life, a way of "waking up" to the very life we are living. The feeling involved in the process is a nonintentional expressivity. Cage poetically states that music brings together sounds and people in a "walk in the woods of music, or in the world itself."

Susanne Langer provides a detailed discussion of the relationship of feeling to life. For her, music sounds as feelings feel. She views music as a vital form, a dynamic form that is organic and characterized by rhythm. Music takes on significance as a semblance of this dynamic structure and expresses the forms of vital experience that language is unfit to convey. Feeling and life constitute music's import. Further, this vital form is the essence of all art (the power of revealing a new sort of truth).

According to Langer, music articulates those forms that are expressive of our emotive, subjective lives. Music is analogous to and reminiscent of the forms of human feeling. These vitally felt expressive forms are worked out in pure, measured sound and silence. Music, she asserts, is a tonal analogue of emotive life.

Langer further states that what is logically expressed in musical experience is not discursive meaning in the usual sense but a wordlessly presented conception of what life feels like (its subjective reality). This she calls vital import, a presence that is never fixed but can be true to life in a way language cannot.

Langer goes on to describe the connecting link between music and subjective reality as sentience. She views the patterns within life itself (repose, tension, speed, excitement) as forms of growth that can awaken feelings that occur in nature, within our subjective lives, and metaphorically in music itself. The awakened feelings are sentient and ineffable.

Langer likens the rhythm implicit in the vital form of music to virtual time — not an image of clock time, but of lived time. The immediate sense of passage, the semblance of one's subjective time, is analogous to virtual time in music. This lived time, the primary illusion of music, is the sonorous image of passage abstracted from reality to become free, plastic, and entirely perceptible.

There is a consensus among these authors that feeling (affect) is a form of cognition. Reid, for example, states that the feeling of an art work has two aspects: the intra-psycho-physical organism (person) and the life situation toward which it is directed. He further clarifies this interaction with the notion that musical meaning (the content of the cognitive feeling of music) is both concretely different from all life feelings and meanings and is related to life feelings and meanings — sometimes suggesting and echoing them, though never reproducing them. The statics and dynamics of some music are related to the statics and dynamics of some life situations.

Reid's work, like Reimer's, expands the view that feeling in music is a metaphor for feeling in life, to add the position that musical experience is more than feeling qua feeling; it is knowledge. For Reid, feeling is actively auxiliary in what we do and think. It is a living process becoming aware of itself; it is a mental happening, not an activity. Reid likens feeling to awareness, though it is more general, more open, more exclusively subjective. Cognition involves focusing, grasping, acting, and reacting functions with respect to the world.

Clifton provides yet another cognitive view of the nature of feeling in musical experience. He calls this nature of feeling *possession*. The constituents of possession are described as acts of belief (which underlie all cognitive and affective acts), freedom (which provides the possibility for either possessing or not possessing), caring (a fundamental feeling stemming from an attitude of concern for the object of possession), and willing (which urges the continuity of the possessed object and the act of possession). Clifton believes that, without this aspect of possession in musical experience, we will not come to "own" the musical meaning that might otherwise be available.

Further, Clifton states that the experience of music is contingent on a belief that there is an object (music) and that it is I who experience it. When we attend to something in which we believe, an act of commitment is involved. We possess the moment that makes meaning possible. Clifton concludes that the structure of musical experience is possible because the idea and the meaning are joined. When this happens, the materials begin to have meaning for us.

Nelson Goodman expands upon the idea that feeling is a form of cognition. He suggests that feeling uses two basic cognitive processes in interaction with music. On the basis of feeling, listeners discriminate between musical elements and events, and they also classify these elements and events. Feelings are the means by which a listener discerns precisely which literal and metaphorical properties a piece of music possesses. Classifying these properties by feeling, he believes, is often more vital than classification by other means.

Several writers, when considering affect in music, address the responsivity of those who listen to music. Mursell's position with regard to listening provides an appropriate foundation for the discussion. He assumes that the sounds heard by listeners should primarily have an emotional effect. Further, he suggests that any refusal to consider these effects or any overemphasis on the clinical analysis of the sounds is likely to be unsatisfactory for understanding musical listening. However, ignorance regarding the relationships of sounds in music can also impede responsiveness in the listener.

Clifton's thesis is that musical listening involves a reciprocal relation, a collaboration between the sounds and the listener that cannot be achieved without the necessary constitutive activities of both feeling and understanding. In addition, he calls for a closer look at human responses to music listening, including acts of willing, thinking, and feeling — all of which are integral to his notions of the possession of and commitment to the musical moment.

Meyer describes the nature of the musical affective experience in the context of his views on affective experience in general. For example, regardless of the nature of the stimulus situation, he believes that affect is aroused when a tendency to respond is arrested or inhibited. While Reid's view of responsivity to musical stimuli is nearly identical to that of Meyer, he approaches the issue in a slightly different way. Whereas Meyer talks of tendency inhibition, Reid speaks of tendency fulfillment. The difference seems to be largely semantic.

Beardsley's view of responsivity to "felt qualities" suggests a different set of conditions for an aesthetic experience. He lists five features that allow aesthetic responsiveness: (1) object-directedness, a willingly accepted guidance over the succession of one's mental states by phenomenally objective properties of a perceptual field, with attention firmly fixed by the belief that things are working out or have worked themselves out fittingly; (2) felt freedom, a sense of freedom from concerns about matters outside the object; (3) detached affect, a notable affect that is detached from practical ends; (4) active discovery, the sense of exercising powers of discovery; and (5) sense of wholeness, an integration of the self and its experience. Of these five features of aesthetic responsiveness, Beardsley insists that the first be present and prefers that the last one also be present.

Langer views responsiveness as primarily a natural gift, but suggests that it may be heightened by experience or reduced by adverse agencies such as intellectual prejudices and false conceptions that inhibit natural intuitive responses. She feels that the free exercise of artistic intuition often depends on clearing the mind of these adverse agencies.

Langer believes that the training of aesthetic responsiveness is achieved by the education of feeling, an education that encourages a tacit, personal, illuminating contact with semblances of feeling (works of art). For her, this is different from (but should be allied to) schooling in factual subjects and logical skills in the education of thought.

Composers have not been silent regarding responsiveness to music. Arnold Schoenberg discusses the impression art gives as being the result of two components — that which the work of art gives to the onlooker and that which the person is able to give to the work of art. The art work, in his view, is the external stimulus that awakens forces sensed by the perceiver. The intensity of an artistic impression depends on the onlooker's ability to receive even while giving. Schoenberg believes that a work of art can produce no greater effect than when it transmits the emotions that raged in the creator to the listener in such a way that they also rage in him.

Leonard Bernstein's view is somewhat different. He describes the type of communication that takes place between composer and listener in a number of ways. For instance, he states that such communication is the tenderness we feel when we recognize and share with another human being a deep, unnameable, elusive, emotional shape or shade. He believes that a composer is never literal or factual when communicating with a listener. The communication is emotional or, more specifically, emotion recollected. Bernstein wants to dispel the notion that agitated music is written by agitated composers, or that despairing music comes from desperate composers.

Another composer, Paul Hindemith, speaks of "the receiving mind." In his view, the mere fact that music is heard is not enough. The receiving mind must be actively engaged in bringing the music to life before affect can become a part of the experience. This engagement on the part of the listener distinguishes mere acoustical perception from a potentially affective musical experience.

Consideration of the development of responsiveness to aesthetic experience brings about the issue of how images of feeling are created. According to Harry Broudy, one must employ a technique that will give form to the sensory content, a process of objectifying feeling closely related to the formal properties and technical peculiarities of the medium. Broudy describes the form of the expressive image as its design or composition and as being the result of conscious choices made by the artist. We respond sympathetically to the designs and rhythms of aesthetic objects because they are also inherent in nature, a part of our world.

Consistent with Broudy's concept of an expressive image is Langer's notion of artistic utterance. Langer suggests that artists strive to create as complete and transparent a symbol as possible. Unlike personal utterance, which contents itself with half-articulated symbols under the stress of actual emotion, artistic utterance is an expression at the deepest levels, having nothing to do with individual moods and anxieties but instead with the element of ardor for the import conveyed. In other words, Langer believes that it is aesthetic emotion that motivates the artist's work and that, in the case of music, is invested in service to the music itself.

Blacking's views, in the context of his social and cultural interests, are similar to those of Broudy and Langer but are expressed in more general terms. He describes the creation of music as a sharing of the expression of inner feelings in a social context through extensions of body movement, in which certain species-specific capabilities are modified and extended through social and cultural experience and influence.

Finally, consideration must be given to the ways in which psychical distance may hinder or promote affect in the musical experience. Most writers agree that psychical distance is a means of avoiding anything that encumbers aesthetic experience. Thus, the ideal psychical distance will allow for optimal affect in the musical experience.

Abraham Maslow, in discussing peak experience, speaks of a moment of noninterference during which there is a mutual feedback between the perceiver and the perceived. This noninterference, which is free of specific orientations to other things, is what makes peak experience possible. He feels that music is one of the most frequent triggers of this experience.

Reid's notion is that placing something at a psychical distance from ourselves ensures the experience will be outside the interference of extraneous needs and wants. Further, he suggests that the amount of distance is relative, not absolute. Aesthetic experience ceases when the psychical distance is too great or too small. A correct balance is needed.

Aaron Copland describes psychical distance as the ability to let music engulf us while never losing control. The listener is both subjective and objective, inside and outside the music at the same time. Schoenberg agrees, making a point of keeping musical ideas at a "decent" distance from the feelings accompanying them.

Bernstein goes a step further. In describing the act of composition, he refers to the composer's need to achieve a trance-like state before anything important can emerge. For him, external nonmusical influences interfere with this unconscious state. The composer and listener must find a balance between these factors and prevent them from interfering with the creative process. Bernstein's remarks are also consistent with Cage's view that music can act of its own accord, once one gets one's mind and desires out of the way.

Having differentiated the various levels at which affect and feeling are said to be present in musical experience, it is clear that affect is integral to the issue of embodied meaning.

IMPLICATIONS FOR RESEARCH

How has affect been viewed throughout the history of Western music in regard to: (a) definition, (b) relationship of affect to emotion, (c) music as a metaphor of feeling, (d) responsivity to affective arousal, (e) the form and expression of affect, and (f) psychical distance?

How might one differentiate between the literal and metaphorical aspects of musical experience? What are the implications of this differentiation for pedagogical and performance practices?

Use concurrent and retrospective protocol analyses to compare the subjective responses of the following as they listen to a new or favorite piece: (a) a professional performer, (b) a professional composer, (c) an experienced listener, and (d) an inexperienced listener.

To what extent can generative theories of music predict tendency-inhibition and tendency-fulfillment? What might a better understanding of these processes tell us about teaching music in nonperformance settings?

How does one educate for both reason and feeling? What might a curriculum designed for this purpose include? What kinds of evaluation could be used to assess the effects of such a curriculum?

What social, musical, or cultural factors contribute to interference in aesthetic responsiveness? Given an understanding of such inhibitions, how might they be avoided in the teaching/learning process?

EXPECTATION

How, precisely, do sounds arranged in vertical and horizontal order cause them to be internalized as affective? This question is among the most important to be raised by writers on musical experience as well as being among the most vexing. A great many explanations are attempted, and it seems clear that an authoritative answer to which all might agree will not soon be forthcoming. One unifying idea does seem to be particularly helpful, however — the idea of *expectation*. Many writers make use of this idea to help explain our subjective involvement with formed sounds. Music sets up tendencies we can recognize when we are familiar with the stylistic context in which particular tendencies exist. We can then anticipate, expect, contemplate, or speculate on how the music might then unfold. Feelings become engaged in this ongoing process. Tensions, uncertainties, fulfillments, instabilities, ambiguities, resolutions, etc., as they occur among sound events, are perceived and responded to by the listener, performer or composer, being internalized as subjectivity brought to awareness.

★ ★ ★

One frequently occurring theme in the discussion of the musical experience is the crucial role of listener expectation in that phenomenon.

Citations for the material in this section of Part II will be found on the following pages of Part I: Meyer, 113–114, 118; Reimer, 154, 157–158; Mursell, 122; Reid, 145, 147; Bernstein, 21–22, 24; Stravinsky, 178–181; Langer, 90–91, 93–95; Sessions, 170–174; Beardsley, 11–12; Lerdahl and Jackendoff, 101–104.

The notion of expectation appears so often, even among the works of writers whose notions are strikingly dissimilar, that one might well conclude it is a particularly central characteristic of the musical experience.

The theorist most frequently associated with the notion of expectation in music is Leonard Meyer. His writings all build from a common theory regarding the role of expectation. To Meyer, an understanding of that theory is central to gaining an understanding of musical meaning, and he has invested more energy in working out the various implications of expectation in music than anyone else.

Meyer believes that the nature of and conditions for musical affective experience are the same as for affective experience in general. Regardless of the nature of the stimulus, affect is aroused when the fulfillment of an expectation is inhibited. This simple proposition provides the basis for most of Meyer's thinking on Western music. The inhibition of an expectation or a tendency (musical or otherwise) is a necessary and sufficient condition for the arousal of affect.

Expectations may take the form of objective consciousness or tacit awareness; they may be general or specific; they may be acquired formally or serendipitously. Expectations are activated in the listener by the progress of the musical stimuli because some musical consequents of given antecedents are perceived as more probable than others. Each unanticipated musical consequent creates tension in the listener. This tension is experienced as affect if the listener's original expectations were tacit or unconscious. Conscious awareness of musical tendencies and their inhibitions leads to a rationalization of response, an "intellectual" experience. The same processes that give rise to musical affective experience also give rise to the objectification of embodied musical meaning. Because the meaning of a musical passage for an experienced listener is the expectation it produces for a set of musically probable events (not just a single event), Meyer later came to use the term *implication* instead of *expectation* to capture the wide range of meaning available to such a listener.

Among other writers on musical response to whom the notion of expectation is key, Bennett Reimer's thoughts are closest to those of Meyer. Reimer holds that musically experienced sounds are perceived as cohesive and interrelated precisely because they generate expectations as to possible future musical events based on past and present events. Like Meyer, Reimer believes that the role of expectation in music is of critical importance in musics of the Western tradition, but he also believes this to be true to some extent of all musics in all cultures.

To be aware of probable musical consequents, that is, to possess specific musical expectations, Reimer claims, as does Meyer, that a sense of style is essential. Style, to Reimer, is the culturally accepted set of inherent probabilities among musical gestures in which possible consequents are inhibited, delayed, and fulfilled in probable ways. Indeed, he holds that the structure of musical experience depends on the dynamic systems of tendencies and resolutions that structure music itself.

This is consistent with the writings of James Mursell, who feels that life obstacles are represented as expectations in sound, which are subsequently satisfied or frustrated. Mursell considers enhancing the ability to perceive the expectations and consequents in music as being a fundamental goal of music education.

Meyer's notions of the generation of musical affect through the inhibition of expectation are also found in the writings of Louis Arnaud Reid. Reid recognizes that in all aesthetic experience there is some release of inner tension, carried out through external behavior for the satisfaction of a conscious desire. Value, he claims, comes from the fulfillment or the frustration of the tendencies of a given musical style. The fulfillment or frustration of musical tendencies engages the listener in imaginative contemplation. As a result of this involvement, the listener values the musical outcome.

Leonard Bernstein includes the concept of expectation in his notion of musical ambiguity, which comes about when a composer deliberately trifles with the listeners' universal instinct for symmetry through transformation processes such as deletion and embedding. The composer purposefully violates the expectations of the listener to create a *controlled ambiguity*. Bernstein believes that these ambiguities are both inherently beautiful and germane to all artistic creation. They enrich our aesthetic response by providing alternate ways of perceiving the aesthetic surface.

Igor Stravinsky does not use the term *expectation*, but he writes often of the role of speculation in music, by which is meant the contemplation of the probabilities of various consequents. To relatively greater or lesser extents, those consequents are "expected." He holds that the phenomenon of music is, in its simplest form, nothing other than speculation. To Stravinsky, the elements with which this speculation deals are sound and time, and music is inconceivable without them. Of the two, speculation in time is the critical determinant. He writes, for example, that "musical creation is an innate complex of intuitions and possibilities based primarily upon an exclusively musical experiencing of time, . . . of which the musical work merely gives us the functional realization."

Stravinsky identifies two kinds of music, discriminated by their use of time. The first, he says, runs parallel to the passing of real time, "embracing and penetrating it and inducing in the mind of the listener a feeling of euphoria and . . . of dynamic calm." The second runs counter to that process and is not self-contained in each momentary unit, but rather dislocates the centers of attraction and "gravity," establishing itself in the realm of the unstable. Stravinsky believes this characteristic makes the second sort of music particularly adaptable to the translation of the composer's emotive impulses, and he suggests that all music in which the will to expression is dominant belongs to this second type. Though expectation is mentioned in neither description, awareness of the passing of real time undoubtedly is consistent with expectation, specifically of continued regular stimuli. Expectation is more readily apparent in the discussion of the second sort of music, for with attraction and gravity come also an expectation of progression toward some other point.

Susanne Langer concurs, at least with the characterization of the second type, as is evident through the description of her concept of virtual time. This, she says, is the primary illusion of music. It is not an image of "clock time" but rather one of "lived time." According to Langer, this lived time can be measured in music by the quality and the volume of tensions and resolutions experienced by the listening individual.

Stravinsky also writes that music is "nothing more than a succession of impulses that converge toward a definite point of repose." With each impulse, one can infer, expectation of the ultimate repose grows. Before the modern era, Stravinsky tells us, dissonance and consonance generated the feelings of impulse and repose, but during the present century a new musical "logic" has introduced musical listeners to sonic riches not previously available. The new logic, as described by Stravinsky, focuses upon the existence of certain "poles of attraction" in the music. Music that moves toward the poles is impulse; music at the poles is repose.

Other writers include the concept of expectation in the descriptions of the musical response but assign it relatively lesser importance. These writers also tend to use other terms. Roger Sessions describes the importance of progression in music, by which he means movement toward a clearly defined goal. That concept clearly incorporates expectation. Monroe Beardsley claims that kinetic pattern is the most fundamental aspect of musical form and specifies four possible qualities of kinetic pattern in music. Three of the four (introduction quality, conclusion quality, and transition quality) are all described as anticipating a specific type of event. Here, anticipation may be viewed as expectation.

One term that relates closely to expectation and is found often in the writings studied is *tension*. Fred Lerdahl and Ray Jackendoff write of tension in outlining their theory of prolongational reductions. These, they feel, assign a hierarchy to the pitches that creates harmonic and melodic tension and relaxation, among other things. This theory enables them to identify "points of relative tension and repose" and to analyze "the way the music progresses from one to another." Tension also plays a minor role in Sessions's concept of continuity, by which he means the logical flow of events in the composition. Continuity encompasses, in part, balance, tension, relaxation, and contrast, and it determines the ultimate character of the music. Langer endorses the concept, if not the term, in her discussion of expressive form. Here she includes patterns of conflict and resolution as typical of the expressive forms worked out in music.

Expectation, then, seems to be a central concept in descriptions of the musical experience. Despite differences in terminology, the thinkers included in this essay all embrace it in their writings.

IMPLICATIONS FOR RESEARCH

To what extent are the notions of expectation and tension present in the concept of musical experience in popular music genres? To what extent are they present in cultures other than those in the West?

To what extent do the various authors in this study agree in regard to their notions of tendency, tension, speculation, implication, attraction, gravity, anticipation, progression, and expectation? How do they differ? To what extent do these notions constitute a common characteristic of Western musical experience?

To what extent is the inhibition of tendency essential to the generation of musical affective response? How does increasing or decreasing the amount of tendency inhibition effect the affective response resulting from it?

What is the relationship between listener age and the role of expectation in the musical experience? How does an awareness of expectation in music develop? What teaching strategies can be used to effectively heighten the awareness of expectation in the less sophisticated music listener?

What is the nature of musical experience when no expectation can be discerned (that is, when listening to wholly unfamiliar music)? What are the implications for musical experience with serial music? With minimalist music?

What is the function of expectation in each of the three traditional modes of musical experience: listening, composing, and performing? How do they compare?

MEANING

Musical awareness, or undergoing, or subjective experience, is meaningful. Musical meaning, it is generally agreed, is different from signification, in which particular referents are assigned to particular signs or symbols, the meaning of the signs or symbols being that to which they refer. Musical meaning, instead, is a function of the quality of experience one undergoes when engaged with sounds organized in expressive interrelationships. If an engagement is devoid of awareness of how sounds interrelate, as in a totally unfamiliar style, the experience is essentially meaningless. Musical meaning, however, is not unrelated to the world in which we live, because it brings to awareness our sense of ourselves undergoing the world in which we live. That awareness is culturally influenced, accounting for the diversity of styles within and across societies and time periods. Further, some aspects of that awareness are dependent on the particular subjectivities of each individual at a specific moment in life. All people in all cultures, it may be inferred, possess the potential to share the kind of cognition, or meaning, music affords.

★　★　★

Many who write about musical experience accept the premise that music carries with it great impact and meaning. It is this meaning,

Citations for the material in this section of Part II will be found on the following pages of Part I: Reid, 148–149; Meyer, 113–116; Reimer, 154–156; Broudy, 38–40; Bernstein, 23–24; Beardsley, 8, 11; Goodman, 74–75; Langer, 88–89; Copland, 62; Mursell, 126–128; Blacking, 27–28; Clifton, 52–54, 57–58; Lerdahl and Jackendoff, 99.

they feel, that makes music a powerful and engaging force in human life. While authors offer various explanations as to what constitutes musical meaning, there seems to be a general consensus that the intrinsic qualities of a piece of music (its dynamic interrelationships) account for its meaningfulness.

According to Louis Arnaud Reid, there is a relationship between the feelings of the statics and dynamics of some music and the feelings that are present in the statics and dynamics of some life situations. He places the psycho-physical organism at the center of that relationship as the common source of all dynamic responses. An important distinction for Reid lies in the fact that musical meaning (the content of the cognitive feeling of music) is both concretely different from all life feelings and meanings and is related to life feelings and meanings, sometimes suggesting and echoing them, but never reproducing them.

Leonard Meyer addresses the issue in more detail, stating that the source of musical meaning is to be found intra-musically through the comprehension of musical relationships. This meaning, which can be communicated to both participants and listeners, is dependent upon three factors. The first is the learned responses of a listener familiar with an established musical style. The second is a universal psychological mechanism that explains a wide range of affective and intellectual responses. Finally, musical meaning is dependent on the fundamental laws of human perception and cognition.

Becoming even more specific, Meyer states that musical meaning (whether affective or intellectual) arises when a musical tendency to respond is inhibited. A musical work takes on meaning if and only if a musical event arouses a listener's expectations for other musical events. Meaningful musical experience depends crucially on a listener's musical expectations.

It follows, then, that with no experience in a given musical style, a listener will have no musical expectations and, consequently, no meaningful experience of any work in that particular style. On the other hand, for an experienced listener there is likely to be not just a single, fully definite musical expectation, but a weighted set of musically probable events. To a large extent, a listener's experience is equivalent to the internalized set of musical expectations that are produced in relation to a given musical passage.

Meyer makes distinctions among three categories of embodied musical meaning. Hypothetical meanings are those sounds expected by the experienced listener. Because these expectations may be confirmed, denied, or amended as a work unfolds, two other types of embodied musical meaning are possible. The first is evident meaning, occurring when a listener retrospectively gleans causal relationships between a musical antecedent and its consequent. The second is determinate meaning, the retrospective consideration and interpretation of all the musical relationships in a piece of music.

When musical expectations are chained together they produce a musical tendency that may take the form of an objective concept or a tacit awareness; it may be general or specific; it may be acquired formally or informally. Each expectation is activated in a listener by the progress of a musical stimulus, and each unexpected musical consequent creates tension in the listener. Such tension is experienced as affect if the listener's original expectations were tacit or unconscious.

More recently, Meyer has used the term *implication* to refer to a weighted set of musically probable events as opposed to a single, fully definite musical event. Meyer's concept of information can be summarized as the inverse of probability. The most probable event produces the least information; the most unlikely event produces the most information. Thus, Meyer's theory of musical meaning can be modified to this: musical meaning arises when a listener, uncertain of the music's progress, objectively or tacitly estimates the probabilities of the music's continuation. When less probable events occur, the music is experienced as meaningful or informative. To Meyer, music is as meaningful as it is informative.

Meyer also suggests that musical value is proportional to musical meaning and, therefore, to musical information. A piece of music is meaningful to the extent it creates a series of expectations. If a work always goes directly to the most probable consequent, it has little or no meaning or value. If it attains its goal only after irrelevant diversions, or if it never attains its goal at all, it has no potential for meaning and value.

Meyer admits that a syntactically simple work may arouse profound response, but attributes the response to extra-musical significance rather than the intrinsic quality of the piece. He also admits that a syntactically simple work, due to its economy of means, may have greater value than a complex work. Currently, Meyer believes that any attempt to assess musical value must include the criterion of relational richness; that is, the degree to which syntactic and statistical musical parameters are appropriately exploited in various styles and individual pieces.

Bennett Reimer agrees that a sense of style, culturally and historically determined (the set of inherent probabilities among musical gestures), is essential in order for possible consequents to be experienced as expected, inhibited, delayed, or fulfilled in probable ways. Musical experience is structured because music is structured by dynamic systems of tendencies and resolutions. These dynamic, organic interrelations are what are experienced as affective (expressive, significant). Sounds and their interactions embody the dynamic qualities that capture a sense of felt life, which is also dynamic, organic, and interrelated.

Further, Reimer states that the experience of music is meaningful in the deepest sense of the word because it is a way of knowing (cognition). This type of knowing, produced by affective responses to perceived sound events, is knowledge *of* or *within* rather than *about*. Aesthetic (musical) cognition is the product of aesthetic experiencing, in which the intrinsic qualities of organic forms are empathetically processed as affective. For Reimer, cognition is multi-faceted with verbal conceptualization being only one possible way of knowing. The cognition of feeling through experiences of music can be developed in depth, refinement, and scope through music education (the education of feeling-cognition).

Reimer's concern for meaning in music is echoed by Harry Broudy, who identifies the formal properties of the aesthetic image as the arrangement of elements and images that is peculiar to a given aesthetic object. The form of the expressive image refers to its design or composition and is the result of conscious choices made by the artist. Certain formal arrangements are powerful and pleasing to us because these designs and rhythms are inherent in nature so that we respond sympathetically to them when they are encountered in the aesthetic object. Such a response makes the aesthetic experience meaningful.

Broudy also identifies the dramatic structure in art as a quality that makes it seem inherently vivid and unified, requiring no further justification. This quality must be present to some degree in all aesthetic objects in order for them to avoid triviality and command the attention of the observer. Broudy also points to the metaphorical nature of art as an important aspect of meaning, because this allows the aesthetic image to present itself as actually being a particular quality of human experience rather than saying that it is *like* something else. In this way, art acquires meaning by taking on a symbolic nature. The metaphorical nature of art (as well as its presentational nature) is a manifestation of the expressiveness (value import) of the aesthetic image, so that the art work is simultaneously direct and indirect.

Leonard Bernstein also speaks to the metaphorical nature of music when addressing the issue of musical semantics (the study of meaning). Noting that semantic ambiguity in language requires that one either reject the statement as illogical or find another level of meaning (a poetic level), Bernstein states that music need not undergo this transformational process. While language must reach a "super-surface, an aesthetic surface," music is already poetic in nature so that there is no need for further transformation. The metaphorical power of music is specific and far-reaching, providing the essence of musical meaning. As a result, music can articulate that which language cannot.

Monroe Beardsley also approaches the topic of meaning in music by way of the musical metaphor. Music, for Beardsley, cannot function as a natural or conventional sign. It is not capable of pointing beyond itself to specific events, emotions, images, or psychological states. Neither is music a mental or physical symbol of time or process. Rather, music *is* process. Those qualities of music (such as tempo, variations of intensity, and impulsiveness) that resemble qualities of human beings may be called human qualities. Such metaphors, when carefully used, can help to name these human (regional) qualities, because we have no other language for describing their existence in works of art. Beardsley believes, however, that music need not refer to anything outside of its own aesthetically notable qualities in order to help us understand our world.

Another feature of Beardsley's discussion of musical meaning centers around the concept of regional qualities — those qualities that result from the combination of elements that form complexes. These complexes take on new qualities that were not part of the constituent elements and allow us to perceive sensory information in art works as aesthetic phenomena. Regional qualities depend for their existence as well as their nature upon relations within and between the elements and complexes that make up aesthetic objects. Critical analysis of aesthetic objects should be concerned only with internal statements (as opposed to external statements, which are concerned with the cause and effects of such objects). Internal statements concentrate first on the parts of the aesthetic object and second on the manner in which the parts contribute to the qualities of the whole.

Nelson Goodman's concept of multiple and complex reference is similar to Beardsley's concept of regional qualities. For Goodman, a musical symbol demonstrates the property of multiple and complex reference when the symbol carries a number of overlapping and difficult-to-separate meanings, each of which contribute to the effects of the whole work. The reference that music makes to aspects of life outside music is often ambiguous, proceeding through twisted chan-nels and traversing several levels of meaning. Metaphoric and imagina-tive qualities associated with the relationships formed among the elements of the medium are an important part of the total meaning of a musical symbol.

Goodman further states that a musical symbol is likely to demon-strate the property of relative repleteness. That is to say, there are multiple aspects of the symbol system that are significant, and any change in any one of these aspects will affect the meaning of the aesthetic object. In music, small changes in one or more of the elements that make up a phrase can convey a quite definite and intended change in feeling tone. Every change will have significant impact on the meaning of the work.

Following this idea of a whole work of art and its constituent parts, it is possible to see the connection with Susanne Langer's concept of expressive form. An expressive form is one that presents parts, aspects, or qualities that, as a whole, may be taken to represent some other whole whose parts have analogous relations. Music articu-lates those forms that are expressive of our emotive, subjective lives. These include forms of growth and attenuation, conflict and resolu-tion. In music, these vitally felt expressive forms are worked out in pure, measured sound and silence. Those patterns of life and growth found in music and within an individual's emotive, subjective reality are the sentient qualities of music. The feelings or sensations that occur in nature, within our subjective lives, and metaphorically in music are sentient and ineffable.

Music is meaningful because it is a significant form, a highly articulated symbol that, by virtue of its dynamic structure, can express the forms of vital experience that language is peculiarly unfit to convey. Feeling, life, emotion, and motion constitute its vital import, a nondiscursive expression of what life feels like. Vital import is dependent on vital form. This is dynamic form that consists of interdependent, interrelated parts that are characterized by rhythm that is set up when one event prepares the next.

Aaron Copland borrows Langer's concept of living form, stating that the process of music and the process of life are quite similar in nature. Copland views music as an essential element of human existence that will exist as long as the human spirit exists on earth. Music is meaningful because of its ability to emulate the human experience. A composer is one who creates values that are primarily aesthetic, but ultimately of the deepest human importance.

James Mursell also speaks to the role of the composer in explaining meaning in music, stating that the composer shapes an idea in order to bring out its meaning. While the idea has its own meaning, the process of shaping it helps to define it and clarify its realization. The process of composition is to mold tones into shapes holding musical meaning. For the performer, musical meaning is facilitated through the integration of bodily movements and mental and emotional apprehensions. The listener may find it helpful to take the music apart in order to better understand the whole through the analysis of the parts. In order for the music to be meaningful, however, it is essential that the music be recombined after the analysis is completed.

John Blacking approaches the topic of meaning in music from the viewpoint of the social anthropologist. For him, music and other cultural phenomena can be said to have no intrinsic meaning. Rather, meanings are assigned by the social and cultural context in which they are found. Therefore, music cannot be transmitted from one culture to another without the loss of some of its meaning. Musical meaning cannot exist without associations among people.

Thomas Clifton holds a similar point of view, believing that music cannot exist apart from the observer. He defines music as an ordered arrangement of sounds and silences whose meaning is presentative rather than denotative. Music is actualized when sound is experienced in the human body, thus presenting a musical meaning to a human being. Music derives meaningfulness not as an auditory experience, but as a synaesthetic perception in which the body is engaged with sound.

In order for musical materials to have meaning for a person, Clifton believes that possession must take place. That is to say that the experience of music is contingent on a belief that there is an object (music) and that I am the one experiencing it. Because it is necessary to commit to something in order to believe it, Clifton holds that we possess music when we believe in it. In other words, we own it; it is ours. At that moment the structure of musical experience is possible because the idea and the meaning are joined. When this happens, the material begins to take on meaning.

Finally, Fred Lerdahl and Ray Jackendoff remind us that there is much we do not know about a listener's understanding of music and, consequently, the meaning and impact it carries for the person who experiences it. However, the authors point to an idealized state of listening (the most developed understanding the experienced listener can have) as the point at which the listener's real time mental process is not in control. More must be known about mental processing before it will be possible to understand the organization that results from the processing. The recent dramatic expansion of attempts to understand the nature of human cognition is likely to increase future understanding of how music acquires meaning.

IMPLICATIONS FOR RESEARCH

By what means can musical meaning be isolated, expressed, and compared? Would such a comparison reveal different results according to cultural influences, personal preferences, personal beliefs, training as a composer, performer, or listener?

Does musical meaning differ according to age and developmental stage of the composer, performer, or listener? Does musical meaning differ according to formal training in the areas of composing, performing, and listening? How might this be measured?

To what extent do extra-musical associations influence the meaningfulness of music? Is there a correlation between this and the amount of formal training in musical skills? What factors might cause a piece of music to be less meaningful to the perceiver or performer?

What are the mental processes and internal representations that play a factor in the meaningfulness of music? To what extent might this be influenced by brain damage or loss of sensory facility?

INTELLIGENCE

The potential to share musical meaning exists in degree. As in other domains of meaning or knowing, the degree of one's potential may be understood as the degree of one's intelligence in that domain. To be musically intelligent is to be able to share and generate musical meaning, and it is reasonable to hypothesize that this capacity is distributed normally — that is, it could be represented by a normal curve. But whatever an individual's level of potential, that potential is unlikely to be fully realized, so that education in music is relevant to all people. It may be that some aspects of musical intelligence are common to all musical engagements (perceptual acuity seems a likely candidate), while some are particular to specific roles (imaginative projection of implications for composers, for example). There is considerable agreement that musical intelligence transcends strictly "ear-related" skills, given that the involvement of feeling as an active, discerning, organizing factor is essential. In musical experience, feeling plays a central role in the creation of meaning, adding to the more common understandings of "intelligence" a dimension peculiar to the aesthetic domain.

★ ★ ★

Citations for the material in this section of Part II will be found on the following pages of Part I: Cage, 47–48; Blacking, 29; Reimer, 154–157; Mursell, 124–125; Hindemith, 81–82, 84; Sessions, 174–175; Goodman, 70–71, 73–74, 76–77; Lerdahl and Jackendoff, 99; Reid, 139–142; Meyer, 111–114.

General theories of human intelligence frequently divide intelligent response to environmental cues into four categories: the sensory, perceptual, memory, and comprehension/meaning levels of intelligence. Some aestheticians argue that intelligent response to art takes place solely at the perceptual and feeling levels. Others argue for a comprehension/meaning level as well. However, it should be noted that when the authors in this study attempt to describe the comprehension/meaning level of musical intelligence, they tend to use the terms *comprehension* and *meaning* in a much broader way than is practiced in general theories of intelligence. In addition, they are inclined to include many more factors at the comprehension level. Imagination, creativity, and feeling all seem to be essentially involved in authors' attempts to describe the musical meanings that result from the interrelationships of tones in a piece and the understanding of those meanings by performers and listeners.

John Cage makes the general claim that open-mindedness is absolutely necessary to musical experience. Yet receptiveness at the perceptual level must include more than mere tones; a listener must perceive and recognize all the expressive materials of the musical work. Open-mindedness and receptiveness enable the listener to explore eventually the entire world of music through avenues such as ethnomusicology, the pluralism of societal beliefs, human resources of mind as yet untapped, and new technologies.

John Blacking prefers the term *competence* to *intelligence*, and the competence of a musician may be assessed in the areas of composing, performing, and listening. Two differing kinds of musical competence are described: (1) particular musical competence and (2) universal musical competence. Particular musical competence refers to the capacity (innate or learned) to create, or to hear and re-create, the patterns of sound recognized as music in a particular cultural tradition. Universal musical competence is a further development of the first ability and refers to the same capacities in the context of all cultural traditions.

Bennett Reimer also provides some basic conceptions of musical intelligence. He suggests that an individual's ability to have musical experiences is a function of that person's musical intelligence. The term *intelligence* is broader than the terms *talent* or *aptitude,* and it refers to the ability to structure sounds perceptually. This perceptual structuring includes the affective dimension of sounds as well as other qualities such as references and social meanings. He suggests that everyone has some measure of musical intelligence and that this ability, like most others, is probably randomly distributed. Musical intelligence manifests itself in varying levels of ability to "think musically," and subjects can demonstrate this type of thinking through listening, composing, and performing. Musical intelligence is educable. A conception of music education as the development of each person's musical intelligence to its fullest potential has much to recommend it, according to Reimer.

Like Reimer, James Mursell makes the claim that musical experience depends on musical intelligence, some aspects of which are teachable. Mursell enlarges on Reimer's conception of the blend of intelligence and feeling that takes place in the musical experience. Musical experience essentially includes feeling, and he argues that musical feeling should be intelligent feeling. Musical feeling is not something arbitrary, ill-disciplined, and wild, contributed to the event for personal pleasure; it is a total response to a fully understood and appreciated situation. This feelingful response is a discriminating but appreciative and emotional response to the beauty of a musical structure.

Mursell also subscribes to a three-level view of musical intelligence: (1) at the perceptual level, the perceived elements are precise, and the ability to perceive them is learned through active experience with music; (2) listeners process the sound events in terms of musical memory; and (3) they hear relationships in tones, shadings, and forms that they can process not only in terms of memory, but also in terms of musical imagination.

In addition, Mursell often focuses in his writings on the relationships of wholes to parts, and he describes the important role this plays in intelligent listening. He suggests that, in listening to the whole, listeners often close their minds to details, yet perceive them subconsciously. Human response when listening to music is such a complex activity that it may be truly said that listeners hear with their minds rather than with their ears.

Paul Hindemith describes the kind of listening that for him characterizes the musically intelligent listener, and like Mursell he focuses on the active and creative aspect of this ability. He suggests that perceptive listening requires an anticipation of musical events and the construction of parallel images to those presented by the music. Because the full range of listeners will, at any given moment, bring only limited energy and ability to the task, he cautions composers that certain limits seem inherent in the ordering of sound meaningfully.

For the composer, Hindemith offers a different description of musical intelligence. A composer must possess a highly developed sense of musical Gestalt and a capacity for musical vision. That is to say, the musical vision enables a composer to grasp the details of a future work in a single moment. Hindemith argues that the hallmark of a genuine creator is the ability to see in a moment of inspiration the composition in its absolute entirety with every pertinent detail in its proper place.

Roger Sessions offers a three-level view of intelligent musical listening. First, at the perceptual level, a "musical ear" will discriminate between sounds with regard to a number of factors such as pitch, tone quality, intensity, timbre, and duration. Second, once these aspects have been discriminated, the musical ear will relate and associate the musical impressions. And finally, the musical ear will order these associations into hierarchical levels that combine to create an overall image of the work.

Nelson Goodman's theory focuses on a different aspect of this phenomenon: the role symbolism plays in the development of all kinds of intelligence. His analysis of various arts is based on a fundamental conception of them as differing symbol systems. For him, one important aspect of musical intelligence is an understanding of how the musical symbol system is variously used. Therefore, the musically intelligent person would need to be a competent, even facile, musical symbol system user and manipulator.

It must be emphasized that Goodman's conception of artistic symbol systems is much broader than any mere system of notation (putting musical sounds down on paper). Intelligent response to music includes sensitivity to and understanding of (the sensitivity and understandings may be tacit as well as explicit) four important features of artistic symbol systems: syntactic density, semantic density, relative repleteness, and multiple and complex reference.

For Goodman, a musical symbol is likely to demonstrate the property of syntactic density. Syntactic density is found when the differences between the elements of a symbol system are extremely fine, and both the manipulator and interpreter of the symbol system need to be highly sensitive to the subtlety of the gradations used. Musical syntactic density would be found when subtle differences in subsequent repetitions of the melodic line of a song convey important distinctions in expressive quality.

A second feature a musical symbol is likely to demonstrate is the property of semantic density. Semantic density is found when the music refers to an object or event or circumstance that is distinguished by very fine, subtle differences in gradations (as Debussy's portayal of an ocean throughout the course of a day in *La Mer*).

A third feature a musical symbol is likely to demonstrate is the property of relative repleteness. That is to say, comparatively many aspects of the symbol system are significant. In a drawing of a mountain range by Katsushika Hokusai, every feature of the shape, line, and thickness contributes to its meaning. The importance of the same line in the context of a chart of daily stock market averages would be expressly restricted. In this latter case, the only significant aspect would be the high and low marks indicating specific numbers. In music, small changes in one or more of the elements making up a phrase can convey a quite definite and intended change in feeling tone, and every single change will have significance.

Finally, a musical symbol is likely to demonstrate the property of multiple and complex reference. Here, the symbol carries a number of overlapping and difficult-to-separate meanings, each of which contributes to the effect of the whole work. The reference music makes to aspects of life outside music is often ambiguous, proceeding through tortuous and extended chains and traversing several levels of meaning. Metaphoric and imaginative qualities associated with the relationships formed among the elements of the medium are an important part of the total meaning of a musical symbol.

No account of any type of intelligence would be complete if it did not attempt to deal with the issue of current information and prior knowledge and the role of the interplay between the two in intelligent behavior. Several authors provide descriptions of this aspect of musical intelligence although the terminology differs. Sometimes the term *knowledge* is used, sometimes authors prefer the more modern term *cognition,* and sometimes the two terms are used almost interchangeably.

Reimer claims that the experience of music is meaningful in the deepest sense of the word and that interaction with music is a mode of knowing or of cognition. But the knowing is *of* or *within* rather than *about.* Musical knowing is produced by perceptual/affective response to perceived sound events. Aesthetic cognition in general, and in music in particular, is the product of aesthetic experiencing. In this experience the intrinsic qualities of organic forms are processed primarily as affective stimuli. Reimer's view of cognition is a multi-faceted one that holds that human beings have many avenues to knowledge. Although our Western culture places particular value on the symbolic/conceptual mode of response, it is not the only mode of response that provides access to knowledge. Cognition or knowledge of feeling through experiences with art and music can be developed in depth, refinement, and scope. He views aesthetic education as the education of feeling/cognition.

Fred Lerdahl and Ray Jackendoff are somewhat more technical in their description of musical knowledge. They suggest that it is the largely unconscious knowledge acquired in previous experiences (perceived now as musical intuitions) that enables a listener to organize what is heard and make coherent the surface patterns of pitch attack, duration, intensity, and timbre presented by the music. This acquired musical knowledge enables a listener to do five important things: (1) identify a previously unknown piece as an example of a specific idiom; (2) recognize elements of a piece as typical or atypical of an idiom; (3) identify a performer's error as possibly producing an ungrammatical configuration within the idiom; (4) recognize various kinds of structural repetitions and variations; and (5) generally comprehend a piece within the idiom. In contrast, a listener without sufficient exposure to a musical idiom will not be able to organize in any rich way the sounds perceived. However, once a listener becomes familiar with the idiom (that is, once a store of largely unconscious knowledge has been acquired), the kind of organization the listener attributes to a given piece will not be arbitrary but will be highly constrained by that knowledge in specific ways.

Louis Arnaud Reid views the knowledge gained and utilized in appreciation of art works as a particular type of knowledge essentially involving feeling. Because aesthetic appreciation can be trained, he argues that aesthetic experience is more than mere feeling. It is knowledge. Indulgent wallowing in emotionalism is contrasted with the disciplined feeling and emotion that is instrumental to finer aesthetic perception, and Reid argues that this disciplined feeling must be present in developed aesthetic experience. He suggests that feeling is actively auxiliary in everything we do and think. Feeling is a living process becoming aware of itself, a mental happening, not an activity. He compares feeling to awareness but describes it as more general, more open, more exclusively subjective. In contrast, the functions of cognition involve focusing, grasping, acting, and reacting to the world. And "feeling" includes feeling all of that.

Reid qualifies the type of feeling involved in art appreciation even further. Attention must be focused on the object rather than the feeling response, and feelings must be relevant to the perceived object. The purpose of the contemplation should be to get a feeling *of* the work of art. The form of the feeling in a work of art can only be the form of the feeling *of* that work of art.

For Reid, feeling is involved in aesthetic knowledge at both the conscious and unconscious levels. When an individual has internalized technical understandings, it is possible to "think with" those understandings without being aware of them. The same applies to feeling. One can also attend to a work of art by "feeling with" it (that is, by feeling cognitively with it). He suggests that tacit feeling and tacit knowing are both part of the same process with regard to works of art.

Goodman is another author who views the type of cognition used in artistic processing as essentially involving feeling. Specifically, he argues that (1)feelings determine two basic cognitive processes in interaction with music. On the basis of feeling, listeners (1) discriminate between musical elements and events and (2) classify them. By this we are to understand that feelings are the means by which a listener discerns precisely which literal and metaphorical properties a piece of music possesses, and (2) in everyday life classification of things by feeling is often more vital than classification by other qualities. It is more important to be skilled in fearing and distrusting the right things than to perceive exact shapes, sizes, or weights of things in our environment. Classifications made in music on the basis of feeling range from simple divisions such as dissonance/consonance dichotomies to more profound ones such as the selection and appreciation of combinations of elements on the basis of their contribution to establishing a desired quality or mood.

Leonard Meyer has developed a theory that focuses upon the kind of meanings music is capable of conveying to its listeners. It is based upon a claim, similar to that of Lerdahl and Jackendoff, that exposure to a given style plays an important part in musical comprehension. The relationship between knowledge and meaning is a fundamental tenet of Meyer's theory. Unless a listener has knowledge of the stylistic tendencies of the piece of music being listened to, it will have no meaning.

In general, Meyer claims that the source of musical meaning is found intra-musically through the comprehension of musical relationships in a work of music. Musical meaning pivots upon three important elements: (1) the learned response of a listener familiar with an established musical style; (2) a universal psychological mechanism that explains a wide range of affective and intellectual responses; and (3) fundamental laws of human perception and cognition.

More specifically, Meyer suggests that affective or intellectual musical meaning arises when a psychological tendency to respond in a particular way is inhibited. A musical work is meaningful, therefore, if and only if a musical event arouses a listener's expectations with regard to the musical events that will follow. This explanation underlines the fact that meaningful musical experience depends crucially upon the musical expectations of listeners. In fact, to a large extent, a listener's musical experience is equivalent to an internalized set of musical expectations (those probabilities considered or hypotheses generated in response to the musical passages heard).

Meyer defines a tendency as an automatic response pattern, a chain of expectations. Three claims are made regarding expectations: (1) they may take the form of objective (self-conscious) concepts or tacit awarenesses; (2) they may be general or specific; and (3) they may be formally or informally acquired. Expectations are activated in a listener by the progress of the musical stimuli because some musical consequents of given antecedents are more probable than others.

When a musical consequent contradicts the listener's expectations, this creates tension in the listener. If the original expectations were tacit or unconscious, the tension is experienced as affect. When the expectations regarding musical tendencies and their inhibitions are conscious and conceptualized, the tension caused by contradictions leads to a rationalization of response or an "intellectual" response to the music. The listener's attitude in the latter case structures a quite different experience. So Meyer claims that the same processes that give rise to musical affective experience also give rise to the objectification of embodied musical meaning.

In later writings Meyer begins to use the term *implication* instead of *expectation* because he feels it better captures the wide range of meanings available to an experienced listener. That is to say, the experienced listener seldom expects a single and specific musical event, but the musical passage produces expectations for a weighted set of musically probable events. Put more simply, the music sets up tendencies the experienced listener realizes can be resolved in a variety of ways.

To summarize, the authors considered here describe a variety of features of musical intelligence. On the basis of their descriptions, it seems likely that musical intelligence is a highly complex mental activity involving multi-level processing, and the extent to which listeners can cope with this multi-level processing determines the level of quality of their musical experiences.

More specifically, these authors cumulatively suggest that a musically intelligent person will be able to:

1. Be open to, or perceive and recognize, not only tones but the expressive qualities of the musical work.

2. Create, or hear and re-create, the patterns of sound recognized as music in a particular culture or in a variety of cultures.

3. Anticipate musical events in listening and construct inner sonorous images parallel to those presented by the music.

4. Discriminate between sounds with regard to pitch, tone quality, intensity, timbre and duration; relate and associate the musical impressions; and order the associations into hierarchical levels that combine to create an overall image of the work.

5. Use or manipulate the musical symbol system competently, and understand the four important features of artistic symbol systems: syntactic density, semantic density, relative repleteness, and multiple and complex reference.

6. Display knowledge *of* music rather than *about* music, such knowledge being obtained by affective response to perceived sound events.

7. Use feeling cognitively to discriminate more sensitively among the various aspects of the work of art and to apprehend finer meanings. This is achieved on the basis of previously acquired information in both the feeling and knowledge realms and at both conscious and tacit levels.

8. Discriminate between musical elements and events, and classify them on the basis of feeling.

9. Comprehend musical relationships in a piece of music based on knowledge of an established musical style and on expectations (conscious or tacit) for a weighted set of musically probable events to follow.

IMPLICATIONS FOR RESEARCH

How are musical stimuli perceived, processed and recognized in relationship to each other? What effect might this have on strategies for the development of listening skills?

Is there a universal musical competence or capacity? If so, how is it manifested in different cultures and in different historical eras?

Is there a relationship between feeling and thinking? How does each relate to musical experience? Is it possible to clarify the role of cognition in emotion and feeling?

A detailed analysis is needed of the diversity and commonalities of musical intelligence and cognition as they relate to particular age groups and developmental stages.

LISTENING

The foundational interaction with music is listening. The composer listens while composing, the performer while performing, and both produce sounds to which others will listen. The improvement of the ability to listen with perceptual discernment and affective sensibility is fundamental in any notion of improving the quality of musical experience. Meaningful listening is both active and creative, the listener transforming the sounds being heard into a coherent experience being undergone. This transformation involves several mental-emotional operations that, while explained variously by different writers, include attention to aspects of sound (sensuous, technical, structural) and investment of the self in experiencing the expressive implications of what is heard. Musical listening in its richest sense is a work of mind in which mind includes and depends on both perceptual and affective dimensions of experience.

★　★　★

Listening is foundational to the musical experience. To understand how we experience music, it is essential to understand how we listen to music. The writers studied in this monograph have written

---

In addition to the citations found in the notes section at the end of the chapter, citations for the material in this section of Part II will be found on the following pages of Part I: Mursell, 122, 124–125, 127–128, 133, 134–135; Copland, 62–64; Broudy, 34, 36–39; Sessions, 174–175; Reimer, 155–157; Blacking, 29; Hindemith, 81–82; Langer, 86, 88, 90–93; Beardsley, 4–5, 11; Reid, 141, 143, 145–149; Schoenberg, 161, 163; Bernstein, 18–19, 23; Cage, 48–49; Clifton, 52, 57–59; Meyer, 111–115; Lerdahl and Jackendoff, 98–104.

extensively on listening, and they have addressed a broad range of topics related to the act of listening. Because of the wide scope of this essay it has been divided into sections that focus on (1) definitions, (2) the role of the listener, (3) the active involvement of the listener, and (4) the mind of the listener.

DEFINITIONS OF LISTENING

James Mursell differentiates among three different types of listening: intellectual, motor, and emotional. The intellectual listener hears technical factors and analyzes the music without feeling. Pure motor listeners feel rhythm and volume of sound only. Emotional listeners arbitrarily feel moods and feelings that often have nothing to do with the music itself.

Mursell notes that it is important for the listener to remain both subjective and objective throughout the listening process. The perception of objective factors lets the listener feel the music through anticipation and surprise. The listener must find a balance between the technical and emotional aspects of the listening experience; otherwise, an overemphasis on either extreme would result in an unsatisfactory and immature approach to listening. Effective listening, according to Mursell, requires musicianship and sophistication, the ability to discriminate musical details and know their significance. Effective listening requires preparation and improves through education.

Aaron Copland makes a distinction among three planes of musical listening. First, we listen for the sheer pleasure of the musical sound itself on the sensuous plane. Listening at this level is enjoyable, but insufficient. Musical listening, according to Copland, should be active listening, which takes the listener beyond the music's sensuous appeal. The second plane is the expressive. Here we explore the nature of musical meaning and the expressive power of music. Copland raises such questions as: What is expressed in the music? What does the music mean? Can it be put into words? Finally, there is the sheerly musical plane. Most listeners are not sufficiently conscious of this third plane; professional musicians, on the other hand, are all too conscious of this aspect of music. The musical plane involves the awareness of the notes themselves and of their manipulation.

Copland believes that simultaneously and without thinking we listen on all three planes. The ideal listener combines the training of the professional with the innocence of the intuitive amateur. Like Mursell, Copland suggests that the goal of the listener is to remain both subjective and objective, to be inside and outside of the music at the same time. Copland feels consequently that education is essential to developing a better understanding of music:

> No composer believes that there are any short cuts to better appreciation of music. The only thing that one can do for the listener is to point out what actually exists in the music itself and reasonably explain the wherefore and the why of the matter. The listener must do the rest.

In aesthetic scanning, a technique for approaching works of art, Harry Broudy has identified four categories of aesthetic perception that can be applied specifically to the act of listening to music. First, the perceiver becomes aware of the sensory properties of the piece, the qualities that are most evident to our senses when encountering a work of art. Then one responds to the formal properties or the structure and organization of the work. Next the expressive properties become apparent, and one speculates about the possible meanings of an object or event. Finally, the technical properties, or how the art work is produced, are examined. These, combined with the historical, re-creative, and judicial understandings of the work, comprise an informed aesthetic response.

In his discussion of listening, Roger Sessions offers a definition of "the musical ear," a way of hearing music that applies to both musician and nonmusician. First, the musical ear discriminates sounds on a number of levels (pitch, tone quality, intensity, timbre, and duration). Second, the musical ear relates and associates these musical impressions. Third, the ear orders these associations into hierarchical levels that combine to create an overall image of the work.

Sessions proposes that the principal feature that enables the listener to organize the musical impressions is the perception of harmony. Harmony, more than any other element of music, affords the possibility of extension and growth by virtue of the almost inexhaustible variety of tonal relationships. Through the perception of harmony, the musical ear is able to compare areas of tonal contrast and put them into the perspective of the overall design.

For Susanne Langer, listening must involve the experience of the total work as an "expressive form." She points out that the primary activity of musical hearing is not the ability to single out the separate elements of a composition and recognize all its devices; rather, it is to experience the primary illusion, "to recognize at once the commanding form which makes the piece an inviolable whole."

Monroe Beardsley discusses a "parts-whole" approach to a work of art. He uses the term *local qualities* to describe the most elementary parts, which we may or may not perceive when experiencing art. But when elements combine to form complexes, these complexes, or regional qualities, allow us to perceive sensory information in art works as aesthetic phenomena.

According to Louis Arnaud Reid, the aesthetic begins with the experientially indivisible: this is what he calls fusion of the aesthetic experience. Reid stresses that the perceiver/listener should become aware of the subjective aspects of the music only in retrospection, for one cannot attend to the music and the specifics of one's own dynamics simultaneously. Any conscious efforts at introspection while listening not only slows the process but also robs the perceiver of the impact of the whole. The perceiver/listener must be able to bring his or her psycho-physical being to the experience tacitly. It is intrinsic to the musical experience.

THE ROLE OF THE LISTENER

Bennett Reimer states that listening is the essential mode of musical experience — music cannot be experienced if it is not heard. Listening is a part of all aspects of musical involvement, whether through performing, composing, or as an activity by itself. Reimer states that the enhancement of listening ability is a primary function of music education, and listening must be taught directly. Performing and composing are powerful and necessary tools for developing listening abilities, but there are limitations inherent in these processes. Every person is able to listen to more kinds of music and more complex music than he or she can perform or compose; thus, the systematic teaching of listening is an essential component of music education.

According to John Blacking, listening is too often ignored and underrated as an aspect of musical ability. He declares that "listening to music, like comprehending verbal language, is as much a creative act as making it." For musical tradition to flourish, there is a need for both performers and critical listeners. Blacking reminds us that, particularly in societies where music is not written down, accurate and informed listening is of paramount importance. In these societies, listening is as significant a measure of musical ability as performance.

Arnold Schoenberg writes extensively on the communication and interaction that take place between the composer and the listener. According to him, the listener must understand the composer's intent, and it is essential for the composer to communicate his ideas. Idea is defined as "the totality of the piece," and the efforts of the composer are to be directed toward making the idea comprehensible to the listener. A work of art can produce no greater effect than when it transmits the emotion that raged in the creator to the listener, in such a way that they also rage and storm in him or her.

In his writings, Leonard Bernstein also attempts to describe what the composer communicates to the listener. He defines this interaction as a particular type of communication: "I wish there were a better word for communication; I mean by it the tenderness we feel when we recognize and share with another human being a deep, unnameable, elusive emotional shape or shade." In communicating with the listener, the composer is never literal and can never be factual. Bernstein says, "In other words, you can't state facts with F sharps. You can't write music that is going to inform anybody about anything, and, in fact, you can't write music that is going to describe anything unless I tell you what I want the music to be describing." Furthermore, what the composer is saying to the listener must be "emotional" or, more specifically, an emotion recollected. Bernstein wants to dispel the notion that agitated music is written by an agitated composer, or despairing music comes from a desperate composer.

Sessions discusses the collaborative, creative nature of the relationship among the listener, composer, and performer. He points out that the performer and listener are, in many ways, adding to the work of the composer. Further, the listener is often able to "visualize" the composition (with the ears, not the eyes) in a way that surpasses what is conceived by the composer and performer.

John Cage raises the issue that, in the contemporary musical experience, the distinctions among the roles of composer, performer, and listener are breaking down. He cites two factors that are responsible for this change: indeterminacy in composition, which allows for the active participation of the performer and the audience in the creative process, and the development of a more advanced musical technology, which enables any individual to become at once composer, performer, and listener. Rather than the traditional, hierarchical separation of roles, Cage proposes that a more democratic relationship is now possible among composer, performer, and listener.

THE ACTIVE INVOLVEMENT OF THE LISTENER

Mursell defines the listening process as active rather than passive: "Listening should by no means be considered passive reception — not even when the main consideration is the evocation of a mood. The successful listener enters into the music, is possessed by it, and so is inspired and enabled to make it for himself."

Thomas Clifton's phenomenological description of the musical experience focuses largely on the active role of the listener. Music involves a reciprocal relation (a "collaboration") between the listener and real or imagined sounds. According to Clifton, the experience of music cannot result from passive observation or casual encounters. A meaningful musical experience demands the perceiver's personal involvement with the music.

Similarly, Schoenberg discusses the interaction that takes place between a listener and the work of art. He states that an artistic impression is substantially the result of two components — that which the work of art gives to the onlooker, and that which the person is able to give to the work of art. The work of art seems to be merely the external stimulus that awakens those forces sensed by us as an artistic impression. The intensity of an artistic impression depends on the onlooker's ability to give even while receiving.

Paul Hindemith emphasizes the importance of a receiving mind in musical listening. He states that music remains "meaningless noise" unless it touches a receiving mind. The receiving mind must be active in order to transform a mere acoustical perception into a genuine musical experience.

THE MIND OF THE LISTENER

According to Mursell, when music is heard the listener perceives relationships in tones, expressive shadings, and (ultimately) forms, processing them in terms of musical memory and imagination. Listening is a complicated mental process, requiring the ability to attend to music and recognize and discriminate its elements. The critic, the composer, the instrumentalist or vocalist all perform a highly expert act of selective attention: "In all cases it may be truly said that we hear with our minds rather than with our ears."

This type of listening should not be confused with an experience focused solely on knowledge about music. Although knowledge about music is necessary to perceive fully a work of art, the listener must lower his or her level of consciousness of the formal aspects of music, or the experience will become analytical rather than musical. Much like Langer's concept of expressive form, Beardsley's notion of regional qualities, or Reid's idea of fusion of the aesthetic experience, Mursell states that the listener must be able to experience the totality of the work of art: "With or without conscious intention, he closes his mind to its constituent detail and intricate nuance. These matters may be important and interesting enough, but for the time being he agrees with himself to disregard them. And this is something which he must learn to do. . . ."

It is important to emphasize that Mursell believes that such expertness in musical perception can be taught. Listeners can learn how formal elements work, and this learning can enhance the musical experience. He also stresses that learning about the formal elements should take place within the context of the real experience of real music.

To Langer, listening is the primary activity of the musical experience. She differentiates two types of listening — physical or actual hearing, and inward or mental hearing. Physical hearing is the mind's actual sensory perception of sound. Inward hearing is "a work of the mind, that begins with conceptions of form and ends with their complete presentation in imagined sense experience." It is a talent, "a special intelligence of the ear, and like all talents, it develops through exercise." Inward hearing is related to performance as well: "The mind hears, the hand follows, as faithfully as the voice itself obeys the inward ear."

In defining the listening experience, Blacking makes a distinction between external listening and internal listening similar to that made by Langer. External listening is the perception acquired in the course of social and cultural experience, and inner listening is the hypothetical process of hearing music in the head. Blacking also suggests that inner listening must precede performance, for the music must exist in the mind of the performer before it is actualized.

Hindemith refers to the "inner ringing and singing," which is experienced by both the composer and listener. For the listener, this ringing and singing allows for the mental construction of parallel, mirrored musical images from the musical stimuli: "Listening to music or imagining music is based on previous audibly musical or imaginary-musical experiences."

There are limitations, according to Hindemith, in the listener's ability to listen in a meaningful fashion. Listeners are able to bring only limited energy and ability to the task of anticipating and constructing parallel images, and "once he reaches a certain point of versatility in his power of musical co-construction, no further progress seems to be possible."

Reimer also discusses the creative aspect of listening, where listeners construct their own experience by not only noticing musical events as they occur, but by listening forward, anticipating what might occur, and listening backward, checking what is now occurring against what has already occurred. He describes the creative act of listening as involving selective attention at various levels of inclusiveness, anticipatory projection, reflective reappraisal, and affective self-investment.

Leonard Meyer's writings further clarify the process that occurs in listening. He builds his description of the musical experience on this central thesis: musical meaning arises when a musical tendency to respond is inhibited. A musical work is meaningful if and only if a musical event arouses a listener's expectations for other musical events. A meaningful musical experience depends on a listener's musical expectations. The listener objectively or tacitly estimates the probabilities of the music's continuation, and when less probable events occur, the music is experienced as more meaningful.

For a listener to have established a set of expectations, he or she needs to be familiar with a musical style. If a listener has no experience in a given musical style, a meaningful musical experience of any work in that style is unlikely. Thus, a listener's experience is equivalent to the internalized set of musical expectations relative to the musical passages heard.

Fred Lerdahl and Ray Jackendoff also express the importance of exposure to a musical idiom. Without sufficient understanding of a musical style, listeners are not able to organize in any rich way the sounds they perceive. However, once they become familiar with the idiom, the kind of organization they attribute to a given piece will not be arbitrary but will be highly constrained in specific ways. Musical knowledge enables the listener

> to identify a previously unknown piece as an example of the idiom, to recognize elements of a piece as typical or anomalous, to identify a performer's error as producing an ungrammatical configuration, to recognize various kinds of structural repetitions and variations, and, in general, to comprehend a piece within the idiom.

Lerdahl and Jackendoff's book *A Generative Theory of Tonal Music* was written for the purpose of describing "the musical intuitions of a listener who is experienced in a musical idiom." Their goal is to understand "the largely unconscious knowledge that the listener brings to his hearing — a knowledge that enables him to organize and make coherent the surface patterns of pitch, attack, duration, intensity, timbre, and so forth." They have developed a theory of musical grammar that explores the connections between the presentation of music and the listener's mental structuring of that piece.

Their theories have focused upon the "experienced listener" or the idealized state of listening. Lerdahl and Jackendoff do not infer that all human beings are capable of listening to a piece in an identical fashion; rather, they consider there to be a "most natural hearing," taking into account a multiple range of interpretations.

Lerdahl and Jackendoff's interest is in the final state of a listener's understanding as opposed to the listener's real time mental process. They believe that, as theorists, they must first understand the organization, the structure of the music, before theorizing about the mental processing that takes place while listening.

Lerdahl and Jackendoff also address the question of how much of an experienced listener's knowledge is learned and how much of this knowledge is due to innate musical capacity or general cognitive capacity. Toward understanding those aspects of musical understanding that are innate, they have developed a series of musical universals that are principles available to all experienced listeners for organizing the musical surfaces they hear.

Like the linguistic theories of generative-transformational grammar (as proposed by Noam Chomsky), Lerdahl and Jackendoff's generative theory of tonal music attempts to provide a structural description for any tonal piece or, to put it differently, the structure experienced listeners infer when they hear a piece of tonal music. They define four components of the musical structure: grouping structure, metrical structure, time-span reductions, and prolongational reductions. Within each component, they have developed well-formedness rules and preference rules that describe the listener's hearing of a piece.

The subject of listening has occupied a significant portion of the writings on the musical experience included in this monograph. The writers have emphasized various features of musical listening, and an analysis of listening is vital to a description of the musical experience. As Reimer suggests, the active, intelligent, cognitively meaningful, self-generated, feelingful nature of musical listening constitutes the foundational mode of human interaction with the art of music and accounts for the power and ubiquity of musical experience in human history.

IMPLICATIONS FOR RESEARCH

How can various levels of musical listening (sensuous, perceptual, creative, technical) be isolated for study? How can various combinations, or the totality, be examined as they operate in natural (whole) experiences or in separately focused exercises?

What are the developmental factors influencing the ability to process various dimensions of musical listening? Are there different configurations of levels that are natural at different ages?

What specific educational interventions produce identifiable differences in each level separately, in various combinations, or in the totality?

What effects on listening ability are produced by performance experiences, composing experiences, or listening experiences? Are there differences in the content of the listening experiences produced by each?

How can the "creative" or "original" or "self-generated" aspect of listening be assessed and improved?

To what extent does style familiarity affect the ability to process sounds sensuously, perceptively, or creatively in listening? Given a positive correlation, what are ways to teach style familiarity efficiently?

How can necessary "thinking about" learnings be best integrated so they become "thinking with" aspects in listening? That is, what are the details in achieving automaticity or tacit awareness in the listening experience?

SENSUOSITY

Underlying musical experience is an aspect that forms a kind of "grounding" for all that occurs above it — the sensuosity of tone. Sounds have a tangible effect on our bodies and our being; they are "felt" as much as they are "heard." Musical sensuosity is not chaotic. It is a formed, coherent phenomenon contributing to the meaningfulness of the experience as a whole, in a minor way according to some writers and in a major way according to others. Those who emphasize its importance point out the necessary involvement of the body in any meaningful interaction with music, in that feeling is always connected to and dependent on the body in which the self exists. Just as all musics rely on the dimension of sounds in relation to one another, all musics also rely on the dimension of sound as immediately felt within. While some musics emphasize one over the other, both dimensions contribute to the totality of musical experience.

★ ★ ★

A number of authors who write about musical experience mention sensuosity as a component of the experience. Aaron Copland refers to the power of this component as music's primordial appeal. He says that music affects all people, whether musically simple-minded or sophisticated, with a sense of immediacy resulting from its sheer

---

Citations for the material in this section of Part II will be found on the following pages of Part I: Copland, 61–64; Langer, 86–89; Reid, 140–142; Broudy, 34–35; Lerdahl and Jackendoff, 102; Blacking, 28, 30; Clifton, 57–59; Mursell, 122, 127, 129–131; Reimer, 156–157.

rhythmic and sonic impact. This sensuous plane of musical listening consists of listening "for the sheer pleasure of the musical sound itself." This plane is only one of three, however. The others are the expressive plane (which involves the meaning expressed by music) and the musical plane (which involves musical sounds simply for themselves). While Copland believes that the sensuous plane of musical experience is important, he also advocates the teaching of listening skills so that listeners can experience music more fully at all its levels.

Susanne Langer locates the source of musical sensuosity within the significant form of a musical work. A piece of music is a "highly articulated sensuous object" that can convey forms of vital experience that language cannot convey. Its import is a product of life feelings, musical motion, and emotion. Upon hearing musical works that have been cast in significant forms, listeners experience sentience. Tension, repose, speed, and excitement are patterns found both in music and in human subjective experience. Music has a sensuous effect because its tones are a metaphor of feelings or sensations that occur naturally in life.

A slightly different slant on this position is delineated by Louis Arnaud Reid. He claims that the aesthetic in art cannot express life feelings exactly, because the dynamics of musical experience and life experience are not entirely like one another. Nonetheless, the feeling of an art work does involve an intra-psycho-physical content. Aesthetic experience always involves a focus on what transpires on the fringes of consciousness. An aesthetic object expresses functionally the human inner states of mind and body, the untranslatable parts of human experience. According to Reid, music has a sensuous effect but a semiconscious one.

Sensuosity is also acknowledged by Harry Broudy, though he describes it as a minor part of musical experience. He suggests that aesthetic education should include studies in expression, to free students who create music from rigid technical rules and standards. But the intended purpose of this process is to help them discover that feelings must be shaped and that form is a necessary part of the musical medium. Each art work has a particular shape. Broudy points out that certain formal arrangements are powerful and pleasing to listeners because they contain designs and rhythms inherent in nature itself. Thus, listeners respond sympathetically upon encountering them in music. However, he also stresses that sensuous appeal alone is not enough. Music must be carefully formed if it is to cause meaningful musical experience.

Fred Lerdahl and Ray Jackendoff refer to the sensuous elements of music as nonhierarchical relationships. The primary sensuous elements are timbre, dynamics, and motivic-thematic processes. Their theory of music does not address these elements directly. However, they state that these dimensions contribute in crucial ways to the hierarchical structures of musical works.

According to John Blacking, many if not all of music's essential processes can be found in the constitution of the human body and in patterns of interaction between human bodies in society. Music is a metaphor of feeling that draws on man's nature for many of its forms. Both human feelings and musical patterns are structured. When music is created, feelings are transformed into patterns in relation to innate bodily structures, individual musical experience banks, and societal conventions. Thus, when music is heard, patterns are transformed into human feelings.

Thomas Clifton takes a phenomenological view of musical experience. He claims that such experience is based on the feeling within one's body of musical presentative meaning. (By "body" he means a combination of mind, feelings, senses, and will.) Music is not a purely auditory experience. It can only be properly understood as a synaesthetic perception — a bodily engagement with sound. Such perception results from human reactions to musical elements. For example, recognition of tonality is not an intellectual entity. It is a habit, an aptitude acquired by the body, a bodily movement, a sensuous experience, and a feeling, all of which combine for an intuitive sense of tonality.

James Mursell considers the sensuous part of musical experience to be critical. He describes rhythm as the primary element that causes the sensuous response of kinesthetic experience. Evidence of music's direct ties to the human body can be seen in the movements of both performers and listeners. Rhythms are perceived in hierarchical groups, and muscles of various sizes may move sympathetically with various rhythmic levels. While such movements are largely instinctive and are not always visible, they are nonetheless quite literally like real feelings physically felt in life.

Finally, Bennett Reimer defines sensuosity in a way that strikes a balance between and also summarizes some of the above positions. Music always includes a sensuous (as if processed by body-sense) dimension. Listeners react sensuously to sound as such. Certain elements of sound, such as beat, dynamics, tone colors, densities, and accents, have particular sensuous power. While some musics are goal-oriented, others are oriented more toward energy activation and thus emphasize the sensuous response. Sensuous response can be complex, subtle, and affectively profound. As an "indwelling" response within the body, sensuosity is intimately related to musical experience.

IMPLICATIONS FOR RESEARCH

How do each of the elements of music (such as rhythm or melody) contribute to its sensuosity? Does one element possess more sensuous appeal than another? Which element(s) cause the most feelingful response to music? Do quantifiable musical parameters (louder/softer, brighter/darker) affect sensuous appeal?

How does the culture in which one lives affect the perception of sensuosity in music? Through what formal and informal means are such cultural influences learned? Can perception be traced through developmental stages related to age? Does this change from culture to culture?

To what extent does the amount of training in musical listening or performance affect the sensuous response to music? How can this be measured?

If aesthetic experience "transpires on the fringes of consciousness" (as Reid postulates), how is musical perception and sensuous response affected by brain damage, intellectual development, and an individual's intellectual profile?

TIME

The experience of musical process, on which the sense of meaningful interrelations of sounds depends, is itself dependent on the sense of motion we get from music. And motion is intimately connected to the passage of time. We feel musical sounds as being in motion because events occur from moment to moment — not from any direct sensation of literal motion. The moment-to-moment passage of tendencies creates an experience of time as lived or virtual time, as distinguished from real or clock time. Time as experienced psychologically in music relates in complex ways to the real time in which it is embedded. In music, time passes, but with an internal vividness caused by tonal events both existing in time and surpassing any consciousness of literal time.

★   ★   ★

Time in music is a matter that has interested many who write about music and musical experience. While it is an obscure problem that is difficult to penetrate, it is of great importance to those who consider the intricacies of musical experience. One writer to whom this issue is important is Susanne Langer. The relation between time and music is of prime importance to her theory of art: "Music makes time audible, and its form and continuity sensible." This assumption arises from her belief that motion is the essence of music. We experience the movement of music because of the lapse of time.

Citations for the material in this section of Part II will be found on the following pages of Part I: Langer, 90–91; Stravinsky, 178–180; Hindemith, 84; Clifton, 55.

Langer speaks to the classical philosophical conflict between time as "being" (ordinary time) and time as "becoming" (experienced or lived time). She distinguishes between virtual time (which is lived or experienced time) and actual time (which is the one-dimensional, infinite, pure succession of various temporal data, actual happenings, or moments). For Langer, actual time is synonymous with clock time.

On the basis of this distinction, Langer claims that virtual time (musical time) is subjective, dynamic, and dramatic. It embodies the images of the passage of life with which we are acquainted by intuition. Time is "the primary illusion of music." However, musical time is logical. It has the same logical patterns as our tensions which are brought to life by rhythms (the most characteristic principle of vital activity) that can be manipulated by the composer. By stating that musical time is filled with tensions and resolutions, Langer is stressing the psychological aspect of time in music. Musical time is perceptible; it is experienced solely through listening, by "letting our hearing monopolize it, organize, fill, and shape it, all alone."

Concurring with Langer, Igor Stravinsky claims that music is an art of time, presupposing before all else a certain organization in time. In his view, a musical composition involves the functional realization of time. In other words, a musical composition is based on the temporal ordering of the sounds perceived. Stravinsky also distinguishes between two types of time. For him, psychological time is the flow of time that depends on our state of consciousness and the events that influence it. Real time is the normal flow of time (clock time). Stravinsky maintains that it is the interaction of these two types of time that makes up musical time. Unlike Langer, he does not claim that music is perceived exclusively as psychological time. Rather, music "establishes a sort of counterpoint between the passing of time, the music's own duration, and the material and technical means through which the music is made manifest."

Further, Stravinsky states that some music may be mainly grounded in real time, and some music may remain faithful to psychological time. The prevailing characteristic of the first kind of music is similarity, which he believes leads to unity and true solidity in a composition. The creative process of the second kind of music is ruled by contrast, which leads to variety. Stravinsky states, "For myself, I have always considered that in general it is more satisfactory to proceed by similarity rather than by contrast."

Paul Hindemith considers musical time to be a formal feature of music with functional significance. According to him, musical time evokes two different kinds of affect. On the one hand, musical time expressed by meter runs parallel to actual time because of its regularity. On the other hand, musical time expressed by rhythm, because of its incommensurable nature, produces an effect that in normal life is nonexistent.

Thomas Clifton is concerned with the same problem because he views time as a necessary constituent of musical experience. He regards time as "the experience of human consciousness in contact with change." Time is not an absolute medium, but an "experience . . . which is in constant flux." Clifton refers to time as *horizon* (the temporal edge of a single field, which may include multiple events that can be regarded as part of this field).

The distinction between musical time (which is similar to Langer's virtual time) and chronological time is important to Clifton. He points this out in the difference between the time a musical piece takes and the time it presents or evokes. For Clifton, time is in the music; it is presented or evoked by the music, and it is designated by the music.

IMPLICATIONS FOR RESEARCH

What musical parameters affect the perception of musical time? How does a listener perceive, encode, and process musical duration and tempo? Is temporal structure intrinsic to the music, the listener, or the performance?

Are different types of time experienced during the listening process? How does the listener perceive musical duration and tempo?

How can teaching and learning processes of music be affected by considerations of musical time?

REFERENCE

In addition to being made of sounds in relation to one another occurring over time, music can make reference to things, ideas, emotions, and actions in the same way language does — by designation or denotation. None of the writers in this study claims that designation is necessary in order for musical experience to occur, or that when and if designation is present (words in vocal music, programmatic material) the designation itself can be considered the essential meaning of the music. Designation in music is viewed variously from denial that music is capable of it at all to assertions that it can add significantly to the intra-musical experience. While no writer here embraced referentialism in its full sense (that music's nature is language-like in essence), many recognized that reference can and does occur in music and that it must be taken into account (if only to deny its validity) in any treatment of musical experience.

★ ★ ★

According to the referentialist's point of view, the function of an art work is to communicate a message or emotion. Art is a language that serves to convey that which the artist wishes to express. The sounds in music may refer to extra-musical experiences. Therefore, the meaning of that piece of music exists outside the work itself. The

Citations for the material in this section of Part II will be found on the following pages of Part I: Langer, 86–87; Meyer, 111–115; Reimer, 153–156; Reid, 140–144, 147–148; Mursell, 122–123; Beardsley, 8, 10–12; Broudy, 33, 39–40; Bernstein, 18–19, 23–24; Blacking, 27–28. 30; Goodman, 70, 72, 74–75.

story or program of the music constitutes its meaning. According to the referentialists, a piece of music is successful to the degree that the music effectively directs one's attention to its extrinsic (extra-musical) meaning.

For Susanne Langer, artistic creation does not begin with a formulated message. The composer who seeks to communicate rather than create will not produce music. Rather, the result will be a limited expression or "artificial language." The contribution of music is not self-expression or communication; music's gift is insight. Musical structures correspond with the structures of human feeling more so than do the structures of language. Accordingly, music can impart the nature of feeling in a manner that language cannot. Music is a nondiscursive symbol that articulates what is verbally ineffable.

Leonard Meyer believes that musical meaning is intra-musical and can be perceived through the understanding of musical relationships. Musical meaning is communicated to both participants and listeners, and this meaning depends on (among other things) the learned responses of a listener who is familiar with a musical style rather than a composer's intentions or strategies. Meaning in music occurs when a musical tendency to respond is inhibited. A piece of music is meaningful only when (and if) a musical experience arouses a listener's expectations for other musical experiences. Meyer suggests that response to a musical performance could partially be a function of the extra-musical significance that a piece has for the listener, but this has nothing to do with the organization or structuring of the music itself.

Like Meyer, Bennett Reimer believes that musical experience can involve extra-musical components such as the words of vocal music or program material. These components can add to the intra-musical experience. For Reimer, however, when the experience of music becomes entirely a response to the extra-musical (as opposed to music's intrinsic expressiveness), the experience is nonmusical. The arts are unique because, unlike conventional symbols, their meaning comes from their nature as expressive forms. It is neither possible nor desirable for an expressive form to have the same meaning for everyone. An art work needs to be approached, perceived, and responded to as a bearer of insight (that is, for its embodied meaning) rather than for information (designated meaning).

Louis Arnaud Reid also recognizes the presence of extra-musical components. He states that musical association includes two types: the incidental and the transformationally fused. Incidental association (imitation) is likely to be diversionary, distracting, and harmful to the musical experience. When associations are transformed by a fusion of the parts with the whole, nothing is encumbered. For Reid, it is always a matter of context or degree. Reid agrees with Langer that music can reflect the nature of feeling in a manner that nonmusical references cannot. Feeling is a basic mental concept. Emotion is a derived one. Emotion is dependent for its character on distinguishable factors, excitations bound up in our relation to the world. An emotion is an external reference to an objectification, whereas feeling (the ineffable) is the internal base from which emotion springs.

For James Mursell, music's principal expressive devices are intrinsic to the music. Extrinsic associations may enhance the musical experience, but they may also hinder it. Both the intrinsic and extrinsic sources of feeling are helpful when they apply, but the subjective response should never be forced. To Mursell, beauty is embodied as musical ideas, using expressive devices to represent life struggles. The ordering of tones, dynamic shadings, and tempi create moods that are intrinsic.

Monroe Beardsley suggests that music is not capable of pointing beyond itself to specific events, emotions, images, or psychological states. It functions neither as a natural nor conventional sign. Music and mental life share common features such as tempo, variations of intensity, and impulsiveness. Some musical qualities resemble qualities of human beings, their states of mind, traits, actions, or activities. Metaphors, when carefully used, can help us name these human qualities, since we have no other language for describing their existence in art works. However, music need not refer to anything outside of its own intrinsic qualities in order to play its unique role in helping us understand our inner world.

The idea that musical structure corresponds with the structure of human feeling is also held by Harry Broudy. For him, the metaphorical nature of art is the ability of a musical experience to present itself as actually being a particular quality of human experience rather than saying it is like something else. In this way, music takes on a symbolic nature rather than being a sign that points to something outside of itself.

Leonard Bernstein stresses that the musical experience should be focused within the music. He emphasizes that musical analysis should be concerned with musical meaning and what is going on within the music. While Bernstein finds anecdotes, analogies, and figures of speech helpful, he uses these referential devices only to make music clearer or more accessible, and not to entertain or direct the listener's attention away from the music.

John Blacking feels music has no meaning of its own. Music and other cultural phenomena can be said to have no intrinsic meanings. It is possible, therefore, for society to assign any meaning to them. Music requires affiliation with society before it can obtain meaning. Music cannot be transmitted or have meaning without associations among people.

For Blacking, there are two levels at which a relationship between music and society can be expected — the level of ideas and the level of interaction in which ideas are invoked. There are also two areas of action that are involved in every performance situation — the musical and the social. Neither ideas nor musical action can be understood without reference to patterns of social interaction, for ideas and music, like anything cultural, are social facts.

Nelson Goodman states that a musical symbol is likely to demonstrate the properties of multiple and complex reference. Here, the symbol carries a number of overlapping and difficult-to-separate meanings, each of which contributes to the effect of the whole work. The reference music makes to aspects of life outside of music is often ambiguous, proceeding through tortuous and extended chains, and traversing several levels of meaning. Metaphoric and imaginative qualities associated with relationships formed among the elements of the medium are an important part of the total meaning of a musical symbol.

Many writers about the musical experience who are not referentialists recognize that conventional symbols and extra-musical references exist in music. However, there is disagreement as to whether these references are irrelevant to the meaning of music or whether they contribute to music's intra-musical expressiveness.

IMPLICATIONS FOR RESEARCH

To what extent can specific emotions and meanings be transmitted unambiguously from composer to listener? How could evidence of such communication be obtained? Is the communication of emotions and meanings enhanced by any particular musical style, listening practice, or performance experience?

Do trained musicians perceive intra- and extra-musical meaning differently than do nonmusicians? Does the level of musical training or musical education effect perception of meaning? How does teaching for the perception of intra- or extra-musical meaning effect the listener's musical experience?

To what extent do some composers intend communication of specific emotions or meanings to listeners? Through what means could this intent be identified and measured? Do composers of certain musical styles try to convey specific emotions and meanings more than composers of other styles?

How is the musical experience affected by treating music as a conventional symbol rather than an expressive form? Are there correlations here with age and intelligence? Under what conditions do extrinsic associations enhance or hinder musical experience? Through what research methods could such an investigation be carried out?

INSPIRATION AND CREATIVITY

An important aspect of musical experience recognized by many writers is creativity. Several composers recognize the role of inspiration as providing a particularly intense, germinal source for creative activity. But creativity extends to musical imagination as it is exercised not only by composers and performers but also by listeners. While composers tend, naturally, to discuss creativity in terms relating to compositional challenges, other writers apply the concept to all engagements with music, in that all musical experiences require decision-making of one sort or another, including the perceptual/affective decisions regarding which event to attend to in the listening experience. Whether viewed from the perspective of the creative musical specialist or the audience experiencing the product of that specialty, imagination (creativity) is an important dimension of musical experiencing.

★ ★ ★

INSPIRATION

There is general agreement among professional musicians (primarily composers) that inspiration refers to a short burst of insight that helps drive the creative process. Aaron Copland argues that the substance of inspiration can be found in the moment of possession of the germinal musical idea and that the source of this idea may reside in the

---

Citations for the material in this section of Part II will be found on the following pages of Part I: Copland, 62, 65, 66; Hindemith, 84; Sessions, 167–170; Reid, 142–143; Stravinsky, 179; Bernstein, 19–22; Reimer, 157; Beardsley, 8; Cage, 46.

superconscious or subconscious. This is qualitatively different from creative intuition that drives the composer on a daily basis. Inspiration, for Copland, is a much more rare, brief, and exhausting experience.

Paul Hindemith speaks of inspiration in terms of musical vision (a single moment in which the composer grasps the details of a future work). Unlike many, Hindemith is convinced that "if we cannot, in the flash of a single moment, see a composition in its absolute entirety, with every pertinent detail in its proper place, we are not genuine creators."

Roger Sessions adds that inspiration can create momentum for the musical thoughts of the composer, setting in motion the energy necessary to sustain the creative effort. For Sessions, however, the source of inspiration is the music itself. Inspiration gives rise to the "musical idea," which can be viewed as the generative kernel of the composition.

CREATIVITY

The notion of the musical idea as a product of inspiration leads naturally to creativity, the creative process, and the nature of the creative person. Composers, educators, and aesthetic theorists have written extensively about creativity and have done so using the three perspectives of person, process, and product.

Person

The personal quality of imagination occupies much space in these writings. For instance, Copland believes that the freely imaginative mind should be the core of all musical performance and listening. The elements of music (rhythm, melody, form, etc.) are only "meaningful insofar as the imagination is given free play."

Louis Arnaud Reid writes about "imaginative contemplation" as a characteristic of people engaged in composition and in all aesthetic encounters with music. The aesthetic object, contemplated imaginatively, has intrinsic value for its own sake, not for its practical, cognitive, or existential implications. The artist's imaginative contemplation is his or her own. If it becomes public, the connection is not from person to person but from contemplation to contemplation. For Reid, this imaginative aesthetic contemplation requires certain conditions: (1) the apprehension of perceptual data; (2) interest in appearance for the sake of meaning (value that transcends the data itself); (3) the avoidance of extra-musical referents; and (4) feelings relevant to the perceived object.

Igor Stravinsky also speaks of personal characteristics in terms of creative thinking. He writes, "Musical creation is an innate complex of intuitions and possibilities based primarily upon an exclusively musical experiencing of time, . . . of which the musical work merely gives us the functional realization."

This innate complex of intuitions is described in another way by Leonard Bernstein. In describing the act of composition, he refers to the composer's need to achieve "the trancelike, out-of-mind state for anything really important to emerge." Once the composer has reached this mental state, the utmost that can be achieved is "a totality, a Gestalt, a work." He lists other possibilities that can result from this state of mind: (1) a general climate or atmosphere; (2) a theme, the basic idea or motive to be developed; (3) a tune; and (4) a fragment of an idea or effect. Bernstein reminds the reader that certain external, nonmusical influences can interfere with this unconscious state, including such entities as audience, nationalism, prevailing trends, critics, society and social structure, other works of art, a specific performer or conductor or orchestra, and self-criticism. The composer must find a balance among these factors and prevent them from interfering with the creative process.

Process

Bennett Reimer claims that creativity is a decision-making process and that this process is the essential characteristic of creativity. This is true for all aspects of the musical experience, because all musical experience has a creative dimension. Listening requires the exercise of choice, control, and attention in order to create one's own experience. This involves exploring perceptual-affective potentials and discovering their musical implications. Composers explore and discover affective possibilities in compositions, and performers bring them to sonorous completion.

Monroe Beardsley writes in more specific terms about the creative process:

> There are two clearly marked phases [of the creative process] which constantly alternate throughout. . . . There is the inventive phase, traditionally called inspiration, in which new ideas are formed in the preconscious and appear in consciousness. And there is the selective phase, which is nothing more than criticism, in which the conscious chooses or rejects the new idea after perceiving its relationship to what has already tentatively been adopted.

Beardsley refers to inspiration as an ongoing phenomenon that becomes part of the creative process.

In his writing on creative process, Bernstein proposes that theories from linguistics might be appropriate parallels for music. In linguistics, transformation is the process through which basic concepts or bits of information become language. Noam Chomsky and others believe that an understanding of the ways language is created reveals insights into the workings of the human mind. Bernstein claims that the concept of transformational grammar can be applied to music as well as language and that rules such as "deletion" and "embedding" may be used to explain the process of musical creation.

Product

Finally, composers such as John Cage and Roger Sessions have written about creativity from the standpoint of the created product. Cage, for instance, maintains that his compositions are the integration of structure, form, method, and material: "I write in order to hear; never do I hear and then write what I hear." Expressive musical materials are what Cage refers to as the infinite creative possibilities that contemporary technology has made available to each of us with regard to sound and silence.

Sessions writes about the musical idea as the generative kernel of the composition. This kernel may be arrived at easily and quickly, or it may require great amounts of revision. Its formation results from the manipulation of notes that constantly takes place in the mind of the composer. Serving as a point of departure for the composer, it may take any of several forms (such as sonority or rhythm). The spirit and energy of the musical idea must be recaptured in every aspect of the composition. Its execution is the actual "fleshing out" of the music from the previously established skeleton. This execution determines the structure of the musical product.

IMPLICATIONS FOR RESEARCH

What role does inspiration play in the formal processes of creative thought for a composer, a performer, and a listener? Is this role different depending on the creative intention? How is this role affected by age and experience? What conditions, both musical and extra-musical, seem to affect inspirational thought? Is it possible to teach musical material in a way that promotes inspirational thought? If so, how?

For a person to be creative, it is clear that there must be an understanding of musical material (such as facts, techniques, craftsmanship) together with the ability to think divergently in musical terms with these materials. What is this divergency of thought? What role does divergency play in terms of a more general view of musical intelligence? Can divergent thinking be taught? Under what conditions does it occur most often? Is all of this different for each person, or are there generalizations that can be found?

What insights can be gained from a comparative study of the many models of creative process that have been suggested (both formally and informally) by musicians, psychologists, and aestheticians? Is the creative process in music sufficiently unique to be considered apart from creative thinking in other content areas, such as language, art, or science? What evidence is there for this view?

Is it realistic to view the creative product as a measurable entity? What factors should be considered as part of such a measurement, and what should such data actually represent?

GREATNESS

A striking characteristic of musical experience is its ability to provide a sense of depth and profundity of meaning. Music that does so is often said to exemplify greatness. Great music enhances human consciousness by plumbing the essence of the human condition. Full experiences of such music are imbued with awe, in that one feels in touch with the core of being human, of being conscious of ultimate concerns. It may be this potential of music that causes us to regard it with a profound respect transcending more ordinary endeavors.

★ ★ ★

Those who write about the musical experience often address the issue of musical greatness, that is, the ability of the music to reflect the essence of human experience and its power to take this experience to even greater heights. To many, the quality of the musical experience is commensurate with the quality of the music itself. Good music, according to James Mursell, is that which exhibits subtlety of effects and profundity of feelings; good music does more and deeper things with feelings than music of a lesser quality. The level of difficulty, the particular musical style, or its general popularity are all irrelevant in determining its "goodness." To Mursell, meaningful musical experience is possible only if good music is used.

John Blacking agrees when he says there is a difference between music that is occasional and music that enhances human consciousness,

---

Citations for the material in this section of Part II will be found on the following pages of Part I: Mursell, 133–134; Blacking, 27–28; Copland, 66; Beardsley, 5–6, 8; Meyer, 115–118; Maslow, 106–107, 109; Reid, 149.

or, put another way, music that is simply for having and music that is for being. While the former may exhibit good craftsmanship, the latter is art. Aaron Copland seems to have been thinking along the same lines when he said that music is a "haven wherein one makes contact with the essence of human experience" and that a masterwork arouses in us feelings of a spiritual nature that lie dormant, only waiting to be awakened. Therefore, a performance of great music is a "reincarnation of a series of ideas implicit in the work of art."

Monroe Beardsley chooses to stay away from the labels *good* or *great* and instead refers to aesthetic value when discussing artistic quality: "The aesthetic value of anything is its capacity to impart — through cognition of it — a marked aesthetic character to experience. The term 'cognition' here refers to the apprehension (but not the misapprehension) of the thing's qualities and relations, including its semantic properties." A musical composition can be objectively evaluated according to its degree of unity or disunity, complexity or simplicity, and intensity or lack of intensity of regional qualities.

Leonard Meyer addresses both the question of value and greatness. For him, these are two separate issues. While he believes that a syntactic theory such as his may be appropriate for assessing musical value, musical greatness can only be determined by considering the interaction between a work's syntactic structure and the profundity of its associative or extra-musical context (such as aspects of human existence like "man's awareness of his own insignificance and impotence in the face of the magnitude and power of creation"). When both dimensions (syntactic and associative) are superior, "we attain a new level of consciousness, of individualization."

This seems to resonate with Abraham Maslow's notions of peak experience and self-actualization. Indeed, Maslow does address music in his description of these phenomena. He believes that a peak experience can be the result of a variety of different triggers, but that it is always associated with descriptive words such as *awe, ultimate truths, bliss, ecstasy,* or *rapture.* "These were moments of pure, positive happiness when all doubts, all fears, all inhibitions, all tension, all weaknesses, were left behind." Peak experience is a moment of non-interference during which there is a mutual feedback between the perceiver and the perceived. A sense of disorientation in time and space frequently accompanies the experience. According to Maslow, music is one of the most frequent triggers of peak experience.

Maslow believes that learning about one's own identity is an essential part of education and that the arts, particularly music and dance, are an effective way of getting to this biological identity: "In this realm of intrinsic learning . . . the arts . . . are so close to our psychological and biological core, so close to this identity, this biological identity, that rather than think of these as a sort of whipped or luxury cream, they must become basic experiences in education."

Writers who have focused part of their discussion on the issue of musical greatness have not only addressed the issue of aesthetic value (that is, the relative quality of the perceived object), but they have also discussed the unique, often ethereal nature of the perceiver's experience. Perhaps Louis Arnaud Reid expressed it most pointedly when he wrote, "Aesthetic experience is not the stopping or ending of a process, but a life of appetite and satisfaction more intense than ordinary earthly life and rounded to unearthly perfection."

IMPLICATIONS FOR RESEARCH

In what conceptual framework do people who report profound, even spiritual experiences of music express such experiences? Is their language related to age, religious beliefs, cultural background, musical education, or personality characteristics?

Is there a kind or type of music most likely to cause experiences described as ethereal, transcendent, or peak? Do people experience this with only certain types of music? Is familiarity a factor?

Do those who perform or compose report experiences of greatness more often than those who listen? Are their experiences connected to the act of performing or composing? Are they more likely than others to have such experiences?

At what age do experiences of profound musical depth begin to occur? What characteristics of music seem to cause such experiences in young people? How does this compare with those characteristics of music that cause similar experiences among older people?

What do belief systems in cultures other than Western society claim in regard to the deepest levels of musical experience? Are their music education practices related to those belief systems?

UNIVERSALS

Are there universally existent characteristics of people and music that account for the ubiquitous nature of musical experience? One suggestion is that humans are endowed with an innate capacity for language. Another suggestion is that the principles by which sounds can be organized derive from universally existent propensities that govern how sounds can be structured. Underneath the many differences among the world's musics, at present and throughout history, there may be underlying correspondences between mind and sound that universally cause people to experience organized sounds as being sensible and compelling.

★ ★ ★

The question of whether there exist musical universals that permit all people to appreciate and experience a variety of musics is raised in two essays in Part I of this monograph.

Leonard Bernstein attempts to answer this question by comparing music with language, using phonology (the study of the basic units of language) as a point of departure. In *The Unanswered Question,* Bernstein begins his exploration of the connection between language and music by searching for a musical equivalent to the linguistic phoneme. Bernstein's proposal that the "innate musical-grammatical competence which we may all possess universally" is based on our ability to construe the overtone series. Just as different cultures of the world

---

Citations for the material in this section of Part II will be found on the following pages of Part I: Bernstein, 20–24; Lerdahl and Jackendoff, 99–102.

have constructed a large number of grammars or languages from the basic monogenetic materials, Bernstein believes that all types of music from the world's cultures are derived from a common origin that he calls the universal phenomenon of the harmonic series.

Fred Lerdahl and Ray Jackendoff perceive musical universals in a broader context. For them, universal principles of musical grammar (or musical universals) are hypotheses about those aspects of musical understanding that are innate to all humans. The musical universals are principles available to all experienced listeners for organizing the musical surfaces they hear, regardless of the idiom in which they are experienced.

The most natural hearing, they suggest, is the way that the idealized "experienced listener" hears a piece. The theory states that "rarely do two people hear a given piece in precisely the same way or with the same degree of richness." However, Lerdahl and Jackendoff also state that "there is normally considerable agreement on what are the most natural ways to hear a piece." While their theory is primarily concerned with those musical judgments for which there is substantial interpersonal agreement, it is also capable of characterizing situations where there are alternative interpretations.

Specifying the rules of musical organization (that is, musical syntax) can clarify the musical universals present in music. Bernstein analyzes the similarities between musical and linguistic structures and believes that both consist of deep and surface structures. The most basic components of music are the chosen elements such as pitches, tonalities, and meter. From these choices arise what he calls the "underlying strings" or the melodic motives and phrases, chordal progressions, and rhythmic figures. These are then recombined to create the deep structure of the music. Deep structure, or the prose of the music, is defined by Bernstein as "the raw material waiting to be transformed into art."

Lerdahl and Jackendoff claim a rule to be universal if it applies in the same way in every idiom that employs the distinctions to which the rule is sensitive. Formal musical grammar is represented in a system of rules that assigns analyses to pieces of music. Such a system charac-terizes the organization of a composition in a way that models the listener's connection between the aurally presented musical surface and the psychological structure attributed to the piece. The components of this grammar are well-formedness rules and preference rules.

The well-formedness rules specify the possible structural description that can be applied to a piece of music. They are a limited number of short, succinct rules that outline the most basic of all structural descriptions. Preference rules deal with the way the experienced listener mentally interprets the musical sound surface being heard. Furthermore, it is the perception and designation of specific structural descriptions that specify which well-formedness rules become the preference rules for a specific musical example.

Lerdahl and Jackendoff are confident that one of their metrical preference rules (the stress rule) is universal. The comprehension of regular or irregular stress points in music is an innate aspect of hearing and comprehending music. This rule can apply in every idiom and is therefore considered a universal rule.

The universality of tonality is an issue of concern to many writers, especially those who seek to explain contemporary trends in composition to the layman. Throughout his career, Bernstein wrestled with the issue of nontonal music. By the time he delivered the Norton Lectures of 1973, he questioned how ambiguous the composer could be before the clarity of musical meaning was lost altogether. In his opinion, contemporary compositional techniques such as serialism work against our innate sense of tonality. However, he suggests that as long as the twelve tones used are the same twelve tones derived from the natural harmonic series, one cannot destroy their inherent tonal relationship. Thus, Bernstein reaffirms the belief in a worldwide, inborn musical grammar that is firmly rooted in tonality.

Musical universals, according to Bernstein, impose certain expectations in the minds of the perceiver. When this expectation is violated, an ambiguity occurs. Musical ambiguity is created when a composer deliberately takes our universal instinct of symmetry and plays with it through transformational processes such as deletion and embedding. The use of rules of transformational grammar to create a controlled ambiguity results in a violation of the expectations of the perceiver. However, according to Bernstein, these ambiguities are beautiful, and they are germane to all artistic creation.

Controlled ambiguities thus enrich our aesthetic response, whether in music, poetry, or painting, by providing more than one way of perceiving the aesthetic surface. The creative process of bringing ambiguities into musical being, therefore, becomes an integral part of the definition of musical universals.

IMPLICATIONS FOR RESEARCH

Do inexperienced listeners become "experienced listeners" once they are able to perceive some of the deep structure of music as defined by Bernstein? Can this transition from inexperienced to experienced be identified?

Does one lead the inexperienced listener to a perception of the deep structure of music by first illuminating the elements of the surface structure (pitches, tonalities, meter, etc.), or is another approach possible? What is the best strategy to help the listener make the transition from perceiving surface structure to the deep structure of music? Which musical styles are more accessible to inexperienced listeners who are trying to transfer their perception of the surface structure to the deeper structures?

Can universal preference rules, such as the stress rule, be identified as existing in all musical styles and applicable in every idiom? Do listeners from other cultures perceive the same preference rules in a musical style or idiom as the listener from the music's own cultural setting?

Is there a correlation between the inability to perceive a particular universal preference rule (such as the stress rule) in a foreign culture's music and the listener's ability/inability to appreciate or value the music? Can the listener's perception of that particular music be enhanced? Will that enhancement increase the listener's appreciation or valuing of that music?

If we accept Bernstein's theory of an innate sense of tonality derived from the natural harmonic series, then what effect does exposing inexperienced listeners to large quantities of nontonal music produce? Does this result in confusion, ambiguities, stimulation, or have no effect on their future musical expectations of tonality?

Are controlled ambiguities for one listener perceived as uncontrolled ambiguities for another? Is this perception related to certain factors such as the listener's age, intelligence, musical experience, cultural background, or personality type? What process can be used to assist in the transformation of the perception of uncontrolled ambiguities to a degree of controlled ambiguities?

FUNCTIONALITY

Does musical experience serve a special function beyond the gratification of every individual's need for meaningful experience? Music obviously accompanies and enhances a variety of social activities and is used for a variety of purposes not entirely focused on the experience of the music for its own sake. These functional roles are recognized to be important, but underlying them is a deeper contribution musical experience makes to society. This has to do with its power to exemplify that all humans in a culture share modes of feeling common to being human and common to the particular cultural group in which a musical style exists. The social interaction of creating and sharing music both reflects and strengthens bonds of common feeling. Community, at this level, consists of a union of feeling with feeling, person with person, in shared bonds of subjective mutuality. Understood this way, musical experience is an instrument for social communion.

★ ★ ★

Several authors in this volume discuss the social/community aspects of music with respect to musical experience. John Blacking suggests that the value of music may be found in terms of the human experiences involved in its creation. He traces these values to the functions and effects music has in a given society. One of the chief

---

Citations for the material in this section of Part II will be found on the following pages of Part I: Blacking, 28, 30; Langer, 86–87, 89, 95; Reimer, 154–157, 159; Cage, 47–49; Beardsley, 9–12; Mursell, 123, 125–126, 135.

reasons music is to be valued is that it involves people in shared experiences within the framework of their culture. Blacking suggests that through music, patterns of culture and society emerge in the shape of humanly organized sound. Music confirms what is already present in society and culture, adding nothing new except sound. Any analysis of music must begin with an analysis of the social situation in which the music is generated. Blacking presents a socio-physical application of these ideas by discussing the creation of music as a means of sharing inner feelings in a social context. This occurs through extensions of body movement since many (if not all) of music's essential processes may be found in the constitution of the human body and in the patterns of interaction of human bodies in society.

According to Blacking, there are two levels at which a relationship between music and society can be expected: (1) the level of ideas and (2) the level of interaction in which ideas are invoked. The two areas of action that are involved in every performance situation are the musical and the social. Neither ideas nor musical action can be understood without reference to patterns of social interaction, for ideas and music, like anything cultural, are social facts.

While Blacking perceives that the social/community function of music arises from cultural roots, Susanne Langer states that art penetrates deep into personal life because it articulates and gives form to human experience. Artistic training is the education of feeling, just as our schooling in factual subjects and logical skills is the education of thought. The real education of emotion is not the conditioning that results from social approval and disapproval, but the tacit, personal, illuminating contact with symbols of feeling. Furthermore, while responsiveness is primarily a natural gift, it may be heightened by experience or reduced by adverse agencies. Because responsiveness is intuitive, it cannot be taught; but the free exercise of artistic intuition often depends on clearing the mind of intellectual prejudices and false conceptions that inhibit people's natural responsiveness.

Bennett Reimer expands the idea of music's function when he suggests that musical experience has a social function beyond its nature as a group activity in classes and performance situations. The community as formed by musical experience is a cultural group with shared common experiences of inner feeling. Every shared musical experience unites people in a bond of affective experience. Music exemplifies that all humans feel and that at least some feelings are shared by all. The major value of cross-cultural musical experiences is that they broaden one's possibilities of experienced feeling-domains, adding to the breadth of those with whom one can be in community.

Speaking of this broader community, John Cage writes that "music's ancient purpose — to sober and quiet the mind . . . — is now to be practiced in relation to the Mind of which through technological extension we all are part, a Mind, these days, confused, disturbed, and split." In addition, Cage calls for "musical open-mindedness." This involves the recognition of any and all expressive materials as well as the exploration of the entire world (cosmos) of music.

Monroe Beardsley presents another perspective on the social function of art. He discusses the fictive nature of art works that distinguishes them from natural or practical objects. This nature enables them to display expressive or aesthetic qualities that are our mark on the world around us. In the creation of art works, one humanizes the earth in a way that is unique to the arts.

From a slightly different vantage point, James Mursell indicates that the social aspects of music are important, especially in educational settings. He believes that vital musical experience is important for all people. Music embodies the "mission of mankind." It gives people interests, self-discipline, adventure, courage to think, and awareness of talents. Music education effects democracy, free association, cooperation, and preservation of culture. The music educator's purpose is to help people become more human by being able to share more deeply the interactions and experiences that unite person with person in community.

IMPLICATIONS FOR RESEARCH

In what ways do belief systems of a given group of people (cultures, nationality, creed, etc.) affect their perceptions of and responses to music?

Given a homogenous group of people (for example, a particular tribe of Native Americans), in what ways can we gather information to identify the effect of their particular belief system on the nature of musical experience within that group?

Given the identification and measurement of interactions in several homogenous groups of people, can we then compare the information across groups to determine correlations between various factors?

Would short-term changes in people's belief systems, as through intensive study of an alternative system, affect their perception of and reaction to music?

Do gradual changes in people's belief systems, such as what might occur at different age levels, affect their response to music?

Given the claim that some feelings are shared by some or all people involved in a musical experience, how can evidence be gathered that this occurs? What nonmusical influences (social status, cultural heritage, etc.) affect the sharing of musical experience, and to what degree? What shared feelings are a result of other factors?

To what extent do people's extra-musical characteristics (self-discipline, cooperativeness, courage to think, etc.) affect their perceptions and reactions in musical experience?

What effects do functional uses of music, such as therapy, advertising, etc., have on people's intra-musical perceptions and reactions?

MUSICALITY WIDESPREAD

The ability to experience music, and the desire to so so, are generally recognized as inborn. However, most writers recognize also that people have differing capacities for such experience and that, whatever an individual's innate capacity, it can be developed through pertinent education. All agree that music exists not just for musicians or for some musically elite segment of the general population, but for all humans as members of that community of beings who are capable of humanizing their world through aesthetic endeavors. The art of music is an essential mode through which human experience acquires meaning. The function of music education is to develop every human's capacity to share such meaning through musical experience.

★ ★ ★

Many if not most writers on musical experience believe that the ability to experience music is so widespread that it must be considered an inborn capacity for all humans. According to James Mursell, the expressive qualities of music make it inherently enjoyable if the musical experience is not distorted by overemphasis on technical factors. Furthermore, he states that music is enjoyable for all types of people (the musician as well as the nonmusician). While all people are capable of experiencing music, Mursell states that musicality can be developed

---

Citations for the material in this section of Part II will be found on the following pages of Part I: Mursell, 121–122, 125, 127, 129, 131–134; Blacking, 27–28; Reimer, 154; Sessions, 174–175; Hindemith, 84; Copland, 62; Meyer, 111–116; Beardsley, 9–10.

in all people through music education by expanding their perceptive ability and teaching them to be creative, active, and open musical listeners and performers.

In John Blacking's view, the universal existence of music can be explained by the functions and effects music has in a given society. One of the chief functions for which music exists is to involve people in shared experiences within the framework of their cultural experience.

According to Bennett Reimer, musicality (or musical sensitivity) is the ability to have musical experiences. All people — even severely damaged people — can experience music to some degree. Musical experience is not limited to the talented or elite. That is why all cultures have music and all people have musical experience by nature. Like Mursell, Reimer claims that all people can benefit from music education, for the level of every person's musicality can be improved.

Roger Sessions believes that the "musical ear" is not restricted to the musician. The musical ear employs a method of hearing music that permits the listener to discriminate between sounds on a number of levels such as pitch, tone quality, intensity, timbre, and duration. Once discriminated, the musical ear relates and associates the musical impressions. Finally, the musical ear orders these associations into hierarchical levels that combine to create an overall image of the work.

Paul Hindemith identifies a particular quality of music — musical space — which, in its obviousness, is apparent even to the entirely untrained mind. He believes that it is the pitch relation among tones and not the loudness or color of tones that produces this effect of musical space.

Though all people are naturally aware of musical flow, the magnetic forward pull of music raises questions in the mind of the enlightened listener. Aaron Copland believes that to the enlightened listener the time-filling, forward drive has fullest meaning only when accompanied by (1) some conception as to where it is headed; (2) some understanding of what musical-psychological elements are helping to move it to its destination; and (3) an awareness of what formal architectural satisfaction will have been achieved on its arriving there. Musical education can improve every person's capacity to be musically "enlightened."

Leonard Meyer believes that musical meaning is found intra-musically through the comprehension of musical relationships and that the meaning of music is accessible to all people in some degree. Musical meaning pivots on (1) the learned responses of a listener familiar with an established musical style; (2) a universal psychological mechanism that explains a wide range of affective and intellectual responses; and (3) fundamental laws of human perception and cognition.

More specifically, musical meaning (whether affective or intellectual) arises when a musical tendency to respond is inhibited. A musical work is meaningful if a musical event arouses a listener's expectations for other musical events. According to Meyer, meaningful musical experience depends crucially on a listener's musical expectations. A listener with no musical expectations in a given musical style is unlikely to have a meaningful experience of a work in that particular style. With added experience in the style comes added meaning. The experienced listener develops complex sets of musical expectations. Meyer's definition of musical meaning supports the principle that musicality is widespread and that it can be taught.

Monroe Beardsley asks the question of what art works in general, or typically, or at their best, have to contribute to human welfare. In creating art works, people humanize the earth as they can in no other way. The fictive (or seemingly false) nature of art works distinguishes them from the works of nature and objects that are merely tools or machines. This fictive character enables them to feature the expressive or aesthetic qualities that are in a special way the artist's work on the world, for they are the artistic counterparts of those human qualities that give meaning to all human experience.

IMPLICATIONS FOR RESEARCH

If musical expectations of a particular musical style are part of the requirements for the listener's having a meaningful musical experience, then how does one develop expectations for a given style with which one has no experience or expectations? Is there a measurable correlation between the degree of musical expectations necessary in a given musical style and the degree of meaning derived from the musical experience?

What are possible approaches for helping inexperienced listeners develop the complex sets of musical expectations necessary for having a meaningful experience with a particular style of music? What strategies best develop the musical expectations for a particular style: (a) repeated listenings (familiarity), (b) guided listening, (c) direct instruction (verbal, visual), (d) composing and performing in that style, and (e) combinations of the above?

What are the commonalities between the complex sets of musical expectations necessary for meaningful listening to occur in different musical styles? Which musical styles have complex sets with the most in common? Can a logical sequence of instruction with particular musical styles be derived from such information?

Which musical styles are especially suited for young, inexperienced listeners who are just beginning to develop complex sets of musical expectations? Which are more appropriate for older inexperienced listeners? Is suitability partially determined by the artistic counterparts of human qualities found with specific age groups in a particular society? What other factors, such as intelligence, educational level, and cultural background, influence this development?

PART III

RECOMMENDATIONS AND POSTSCRIPT

RECOMMENDATIONS

By examining the thinking on musical experience on the part of the authors involved in this study, and by searching for ideas common among those authors, a description of musical experience has emerged that seems helpful toward understanding its nature. Obviously, however, the insights gained are a function of the particular group of authors included for study, as well as the relative success achieved in gleaning the insights available from their writings. While this group included many thinkers well recognized in the scholarly and musical communities for the excellence of their work, many others could have been included and many other sources of insight could have been examined. Clearly this study represents a first step in what can be an ongoing program of scholarship.

What further steps need to be taken from the perspective of having attempted the first?

1. The present study needs to be replicated (with all due attention to refinements in its methodologies) with other groups of writers representing the fields of aesthetics, composition, performance, theory, and education to determine the extent to which a group of thinkers other than those examined here would yield similar insights.

2. Comparisons need to be made among the subgroups of thinkers represented in the present study to determine if the subgroups understand musical experience differently. Pertinent subgroups would include composers, performers, aestheticians, music theorists, and educators. Close examination of idea clusters within subgroups could illuminate significant idiosyncrasies among their belief systems.

3. The writers included in the present study represent well-established, influential, "mainline" thinkers in recent history. Comparisons

need to be made between descriptions of musical experience that emerged in this study and those that might emerge among such thinkers from different periods of history to determine the extent to which concepts of musical experience are historically determined, to identify striking dissimilarities from period to period, and to seek constants from period to period.

4. In every period of history there are deviants from the well-established norm. In our own period John Cage is generally regarded as an example. He was included in the present study because it was felt he might provide a measure of balance or a critical point of view. It proved difficult to use his thinking for that purpose because doing so would have changed the nature of the study before the study had a chance to establish its nature. Thinkers like Cage, and others whose views are less easily assimilable, deserve separate attention so that their belief systems can be examined on their own terms and as a possible foil to more conventional views.

5. The authors examined in this study represent not only a particular time of history but a particular culture — that of the West. Studies similar to this one need to be conducted of representative thinkers in a diversity of cultures. As with studies of different historical periods, we may find striking dissimilarities, and perhaps equally striking commonalities, among conceptions of musical experience across diverse cultures.

6. Within our present culture in the United States are a diversity of subgroups that may yield alternative conceptions of musical experience needing to be understood. These include not only cultural groupings (Latinos, Native Americans, African Americans, and so forth) but also groupings by age, levels of education, and socioeconomic status. In addition, comparisons need to be made of those at the extreme ends of the music education spectrum — for example, those who were exposed to optimal music instruction in school as opposed to those who were not, and those exposed to particular orientations, such as Orff or Comprehensive Musicianship, as opposed to those who were not. An infinite variety of other groupings also seems possible. Studies at such a "micro" level could further refine our definition of musical experience.

7. A diversity of scholarly and research literatures exists that may throw needed light on, and add dimensionality to, studies such as this

one and those potential studies suggested above. The literatures of psychology — clinical, experimental, developmental, social, speculative — need to be examined for insights they may add. The literature of sociology may also prove fruitful for understandings of belief systems related to musical experience. The literature dealing with music as an aspect of religion might be examined productively. Certainly the research literature in music education deserves study with an eye toward the assumptions it makes as to the nature of musical experience. And the scholarly and research literatures of the other arts education fields, particularly visual art education because of its breadth and depth, need to be examined for the insights-by-analogy they could offer.

In addition to the need for studies as suggested above, there are some practical and methodological issues raised by the present effort.

This work was undertaken by music educators who, underneath any theoretical interest in the nature of musical experience, are driven by the desire to become more effective as enhancers of musical experience for students in schools and for others. When, and how, can efforts be made to draw implications for teaching and learning from the scholarship we have produced or that later will be produced? What does this research tell us about our educational practices, across the broad range of activities in which we are engaged, that might help us improve those practices? The implications for research listed at the end of each common feature essay in Part II begin to move in the direction of educational applications, but we may need to move more quickly, at least in some ways, to put our learnings to practical use. Attention is needed as to how the music education profession might translate the insights gained here into guidelines for improved programs and improved instruction. It is anticipated that at least some doctoral dissertations of present and future members of the Center for the Study of Education and the Musical Experience will be devoted to this task. It is hoped that dissertations by students at other universities might also contribute to this work of putting theory into fruitful practice.

POSTSCRIPT: THE NEED FOR
COORDINATED RESEARCH

This study may well be the first in the history of music education in which an ongoing research center of doctoral students and faculty have cooperated, as a group and over a period of several years, to produce a scholarly work more inclusive than any single member could have accomplished. The inclusivity is not just a function of quantity of material. It is also, more importantly, a function of shared ideas and shared learning processes. The ideal image of intellectual work in our culture has been that of the individual scholar or researcher working in splendid isolation, creating products of his or her mind for others to admire and use. Now we are beginning to recognize that human knowing is, in fact, communal, and that cooperative scholarship can produce understandings larger and deeper than the sum of individual contributions. Those who were engaged in the present study can attest to the accuracy of that assertion. Our very "groupness" touched, informed, and vivified our individual contributions in ways that transformed them from what they would have been, or could have been, had they not been carried out as part of a larger endeavor to which each of us was devoted.

This is not to suggest that cooperative scholarship is without its hazards or that it is some sort of panacea. It is certainly not to suggest, either, that individual work is not necessary. What it does bring to consciousness is the need for an alternative to the one mode of scholarly production on which we have modeled our efforts. This alternative has implications both for methodologies for accomplishing research and subject matters for research.

As to research methodologies, we would suggest that our present, relentless dependence on individual, isolated studies is unfortunate. This is especially the case when most of these studies are the first (and last) being attempted by the researcher, as is true of the vast majority of doctoral dissertations. It would seem beneficial if young scholars embarking on a first large project were to do so in the context of a supporting research community.

A research center such as the Center for the Study of Education and the Musical Experience provides an environment within which an individual's work can flourish as both individual and contextual. On the side of the individual, research does require that, at many points along the way, a person take responsibility for important decisions. No matter how interactive a cooperative effort might be, individuals will still have to act individually, a reality to be both accepted and cherished. Yet it is not the same thing to act individually and to act disconnectedly. The disconnectedness of our research activities is what tends to make them both humanly frigid and intellectually arid.

On the side of context, a full adoption of a research center model is not necessary in order to achieve a better balance between isolation and cooperation. Small groupings of students or faculty, or combinations of the two, could be assigned to work with an individual as a resource group, not just to check and finally accept a project, as faculty committees now tend to function, but as active participants in the formulation of a proposal, the initial steps toward implementation, the ongoing decision-making process, and the drawing of conclusions. It would be possible for each researcher to be the center of a small support circle, all the research being done at a particular institution forming a cluster of overlapping circles.

The transformation in the scholarly atmosphere produced by such an organization would be dramatic, not just psychologically, but also in the richness of intellectual sharing it would foster. A research center includes this sharing but organizes it into a unifying circle in which all individual efforts reside, every member of the group both participating in each individual study as a resource and carrying out an individual study as primary scholar for whom others are a resource.

No doubt there are midpoint organizational models and alternative models that would accomplish these ends appropriately for the size and nature of particular institutions. What is being suggested here, as a recommendation stemming from the present study, is not a specific organization, but that some attention be paid to the significant gains that could be made by providing some sort of cooperative structure for the research enterprise.

The second implication of considering a change in the traditional way we have conducted research is for the topics chosen to be researched. Presently, we tend to assume that every study must be "original," in the sense of not having been carried out before. Doctoral students typically worry a great deal about finding a topic nobody else has dealt with and, when such a topic is finally located, that it gets done before someone else gets ahold of it and takes it away. This attitude directly reflects a concept of knowledge as existing of a fixed entity, each bit of research shining a separate ray of light on that existent entity. It also reflects the myth previously mentioned, that the scientist or scholar must work independently. Each topic chosen to be researched, therefore, is likely to be unconnected to any other, or to be connected only in inconsequential ways, or to be similar in research modality (a "historical" study, or an "experimental" study), but not in substance, with others.

It is important for the viability of musical and educational scholarship that we recognize what the philosophy of science has been explaining for some three decades: that knowledge is humanly constructed, reflecting human capacities and interests and needs, and that human knowledge is historically, socially, and psychologically embedded. We create what we know, and we do so according to what we need to know in order to make our individual and social lives more meaningful. This suggests that our attempts to generate knowledge should focus on knowledge that has meaning for us — that matters to us. Certainly there are isolated facts and pieces of knowing that are useful. But just as certainly there are compelling issues still unaddressed and significant problems still unresolved. These issues and problems need to engage us, because they guide us as we try to be the professionals we want to be. There is simply no good reason for studying something unimportant when so many important matters confront us.

Important matters, however, are complex. Few scholars will be able, by themselves, to tackle major issues and wrestle them to productive solutions. We can hope for the occasional Newton or Einstein or Dewey or Freud to change our minds about the nature and content of knowing, but most of us will labor modestly to improve our daily lot in small increments. These increments, themselves, can be meaningful, if and when they are tied directly to issues that are meaningful, and contribute, however incrementally, to the resolution of such issues.

Our research needs to be, and can be, structured to deal with meaningful issues. That suggests, of course, a group of researchers clustered around an issue, with some mechanism to allow for attention to the issue over longer or shorter periods of time and to coordinate separate studies so that each can contribute to an accumulating base of knowledge. Our ingenuity will be exercised to the fullest as we invent such structures, because we have little or no experience at doing so. Each of the contributors to the present study hopes that his or her work has helped clarify the nature of musical experience, however incrementally, and has also demonstrated, to some degree, the feasibility and desirability of cooperative scholarship.

BIBLIOGRAPHY

Auden, Wystan H. "Some Reflections on Opera as a Medium." *Partisan Review* (January/February 1952): 10–18.

Beardsley, Monroe C. "Aesthetic Experience Regained." *Journal of Aesthetics and Art Criticism* 28 (1969): 3–11.

———. *The Aesthetic Point of View: Selected Essays.* Edited by Michael J. Wreen and Donald M. Callen. Ithaca, NY: Cornell University Press, 1982.

———. *Aesthetics: Problems in the Philosophy of Criticism.* New York: Harcourt, Brace, and World, 1958.

———. "On the Creation of Art." In *Aesthetic Inquiry: Essays on Art Criticism and the Philosophy of Art.* Edited by Monroe C. Beardsley and Herbert M. Schueller. Belmont, CA: Dickenson, 1967.

———. "Postscript 1980 — Some Old Problems in New Perspectives." Preface to *Aesthetics: Problems in the Philosophy of Criticism.* 2nd ed. Indianapolis: Hackett, 1981.

———. "Understanding Music." In *On Criticizing Music: Five Philosophical Perspectives.* Edited by Kingsley Price. Baltimore: Johns Hopkins University Press, 1981.

Bell, Clive. *Art.* London: Chatto and Windus, 1914.

Bernstein, Leonard. *Findings.* New York: Simon and Schuster, 1982.

———. *The Infinite Variety of Music.* New York: Simon and Schuster, 1966.

———. *The Joy of Music.* New York: Simon and Schuster, 1959.

———. *The Unanswered Question.* Cambridge, MA: Harvard University Press, 1976.

Blacking, John. "Can Musical Universals Be Heard?" *The Worlds of Music* 19 (1975): 14–29.

———. *How Musical Is Man?* Seattle: University of Washington Press, 1973.

———. "The Study of Man as Music Maker." In *The Performing Arts.* Edited by John Blacking and Joann Kealiinohomoku. The Hague: Mouton, 1979.

———. "Towards a Theory of Musical Competence." In *Man: Anthropological Essays to O. F. Raum.* Edited by E. J. DeJager. Cape Town, South Africa: C. Struik, 1971.

Boethius. *De Institutione Musica.* Translated by Calvin Bower. Edited by Claude Palisca. New Haven: Yale University Press, 1989.

Broudy, Harry S. "Arts Education: Necessary or Just Nice?" *Phi Delta Kappan* (January 1979): 347–348.

———. "Arts in Education." Address delivered to the Annual Conference of the Pennsylvania Music Educator's Association, Pittsburgh, Pennsylvania. January 3, 1974.

————. *Enlightened Cherishing: An Essay on Aesthetic Education*. Urbana: University of Illinois Press, 1972.

————. *Paradox and Promise: Essays on American Life and Education*. Englewood Cliffs, NJ: Prentice-Hall, 1961.

————. "Quality Education in the Arts." Unpublished manuscript. 18 pp.

————. *The Real World of the Public Schools*. New York: Harcourt Brace Janovich, 1972.

————. *The Role of Imagery in Learning*. Los Angeles: Getty Center for Education in the Arts, 1987.

————. "Some Reactions to a Concept of Aesthetic Education." *Journal of Aesthetic Education* (July/October 1976): 29–37.

————. *Truth and Credibility: The Citizen's Dilemma*. New York: Longman, 1981.

Broudy, Harry S. and John R. Palmer. *Exemplars of Teaching Method*. Chicago: Rand McNally, 1965.

Broudy, Harry S., B. Othanel Smith, and Joe R. Burnett. *Democracy and Excellence in American Secondary Education: A Study in Curriculum Theory*. Chicago: Rand McNally, 1964.

Buber, Martin. *I and Thou*. New York: Charles Scribner's Sons, 1958.

Bullough, Edward. " 'Psychical Distance' as a Factor in Art and as an Aesthetic Principle," *British Journal of Psychology* V (1912):87–118.

Cage, John. *Empty Words*. Middletown, CT: Wesleyan University Press, 1979.

————. *Silence*. Middletown, CT: Wesleyan University Press, 1961.

————. *A Year From Monday*. Middletown, CT: Wesleyan University Press, 1967.

Chomsky, Noam. *Aspects of the Theory of Syntax*. Cambridge, MA: MIT Press, 1965.

————. *Language and Mind*. Enlarged edition. New York: Harcourt Brace Jovanovich, 1972.

————. *Reflections on Language*. New York: Pantheon, 1975.

Chomsky, Noam and Moris Halle. *The Sound Pattern of English*. New York: Harper and Row, 1968.

Clifton, Thomas. "Music and the A Priori." *Journal of Music Theory* 17 (Spring 1973):66–85.

————. "Music as Constituted Object." *Music and Man* 2 (1976):73–98.

————. *Music as Heard: A Study in Applied Phenomenology*. New Haven: Yale University Press, 1983.

————. "Review of: Alfred Pike's A Phenomenological Analysis of Musical Experience and Other Related Essays." *Journal of Music Theory* 14 (Winter 1970):73–98.

————. "The Poetics of Musical Silence." *Musical Quarterly* 62 (April 1976):237–246.

————. "Some Comparisons Between Intuitive and Scientific Descriptions of Music." *Journal of Music Theory* 19 (Spring 1975):66–111.

Cohen, Marshall. "Aesthetic Experience as Lacking Any Common Denominator." In *Varieties of Aesthetic Experience*. Edited by Earle J. Coleman. Lanham, MD: University Press of America, 1983.

Coleman, Earle J., ed. *Varieties of Aesthetic Experience*. Lanham, MD: University Press of America, 1983.

Coomaraswany, Ananda K. *The Transformation of Nature in Art*. 2nd ed. Cambridge, MA: Harvard University Press, 1935.

Copland, Aaron. *Copland on Music*. New York: W. W. Norton, 1944.

———. *Music and Imagination*. Cambridge, MA: Harvard University Press, 1952.

———. *The New Music*. New York: W. W. Norton, 1968.

———. *What to Listen for in Music*. New York: McGraw-Hill, 1939.

Dewey, John. *Art as Experience*. New York: Capricorn Books, 1958; New York: Paragon Books, G. P. Putnam's Sons, 1934, 1979.

Gardner, Howard. *Art, Mind, and Brain*. New York: Basic Books, 1982.

Glaser, Barney G. *The Discovery of Grounded Theory*. New York: Aldine DeGruzter: 1967.

Goodman, Nelson. *Languages of Art*. Indianapolis: Bobbs-Merrill, 1968. (2nd ed. Indianapolis: Hackett, 1976.)

———. *Of Mind and Other Matters*. Cambridge, MA: Harvard University Press, 1984.

———. *Ways of Worldmaking*. Indianapolis: Hackett, 1978.

Hanslick, Eduard. *The Beautiful in Music*. Translated by G. Cohen. New York: Da Capo Press, 1974. Originally published in 1885.

Heidegger, Martin. *Being and Time*. Translated by J. Macquarrie and E. Robinson. New York: Harper and Row, 1962.

———. *Existence and Being*. Chicago: Henry Regnery Co., 1970.

Helmholz, Hermann von. *Epistemological Writings*. Translated by Malcolm F. Lowe. Edited by Robert S. Cohen and Yehuda Elkana. Boston: D. Reidel, 1977.

Hewett, Gloria J., and Jean C. Rush. "Finding Buried Treasure." *Art Education* (January 1987):41–43.

Hindemith, Paul. *A Composer's World: Horizons and Limitations*. Cambridge, MA: Harvard University Press, 1952.

———. *A Concentrated Course in Traditional Harmony*. New York: Associated Music Publishers, 1943.

———. *A Concentrated Course in Traditional Harmony II: A Course for Advanced Students*. New York: Associated Music Publishers, 1953.

———. *The Craft of Musical Composition*. 4th ed. New York: Associated Music Publishers, 1945.

———. *Elementary Training for Musicians*. 2nd ed. New York: Associated Music Publishers, 1949.

————. *Johann Sebastian Bach: Heritage and Obligation.* New Haven: Yale University Press, 1952.

Husserl, Edmund. *Logical Investigations.* Translated by J. N. Findlay. New York: Humanities Press, 1970.

————. *The Pans Lectures.* Translated by Peter Koestenbaum. The Hague: Martinus Nijhoff, 1967.

————. *Phenomenology and the Crisis of Philosophy.* Translated and with Introduction by Quentin Lauer. New York: Harper and Row, Harper Torchbooks, 1965.

————. *Phenomenology of Internal Time-Consciousness.* Translated by James S. Churchill. Bloomington, IN: Indiana University Press, 1969.

Keiler, Allan. "Bernstein's 'The Unanswered Question' and the Problem of Musical Competence." *Musical Quarterly* 64 (1978): 195–222.

Koffka, Kurt. *Principles of Gestalt Psychology.* New York: Harcourt Brace and Co., 1935.

Langer, Susanne K. *Feeling and Form.* New York: Charles Scribner's Sons, 1953.

————. *Philosophy in a New Key: A Study in the Symbolism of Reason, Rite, and Art.* New York: Mentor Books, 1956.

————. *Problems of Art.* New York: Charles Scribner's Sons, 1957.

Lerdahl, Fred, and Ray Jackendoff. "Discovery Procedures vs. Rules of Musical Grammar in a Generative Music Theory." *Perspectives of New Music* 25 (1980): 503–510.

————. "Generative Music Theory and Its Relation to Psychology." *Journal of Music Theory* 25 (1985): 45–90.

————. *A Generative Theory of Tonal Music.* Cambridge, MA: MIT Press, 1983.

————. "On the Theory of Grouping and Meter." *The Musical Quarterly* 67 (1981): 479–506.

————. "Toward a Formal Theory of Tonal Music." *Journal of Music Theory* 21 (1977): 111–171.

Levi, Albert William. *Varieties of Experience: An Introduction to Philosophy.* New York: The Ronald Press, 1957.

Maslow, Abraham. *The Farther Reaches of Human Nature.* New York: Viking, 1971.

————. "Lessons from the Peak Experiences." *Journal of Humanistic Psychology* 2 (Spring 1962):9–18.

————. *Motivation and Personality.* 2nd ed. New York: Harper and Row, 1970.

————. "Music, Education, and Peak Experience." In *A Documentary Report of the Tanglewood Symposium.* Edited by Robert Choate. Reston, VA: Music Educators National Conference, 1968.

————. *Religions, Values, and Peak Experiences.* Columbus: Ohio State University Press, 1964.

————. *Toward a Psychology of Being.* Princeton, NJ: Van Nostrand, 1962.

Merleau-Ponty, Maurice. *Phenomenology of Perception.* Translated by Colin Smith. New York: Humanities Press, 1967.

Meyer, Leonard B. *Emotion and Meaning in Music.* Chicago: University of Chicago Press, 1956.

———. *Explaining Music: Essays and Explorations.* Berkeley: University of California Press, 1973.

———. "Exploring Limits: Creation, Archetypes, and Style Change." *Daedalus* 109 (1980):177–205.

———. "Grammatical Simplicity and Relational Richness: The Trio of Mozart's G Minor Symphony." *Critical Inquiry* 2 (1976): 693–761.

———. "Innovation, Choice, and the History of Music." *Critical Inquiry* 9 (1983): 517–544.

———. *Music, the Arts, and Ideas: Patterns and Predictions in Twentieth-Century Culture.* Chicago: University of Chicago Press, 1967.

———. "Review of: Donald N. Ferguson, *Music as Metaphor*" (Minneapolis: University of Minnesota Press, 1960) in *Journal of American Musicological Society* 15 (1962): 234–236.

———. "Toward a Theory of Style." In *The Concept of Style.* Edited by B. Lang. Philadelphia: University of Pennsylvania Press, 1979.

Mursell, James. *Education for Musical Growth.* Boston: Ginn, 1948.

———. *Human Values in Music Education.* New York: Silver Burdett, 1934.

———. "Music and the Redefinition of Education in Postwar America." Reprint of first address delivered at the Eastern Music Educators Wartime Institute in Rochester, NY, on March 20–23, 1943. *Music Educators Journal* 29 (April 1943): 15.

———. "Music and the Redefinition of Education in Postwar America." Reprint of second address delivered at the Eastern Music Educators Wartime Institute in Rochester, NY, on March 20–23, 1943. *Music Educators Journal* 29 (April 1943):8–11.

———. *Music Education: Principles and Programs.* Morristown, NJ: Silver Burdett, 1956.

———. *Music in American Schools.* New York: Silver Burdett, 1943.

———. *Principles of Musical Education.* New York: Macmillan, 1927.

———. *The Psychology of Music.* New York: Norton, 1937.

Pike, Alfred. *A Phenomenological Analysis of Musical Experience and Other Related Essays.* New York: St. John's University Press, 1970.

Polanyi, Michael. *Personal Knowledge.* Chicago: University of Chicago Press, 1958.

Rapaport, David. *Emotion and Memory.* New York: International Universities Press, Inc., 1950.

Reid, Louis Arnaud. *Creative Morality.* London: Allen and Unwin, 1937.

———. *Meaning in the Arts.* New York: Humanities Press, 1969.

————. *Philosophy and Education.* New York: Random House, 1962.

————. *Preface to Faith.* London: Allen and Unwin, 1939.

————. *The Rediscovery of Belief.* London: The Lindsey Press, 1946.

————. *A Study in Aesthetics.* Westport, CT: Greenwood Press, 1931.

————. *Ways of Knowledge and Experience.* London: Allen and Unwin, 1961.

————. *Ways of Understanding and Education.* London: University of London Press, 1986.

Reimer, Bennett. "Aesthetic Behaviors in Music." In *Toward an Aesthetic Education.* Edited by Bennett Reimer. Reston, VA: Music Educators National Conference, 1971.

————. *Developing the Experience of Music.* Englewood Cliffs, NJ: Prentice-Hall, 1984.

————. "Essential and Nonessential Characteristics of Aesthetic Education." *The Journal of Aesthetic Education* 25:3 (Fall 1991): 193–214.

————. *Learning to Listen to Music.* Englewood Cliffs, NJ: Prentice-Hall, 1970.

————. "Music Education and Music in China: An Overview and Some Issues." *Journal of Aesthetic Education* 23:1 (Spring 1989): 65–83.

————. "The Nonconceptual Nature of Aesthetic Cognition." *Journal of Aesthetic Education* 20:4 (Winter 1986): 111–117.

————. *A Philosophy of Music Education.* 2nd ed. Englewood Cliffs, NJ: Prentice-Hall, 1989.

————. "Selfness and Otherness in Experiencing Music of Foreign Cultures." *The Quarterly Journal of Music Teaching and Learning* (Fall 1991): 4–13.

————. "Toward a More Scientific Approach to Music Education Research." *Council for Research in Music Education* (Summer 1985).

————. "What Knowledge Is of Most Worth in the Arts?" In *The Arts, Education, and Aesthetic Knowing.* Edited by Bennett Reimer and Ralph A. Smith. Chicago: University of Chicago Press, 1992.

Reimer, Bennett and Edward G. Evans. *The Experience of Music, Developing the Experience of Music, Teaching the Experience of Music.* Englewood Cliffs, NJ: Prentice-Hall, 1973.

Reimer, Bennett, Elizabeth Crook, Mary Hoffman, Al McNeil, and David Walker. *Silver Burdett MUSIC.* Morristown, NJ: Silver Burdett Co., 1974, 1978, 1981, 1985.

Saint Augustine, Bishop of Hippo. *Musik: De musica libri sex.* Sprache von Carl Johann Perl. Paderborn: F. Schoningh, 1962.

Schoenberg, Arnold. *Style and Idea.* Translated by Leo Black. Edited by Leonard Stein. Berkeley: University of California Press, 1984.

Sessions, Roger. *Harmonic Practice.* New York: Harcourt Brace, 1951.

————. *The Musical Experience of Composer, Performer, Listener.* Princeton, NJ: Princeton University Press, 1950.

————. *Questions About Music*. New York: W. W. Norton, 1970.

————. *Roger Sessions on Music*. Edited by Edward T. Cone. Princeton, NJ: Princeton University Press, 1979.

Stapledon, W. Olaf. *A Modern Theory of Ethics, a Study of the Relations of Ethics and Psychology*. London: Methuen and Co., 1929.

Stravinsky, Igor. *An Autobiography*. New York: W. W. Norton, 1936.

————. *Poetics of Music*. New York: Random House, 1947.

Stravinsky, Igor, and Robert Craft. *Conversations with Igor Stravinsky*. London: Faber Music Ltd., 1959.

————. *Dialogues and a Diary*. New York: Doubleday, 1963.

————. *Expositions and Developments*. New York: Doubleday, 1962.

————. *Memories and Commentaries*. New York: Doubleday, 1960.

————. *Retrospectives and Conclusions*. New York: A. A. Knopf, 1969.

————. *Themes and Episodes*. New York: A. A. Knopf, 1966.

Stumpf, Karl. *Die pseudo-aristotelischen Problem über Musik*. Berlin, Königl. Akademie der Wissenshaften, 1897.

————. *Tonpsychologie*. Liepzig: S. Hirzel, 1883.

Wertheimer, Max. *Productive Thinking*. New York: Harper and Bros., 1945.

Wundt, Wilhelm. *Einleitung in die Philosophie*. Leipzig: W. Englemann, 1906.

Wolff, Christian. "Under the Influence." In Reginald Gibbons (ed.) *Triquarterly* 54, "A John Cage Reader" (Spring 1982):145–147.

INDEX

217, 224–225; multiple reference, 73, 74–75, 217, 224–225; process, 10–12; referentialism, 63, 86–87, 122–123, 153–156; symbols, 70, 72. *See also* Musical meaning
Regional qualities, 5–6, 11, 188
Reid, Louis A., 138–149; affect, 139–142, 145, 147, 148–149, 197–198, 199–200, 201, 203; cognition, 139–142; embodied meaning, 143–145, 148–149, 191; expectation, 145, 147, 208; greatness, 149, 261; imitation, 147–148; inspiration and creativity, 142–143, 255–256; intelligence, 139–142, 227; intrinsicality, 142–145, 191–192; listening, 141, 143, 145–149, 234, 237; meaning, 148, 213; reference, 140–144, 147–148, 251; sensuosity, 140–142, 243; tendency-fulfillment, 145
Reimer, Bennett, 152–159; affect, 153–154, 197, 199–200; cultural dimension, 157–159; expectation, 154, 157–158, 207–208; functionality, 154–157, 159, 269–270; inspiration and creativity, 157, 256; intelligence, 154–157, 222–223, 226; intrinsicality, 153–156, 188; key features, xvii; listening, 155–157, 234–235, 238, 240; meaning, 154–156, 215; musicality widespread, 154, 273; music research, vii; perceptual structuring, 155–156, 188; reference, 153–156, 250; sensuosity, 156–157, 245
Relative repleteness, 73, 74, 224–225
Repetition, 164
Representation, 72–73
Retention, 55
Rhythm, 129–131, 172
Ritual, 56–57
Ruggles, Carl, 47–48

Saint Augustine: musical perception, 80–81; philosophical categorization of experience, x–xi

Schoenberg, Arnold, 17, 46, 161–164; affect, 163, 202, 204; and John Cage, 44; Leonard Bernstein on, 24; listening, 161, 163, 235, 236
Selective attention, 157
Selective phase, 8–9
Self-actualization, 106, 109
Semantics: density, 73–74, 224–225; disjointedness, 70–71; finite differentiation, 70–71; musical metaphor, 23–24; music compared to language, 20; unambiguity, 70–71. *See also* Musical grammar; Musical metaphor
Sensory perception, 35, 37–38
Sensory properties, 37–38, 192
Sensory stimulation, 34–35, 156–157
Sensuosity, 242–245; emotion, 86–89, 122, 140–142; physical appeal, 129–131; physical excitement, 163–164; sensitive amateur, 64; structure, 102. *See also* Feelings
Serious art, 34
Sessions, Roger, 166–175; affect, 173–174, 197; expectation, 170–174, 210; inspiration and creativity, 167–170, 255, 257–258; intelligence, 174–175, 224; intrinsicality, 171–174, 190; listening, 174–175, 233–234, 235–236; movement, 171–174; musicality widespread, 174–175, 273
Signification theory, 10
Sonorous imagination, 94
Sound: as human expression, 172; intrinsicality, 187–195; meter, 178–179; patterns, 154
Souvtchinsky, Pierre: influence on Igor Stravinsky, 179
Spirtual nature of music, 65–66
Stapledon, W. Olaf, 145
Stravinsky, Igor, 177–181; expectation, 178–181, 208–210; inspiration and creativity, 179, 256; time, 178–180, 247–248
Stumpf, Karl, 112